Adam Graham

D0996418

ASSESSING ECONOMIC PERFORMANCE

MICHAEL LIPTON

Assessing Economic Performance

Some features of British economic development 1950-1965
in the light of economic theory and the
principles of economic planning

STAPLES PRESS · LONDON

First published 1968 by Staples Press
Copyright © Michael Lipton 1968
Printed in Great Britain
by C. Tinling & Co. Ltd
Liverpool, London and Prescot

ACKNOWLEDGEMENTS

I am grateful to Aaron Sloman and Len Joy for extremely valuable comments on the Introduction and Chapters 1 and 2; to Professor Alan Day, of the London School of Economics, for his careful reading of the book; to David Hitchens for computing pages 246–9; to Rosalyn Douse for indexing, and above all to my wife Merle, for persuading me to translate some of the jargon into English, and for her patience and perseverance as an unpaid editor.

CONTENTS

Contents

Contents

A*

Contents

LIST OF TABLES AND DIAGRAMS

DIAGRAMS (INCLUDING GRAPHS, ETC.)

List of Tables and Diagrams

Introduction

At the University of Sussex, lecturers and students in the Schools of English and Social Studies have been participating in an experiment: a unified course on contemporary Britain. Third-year undergraduates with some training in their special fields—say an economist, a sociologist, a historian, a couple of specialists in English literature and one in politics—join a lecturer from each School for a series of seminars. For each seminar three or four students prepare papers on a central topic. The papers point towards a common discipline created by an area of joint study; the novel and the statistical yearbook, the economic theorist and the applied sociologist, each can enlarge the other's understanding of the old, of education, or of power, in Britain today.

During this course, many students felt the need for instruction in some major organisational features of the contemporary British economy. So I prepared a series of lectures. However, it soon became clear that economic performance could not be properly assessed without clearly articulated criteria for assessment, and study of the conflicts that might arise among such criteria. The preparation of this book thus grew naturally out of problems of teaching and research. For it became clear that existing economic theory, while providing frequently plausible accounts of business, consumer and governmental behaviour and motivation, is seldom much help in deciding whether an economy has performed well or badly during a given period. We find ourselves left with a number of plus scores, a few minuses, many disagreements, and no way of striking a balance.

Yet economics is nearer now than ever to 'furnishing a body of settled conclusions immediately applicable to policy'.[1] It was Keynes who denied this; it is a measure of his achievement that the old joke 'Six economists, seven opinions', now amuses where once it enraged. Once the main features of an economy are determined by empirical enquiry, most contemporary economists would reach similar conclusions regarding the effects of most possible economic policies or events. They would differ, like other people, on what effects were *desirable* (or even on what policies should be rejected whatever their effects). But in *analysis* they would apply similar methods and reach similar conclusions and predictions. Therefore, the time is ripe to look for the evaluative criteria to apply to these agreed results.

2. ECONOMICS AS A SCIENCE

Much of the excitement of economics today comes from its status as an emerging science. But, as a science, it has special difficulties to overcome.

(i) Controlled experiment is difficult; instead, one must see what happens and draw conclusions. The physicist can vary the volume and temperature of a gas, and measure the pressure under adjusted conditions. The economist cannot expect the Government to vary the volume of employment so that he may observe the consequences. He has to rely on theory, together with conclusions drawn from past statistical series.

(ii) Economics is involved, as physics is not, with value-judgments. Such apparently neutral formulae as 'Never interfere with market price formation' or 'Allow democratic decisions at elections to determine economic structure' are not genuinely value-free. Voters have values; market prices reflect existing economic power, and are only right if that is right.

(iii) The great revolutions in physics—those of Newton and Einstein —depended on the development of new mathematical tools to express new concepts derived from experimental evidence. Economics has only recently begun to make its own tools for its own problems, instead of borrowing hopefully from more developed sciences.

---

[1] Keynes denies that this is the object of economic analysis in the introduction to the pre-war series of *Cambridge Economic Handbooks*, e.g. Robertson, *Money*, Nisbet, 1922, p.v.

(iv) Physicists co-operate with other sciences in more or less equally advanced stages of sophistication. Economists share their *methods* with more deterministic, developed disciplines like engineering and mathematics, but their *interests* are closer to much younger studies, such as sociology, which lack highly-developed and testable theories.

For these and other reasons, superficial analogies between economics and physics should be avoided.

However, in a crucial sense, economics is a science, capable of giving answers needed in policy formulation. As physical scientists constantly remind laymen, the essence of a science is not the mechanical, judgment-free transformation of data into results by known rules. It is a set of methods, constantly being enlarged and improved, for transferring knowledge about the past into judgments about the future. Scientific advance consists of making such judgments more precise, and the body of theory underlying them more simple and more general. The three lines of advance in modern economics are marginal, linear, and Keynesian.

3. MARGINALISM REVIEWED

Marginal analysis considers the response of consumers, firms and economies to small changes, on certain assumptions regarding their motives. In a world of large changes, this method is subject both to abuse and to cheap parody. Properly considered, it consists of truths of logic —statements of the status of 'All bachelors are unmarried' or 'Twice two are four', though far less obvious. It is a fallacy that truths of logic are useless in describing the world. Even a mathematical tautology like $e^{i\pi} + 1 = 0$, while implicit in the definitions of the terms,[1] is subtle and important. The severity of the depression of the early 1930s in Britain was largely due to the failure of governments and economists to recognise that budget deficits, in slump, are usually necessary and sufficient for at least some recovery, while surpluses impede it[2]; yet, given a few (almost certainly true) assumptions, this statement is a tautology! The central tautology of marginal analysis is this: to have as much as

---

[1] If we define e as the limit of $\left(1 + \dfrac{1}{n}\right)^n$ as n becomes very large and give i and π suitably related definitions, the statement can be proved by pure logic.

[2] Keynes and Bevin and McKenna stood out on the Macmillan Committee (set up in the late 1920s to investigate the monetary system) against fiscal 'economies' as a cure for recession. See Bullock, *Bevin*, Vol. 1, Heinemann, 1960, pp. 423-35.

possible of anything, it must be impossible to increase the quantity by any small variation in the balance among resources used to get it.[1] This implies subtler tautologies about resource use. For example:

(a) Assuming for simplicity that we can measure and add up the 'utilities' that we enjoy from each unit of each commodity consumed,[2] an *individual* maximises his total utility only if he consumes such quantities of each product as will equate the addition to utility made by the last pennyworth of each. For only then can he make no gain in his position by any small transfer of spending.

(b) A *firm* maximises profit when the return on the last ('marginal') penny spent is the same irrespective of where it is spent (on advertising or production; on making cars or making tractors; on skilled workers or machines; and so on). For otherwise profit can be raised by transferring that last penny, from the line where it earns less to the more fruitful use.

(c) At any given set of relative prices of goods and services, a *community* cannot maximise output unless any two workers, in similar places and conditions, receive identical rewards for identical work. Otherwise, since wages reflect extra product, workers could raise total output by moving from low-wage to high-wage jobs. (Notice that they will tend to do just this; and that, by moving, workers raise the wage in the line of production where they are becoming scarcer, and lower it where they are getting more plentiful, until equilibrium is reached.)

The general principle is called *Pareto optimality*[3]. It indicates that, to guarantee a best solution to any problem, we need to know that no small change can improve the solution. (Clearly this is not *sufficient*: a big change might.)

Marginalism, then, is tautologous but useful. It tells us what we need, but what suffices, for efficiency. When applied to the assessment of an economy, marginalism has one great advantage and one great disadvantage compared to its application to consumer or firm. The advantage is that indivisibilities become far less important. The disadvantage is that valuations (which could reasonably be assumed given to firms or consumers, as relative prices) become either policy variables or determined by the system.

[1] Cf. I. M. D. Little, *Critique of Welfare Economics*, 2nd ed., Oxford, 1957, chapter VIII.

[2] All the important results obtained with these assumptions can be reached, with more effort, by much weaker ones. Little, op. cit., chs. 1-2; J. R. Hicks, *Revision of Demand Theory*, Oxford, 1958.

[3] Little, op. cit., pp. 85-87.

Indivisibilities arise for the firm when equalisation of the marginal return of expenditures tells a small business, for instance, to hire 0·3 accountants per week. If it tells the community to employ 100,000·3 the approximations involved are less important. As regards valuations, an individual firm or consumer is usually too small a part of the market to affect prices much. In optimising, he takes them as given. But the prices created by the relative strengths of supply and demand do not necessarily reflect a true estimate either of the relative scarcity of factors and products, or of the relative need for them; market power of producers (degree of monopoly) and of consumers (income distribution) bias this estimate.

Marginalism can interpret but not justify economic behaviour. It can never justify an economic system. For example, it is sometimes mistakenly argued that, since employers go on hiring each type of worker until the last hour hired adds so little to output as to fall to the same level as the wage-cost, the wage measures some sort of 'real value' of the worker, his 'contribution to output'[1]. Of course, both average and marginal productivity of labour—and hence wages and employment—depend on mechanisation more than morality. All marginalism tells us about wages is that, once they are set in the market (or by contract or bargain or Government), their level determines a unique profit-maximising employment for each firm.[2]

4. KEYNESIANISM REVIEWED

Keynesian methods begin by rejecting the 'fallacy of composition'[3]—the belief that what is true of (or good for) the part must also apply to the whole. Some neo-classical economists seemed to argue that long-term structural unemployment was impossible even in slump, because workers could always make it worth businessmen's while to employ them by accepting wage cuts. Keynes pointed out that, while a fall in the money wage of a small group of workers would indeed raise the employment

[1] J. K. Galbraith, *The Affluent Society*, Pelican, 1962, chapter 4, attributes this view to far more economists than really ever held it. Cf. M. Lipton, The Mythology of Affluence, *New Left Review*, Jan.-Feb. 1966.

[2] A firm, to maximise profit in the short run, will 'saturate' its capital with labour at the ruling (market-determined or union-negotiated) wage, until the value of the (diminishing) addition to the product, by the worker whom it is just worthwhile to employ, is as low as the (non-diminishing) wage.

[3] P. Samuelson, *Economics: An Introductory Analysis*, 6th edn., 1964, p. 11.

opportunities of that group, a fall in money wages as a whole would lead to competitive price-cutting. Thus real wages would not fall. Even if monopolistic practices impeded price cuts, the fall in the general level of real wages would reduce the purchasing power of the workers. These form the main buying group (a) by sheer weight of numbers and (b) because they spend a larger share of income than their employers. A fall in real wages, therefore, could as well cut as raise employment levels. Keynes argued that lower rates of interest, in slump conditions, were as unlikely as lower wages to restore business confidence enough to revive investment and bring about the upturn.[1]

The central Keynesian argument is as follows.

(a) Tautologically, the *earnings* of workers and profit-and-rent-receivers in any year must equal the value of their *product*. But people can use earnings only to save, to consume domestic output, or to buy imports; and the product can be only investment goods (machines, buildings), consumer goods, or export goods. If exports equal imports (and if changes in consumer goods stocks are negligible[2]), then actual savings must equal the value of investment goods produced in the year. 'Savings equals investment' is an identity (truth of logic, tautology).

(b) However, no tautology equates *planned* saving and *planned* investment—not in an advanced monetary economy with little central planning. The farmer who uses some of his time to dig an irrigation canal devotes that proportion of his income and output, automatically, to saving and to investment. The dictatorship that forces producers to set aside effort to make investment-goods does the same. But when one man plans to save in an economy of decentralised decisions, there is no guarantee that someone else plans to invest the same amount.

(c) In such an economy, therefore, the community's savings plans can be frustrated. If savers try to set aside more than investment planners, public and private, are prepared to invest, savers cut their own demand for consumer goods without creating compensatory demand for investment goods. So the people who made those consumer goods find

---

[1] J. M. Keynes, *General Theory of Employment, Interest and Money*, Macmillan, 1936, pp. 219-20.

[2] Alternatively we can treat additions to stocks as investment, and the use of money to buy these additions as saving. For Keynes, physical investment, export surplus or stock accumulation have a main feature in common: provision of current incomes (and hence consumer demand) ahead of output for those incomes to buy (supply)

themselves jobless. They therefore spend less and cause a *multiplier*[1] reduction in employment because the workers who made goods for them find themselves jobless, spend less, and so on. This process goes on until the national income has fallen enough to lower savings plans sufficiently to equal investment plans. This equilibrium level of national income, where savings plans equal investment plans (so that both sets of plans can be satisfied consistently), may be well below full employment.[2] Since neither wage nor interest-rate reductions suffice to produce equilibrium, it is restored by movements in the level of national product (income). One type of inflation is caused by an excess, at full employment, of planned investment over planned saving; it can be described in the same multiplier terms.

The multiplier—the ratio between extra investment and the extra final incomes created through the process of spending and employing —tells the government how much it must spend, to create full employment; or draw in by taxation, to slow down some forms of inflation. Such methods fail unless the unbalance between goods and money, which causes unemployment (not enough money) or inflation (not enough goods), is caused by general and widespread unbalance between demand and supply. For example, the British economy in recent years has featured unemployment 'black spots' in Northern Ireland along

---

[1] R. F. Kahn, The Relation between Home Investment and Unemployment, *Economic Journal*, 1931, pp. 173-98. Suppose everyone spends $\frac{2}{3}$ of extra income on home-produced output, and saves the rest (or uses it to buy imports). Then a new building, costing £1 million in incomes (wages and profits), will produce $\frac{2}{3}$ of £1 million more domestic incomes as the initial incomes are spent; ($\frac{2}{3}$ of $\frac{2}{3}$) of £1 million as the second round of incomes is spent; and so on. 'Ultimately' the total income will be £1 million multiplied by $(1 + \frac{2}{3} + (\frac{2}{3})^2 + (\frac{2}{3})^3 \ldots)$

which adds up, after an infinite number of rounds of spending, to $\dfrac{1}{1 - \frac{2}{3}}$, i.e. £3 million. In this case the multiplier is 3. None of this tells us if the new income is matched by more goods or by higher prices (what does this depend on?) nor does it take account of the *accelerator* effect of rising demand on businessmen's investment plans. This is done by P. Samuelson, Interaction between the Multiplier Analysis and the Principle of Acceleration, *Review of Economics and Statistics*, May 1939.

[2] To apply his analysis to employment as well as to income, Keynes measures income in 'wage-units'; he assumes there is only one possible level of employment for each level of real gross national product. In the very short run, with little mobility of labour (let alone of capital) among industries, the assumption is reasonable. In the long run, with technical change, it is not. Keynesian analysis cannot explain both income and employment as part of the same process without specifying a long-run relationship between capital and labour (causes) and output (effect).

with booming regions in Southern England. General reflation along Keynesian lines affects both areas. Even specific public works in depressed Northern Ireland might not have the desired regional impact if the newly employed workers spent their incomes on goods made in booming Southern England. Different, even opposite, problems prevail in different parts of the British economy. Smooth, general, minimally interventionist Keynesian techniques are unlikely to suffice to solve them.

What is more, great care must be used in applying Keynesian techniques by governments, not only for the rather academic reason that ill-timed intervention might worsen economic instability,[1] but because assessment of the impact of government measures is very complicated. We often read that the government, by budgeting for a deficit (or surplus), pumps money into (or out of) the economy and thus fights slump (or inflation). Our regional example shows this is over-simple, but it may even be false. A budget may have a big deficit, but collect its taxes mainly from the poor and distribute outlays mainly to the rich, thus causing the economy to save more and spend less. This may outweigh the direct 'money-creating' effect of the deficit.

Nevertheless, Keynesian multiplier analysis is a powerful tool in advanced economies, as long as demand fluctuation rather than resource imbalance (or shortage) is the major hindrance to economic progress. The analysis applies to any aggregate relation between money and goods. Investment means money-now (wages to workers making the machinery or buildings) without goods-now; so do exports, or the printing of money, or the easing of credit. All these will raise the level of output if there are idle resources in several parts of the economy, or good mobility of workers or machines from slack to busy sectors. Otherwise the income rise will be confined mainly to prices, and will affect money incomes, not real output.

5. LINEAR METHODS

The methods of splitting the economy into sectors that enable us to

---

[1] M. Friedman, *Essays in Positive Economics*, paints a horrifying picture of Government counter-cyclical policies making things worse and worse unless perfectly timed; and Little, in Worswick and Ady, *The British Economy in the 1950s*, Oxford 1962, pp. 71, 274-6, seems to suggest that British interventions worsened fluctuation by such mistiming. But surely this is far too strong; a comparison of the relatively uncontrolled U.S. recessions of the 1950s with those in the U.K., in their effects on both income and employment, makes it clear that imperfect intervention is better than none.

apply marginal and Keynesian techniques to calculating policy consequences are related to *linear economics*, because they make simplifying assumptions that enable the familiar curves of economic analysis (showing quantity demanded or supplied as varying with price or cost) to be approximated by straight lines. In *input-output analysis*, considered in a little more detail on pp. 168–74 below, the economy is represented as a table showing the flows of commodities among industries (steel to machine-tool makers, coal to steelmakers, etc.) as well as to final consumers. To use this table for prediction as well as description, we need assumptions about the implications, for flows among industries, of changes in the size and composition of final consumer demand. The simplest assumption is that output is a *linear function* of input, i.e.

(a) constant cost: to double steel output doubles the cost of production; and

(b) fixed proportions: such doubling does not alter the best proportions of combining labour, coal, iron, sulphuric acid, etc., in steel manufacture.

Similar assumptions are made in *linear programming*, in which efficient points of production are found. These will be Pareto optimal (p.4), provided that production is a linear function of factor inputs. In *growth theory*, smooth growth (100, 110, 121, 133·1, . . .) is usually assumed, because it is hard to predict fluctuations—but also because smooth growth can easily be given linear representation.[1]

It is surprising how close a fit to reality these naïve linear assumptions represent. Theory is increasingly able to take account of non-linearities, and though those caused by increasing returns to scale are still a serious problem. However, experimental work in input-output analysis shows that non-linearities are generally fairly small in the short run.[2]

---

[1] Suppose our model yields a steady-growth prediction. Then, if Y_t is output in year t, we expect
$$Y_t = Y_o e^{rt}.$$
This looks non-linear and thus awkward to test: but
$$Y_t / Y_{t-1} = e^r,$$
and taking natural logarithms
$$\ln Y_t - \ln Y_{t-1} = r \ln e = r$$
and that prediction can be checked. Of course this is an absurdly simple case, but the principle is the same for all relations like this.

[2] In a lecture to the Oxford Economic Society in 1962, Professor Richard Stone showed that, in ten years of Belgian input-output data, fewer than 1 per cent of the hundreds of coefficients had changed by as much as 2 per cent. (Belgium and the U.K. are both slow growers!)

6. SOME WARNINGS: SCIENTISM

Economics is developing the techniques required of a science. The underdeveloped theory behind some of these techniques means that applied economics demands judgment even more than does the application of more advanced sciences. Some of the dangers will now be spelled out, mainly so that the reader may be warned against possible aberrations in this and other books, but also as a reminder to the writer. The three forces that threaten fruitful application of economics from within (as opposed to the misguided amateurism that impedes it from without)[1] are scientism, theorism and cynicism. The atmosphere in which these evils flourish is a morbid fear of value-judgments: an unnatural child of half-understood philosophy and misplaced intellectual politeness.

Scientism is the doctrine that all sciences should be modelled on the 'hypothetico-deductive' method allegedly typical of physics. Theory is to grow from observation alone, and elaborate structures are out of place unless tested at once. Some economists sometimes act as if they believed economics to be a fully developed science (as nineteenth-century physicists thought their discipline was). A celebrated American research group is alleged to have the motto over its door: 'Take the facts into the basement and beat the theory out of them'.[2] In other words, feed all the data (prices, outputs, purchases, etc.) into a computer, and let the facts make hypotheses for you. This approach is a naïve misconception of the methods of physical science. Its outgrowths in economics are:

(a) The belief that enough observations produce conclusions of limitless generality, applicable even to the Martian economy;[3]

(b) Neglect of the fact, stressed by Professor Hicks, that 'economics is above all a *social* science' that has to co-operate with politics, psychology, sociology and anthropology at important points, together with misplaced nouveau-riche contempt for the 'primitive' state of quantitative methods in some neighbouring disciplines; and

(c) Excessive attachment to mathematical methods as ends rather than means.

The main danger of economic scientism is that it may discredit economic science. When one of the most distinguished economists in

---

[1] Even the better sources are highly fallible; a commentator on German affairs suggested in *The Guardian* that rising imports in Germany in 1964 were increasing the dangers of inflation!

[2] This excellent joke is due to F. M. Fisher.

[3] This suggestion was made in complete seriousness (in discussion), to Professor Myrdal by a leading American economist.

the Western world hands the President of Egypt the solution to his nation's problems in twenty-two equations, tears as well as laughter are in order. The use of quantitative methods, and advanced mathematical techniques, could easily be discredited by such procedures. Even techniques of physical simulation and engineering-analogy models, as properly used by Phillips, Goodwin, Orcutt and others,[1] are immensely valuable additions to the economist's toolbox.

Even in methodology, scientism can harden useful advice to researchers into harsh and inappropriate prescriptions. The Popper-Samuelson operational approach, in its most flexible and useful form, holds that the authority of social, or other, scientists is limited to statements that could, in principle, be tested and, if false, disproved by any experimenter.[2] This useful guide to empirical research, if pushed too far, turns into a dogma that inhibits fruitful theorising by confronting it too early with a reality that is too complex. Rigour is not the same as *rigor mortis*.

Scientism is easily accounted for. Economics has advanced further since 1880 than in the two thousand years before that date. But in the explanation of the facts, motivations and interactions of personal, group and governmental behaviour, it is rather like post-Renaissance astrophysics. Economics has had its Tycho Brahe and Kepler, Copernicus and Galileo, in such figures as Marx, Marshall, Walras, Wicksell and Keynes; it still awaits its Newtons. Yet economists rightly use the latest post-Einsteinian mathematics to express their pre-Newtonian theoretical insights. The techniques are brilliant, and there is a danger of being so blinded by glare as to mistake light for landscape.

7. THEORISTS AND CYNICS

Theorism, like scientism, sometimes appears to cultivate mathematics as end rather than means, but otherwise the two are poles apart. The victim of theorism is less concerned with generality or operationalism than with imposing upon the unfortunate facts whatever pet dodge,

---

[1] G. Orcutt, *Microanalysis of Socio-economic Systems: a Simulation Study*, Harper, 1961; Phillips's use of hydro-dynamic models to simulate the flows of money among economic sectors; and the use of computers to see what happens to complicated methods of prediction as the sample of observations, on which the prediction is based, is reduced.

[2] K. Popper, *The Logic of Scientific Discovery*, Hutchinson, 1962, *passim*; P. Samuelson, *Foundations of Economic Analysis*, Harvard, 1957, preface.

curve or equation takes his fancy. Every economist (if he is any good) sometimes falls into this trap, because he should enjoy his work, appreciate intellectual beauty, and seek to combine both, through theorism, with the pleasure Father gets from playing with his son's toy trains. But this theoretical self-indulgence is as damaging to public respect for economics as its more obvious political counterpart, the use of analysis to disguise the convictions of the analyst. Moreover, love of gadgetry often leads a writer to mistake his gadgets for originality. A great deal of modern development economics, even when it has something really important to say about interactions between population growth and economic change, seems so devoted to graphical techniques that almost every page is decorated by graphs in which two unmeasurable variables are connected by an untestable curve (often intersecting with another, at a putative 'equilibrium').

Professional cynicism is in part a healthy reaction against the aberrations described above. If economists, captivated by tricks, tools or tomorrows, produce beautiful, rigorous or ultra-general theories of no conceivable relevance, they deserve a little mockery. But great care is needed. Most of the mockers (including some of the most celebrated) are not themselves capable of deep abstract logic; and such logic underlies much of pure economic theory, whose relevance to practical problems may be real though hidden. The greatest theorists always recognise the need to keep practical application in mind[1]—even if sometimes right at the back of it. But professional cynics, who often contribute little or nothing, may by their mockery of what they popularise damage the self-confidence, and thus the productivity, of their more fruitful colleagues.

There is a group of cynics more worthy of respect: not frustrated theorists, but people who, after making real contributions, conclude that their tools are faulty beyond repair. This has happened with the technique of fitting observations (and thus explaining them) known as regression analysis and with the 'insoluble' problem of comparing differently structured bundles of outputs (pp. 30–34). In both cases, the cynic is disillusioned because he expected techniques to do too much: to fill the role of theories.

8. CAUSATION AND REGRESSION

Suppose we try to explain yearly changes in butter consumption by

[1] J. R. Hicks, *Value and Capital* (1st edn.), Oxford 1938: end of Preface.

price changes. The *regression equation* is the 'best fit' linking dependent to explanatory variable. The *correlation coefficient* tells us how strong the relation is. If it is significant (in the sense that the risk of a chance relation is small enough) we must assume that it is *in some sense* causal. For example, in Britain, yearly figures show a correlation between wireless licenses issued and road accidents; not because drivers are distracted by car radios, but because the same phenomenon, growing affluence, causes more purchases of both cars and wireless sets. If, as is alleged, the Swedish birth rate is correlated with certain variables indicating stork migration, then some complicated causal chain links the two—though as brothers or cousins, not father and son, in the family of facts.

However, from the scientifically necessary assumption that strong statistical relationships are causal, we must never infer that they are explanatory. Only theories can explain. No matter how often we observe the fizzing of sodium when water is added, we have not explained the relationship by demonstrating it.

This confusion between explanation and demonstration is central in the worries felt by even the mildest of cynics about *collinearity*. When we attempt the statistical explanation of a phenomenon in terms of several other measurable phenomena, we usually explain too much. Suppose I measure British production, for a number of years, and estimate an equation linking it to inputs of labour and machinery; the trouble is that rises in labour inputs are themselves related (as cause, effect and joint decision) to rises in machinery inputs, so that my causal explanations of output rises are not independent. Blaming the statistical tools in cases of collinearity is a bad substitute for finding a better theory to test: one in which the causal factors are either independent or related in a specified way.

A similar error, which leads us into the whole problem of value-judgments, is despondency in face of index-number problems (see pp. 30–34 below). Essentially the problem is that we cannot compare two differently composed bundles of goods if the prices of goods, relative to each other, are not the same in both bundles. Are 2 apples + 3 oranges better than 3 apples + 2 oranges? The answer depends on the relative valuation of apples and oranges. If tastes and production patterns are fairly stable, this relative valuation will change little, so that the comparison can be made in terms of the ruling prices. Even then, however, our comparison assumes that the price system somehow reflects community preference, and is hence 'right'. But prices in fact reflect the tastes of the rich more than the poor, of spenders more than of savers; and the per-unit production costs of a strong monopolist far more than those of a small competitor. So we should beware of using relative prices as tests of comparative values. This should worry us before the question of how to make such comparisons when relative orange and apple prices change. These changes are likely to reflect changes in costs or tastes—but also in distribution of income or monopoly power, so that our index-number problem is really a restatement of the fact that different arrangements of income and power in an economy lead to different patterns of preference and production. The only way to choose among such patterns is to make a choice. The price system is never a substitute for judgments of value, even when all prices are stable between the periods whose welfare we are comparing. The index-number problem merely reflects this fact, which is logically prior to it.

This book attempts to develop criteria for the performance of an economy and to look at the British performance since 1955, by the standards of its past and of other countries, in the light of these criteria. There are important alternative approaches to industrial economics[1] and economic policy[2]. The approach of this book has been chosen because it was felt necessary to analyse the criteria by which we assess economic performance, and to discuss policy in the light of such criteria; and because criteria of performance and principles of economic planning are the same. A discussion of performance in the light of these principles may dispel the emotive fog that surrounds 'planning' as a God-word in contemporary rhetoric.

[1] D. Burn, *Structure of British Industry* (2 vols), C.U.P., 1958; G. C. Allen, *British Industries and their Organization*, Longmans, 1961.

[2] Worswick and Ady (ed.), *The British Economy 1945-50*, O.U.P., 1952, and op cit.; C. Dow, *The Management of the British Economy*, C.U.P., 1963; W. Beckerman and associates, *The British Economy in 1975*, C.U.P., 1965.

CHAPTER ONE

Policy Aims, Performance Criteria and Planning Structure

I. THE AIMS OF ECONOMIC POLICY

(a) Five attitudes to evaluation

To his technical and professional equipment, the economist must add the ability—and will—to analyse carefully the logic of evaluative utterances, and to state explicitly the moral premises of his argument. The other four common approaches to value-judgments by the economist are the acceptance of *ad hoc* moralising, subservience to external moral authority, positivism and 'welfare minimalism'. The first view is distressingly common. Not merely the Sunday papers but also the best articles in the best technical journals are full of dogmatic (if implicit) moralising. A moment's thought concerning the emotive, advertising connotations of two of the commonest terms in an economic Great Debate—free trade and protection—will make this clear. More often, *ad hoc* moralising is disguised in the assumption that the reader will accept, without argument, that any policy stabilising prices or raising the growth rate is *ipso facto* good; or that the economic good is some sort of coherent absolute, so that a policy either promotes it or does not, without possibility of ambiguities.

Subservience to external moral authority is the commonest position of the student of society. Whether that authority be the New Testament on camels and needles, the Buddha on asceticism, Marx on the immorality of private property or a contemporary pundit on the natural moral virtue of stable prices, the position is the same. There is nothing unscientific about explicitly accepting certain moral criteria, provided they are consistent. However, as Kant showed,[1] such acceptance is amoral. There is no element of moral decision in commending something just because it is the will of God, Marx, Henry Ford, or the majority, whose will is defined as good. Since humans are creatures of environment, economists often accept external moral dogma without fully realising it. In such moments they risk being blinkered to reality: as when they seek to punish the thriftless poor by hunger in old age, to make incentives towards providence. Moreover, semi-conscious acceptance of dogma seldom leads to consistency. If it does not, scientific analysis may become impossible (if, for example, one tries to maximise price stability and economic growth at once, because both are Right).

Positivism in philosophy involves many things, but the characteristic most appealing to social scientists is the rejection of statements unverifiable in principle as meaningless. Linked to this is the claim that judgments of value are no more than emotive utterances like 'Hurrah' or 'Boo'.[2] This view limits the economist's role to analysing the consequences of various forms of behaviour, i.e. to if-then statements. Most of economics does demand pure analysis of this type. But the positivist approach is still very dangerous. Everybody has a structure of values. This structure determines what is chosen for analysis, what facts are selected as relevant (especially in a social context, where the multitude of variables often means there is no right or wrong choice of relevant facts, as there is in physics), and what implicit values are inculcated in the analysis.

For example, supporters of extensive state intervention in the economic system usually believe that substantial economies of scale exist in industry, so that private ownership involves the choice between wastefully small-scale operation and dangerous concentration of power. Opponents of state action believe that few such economies of scale exist. They argue that unification of control (especially in state hands) produces unwieldy, top-heavy administrative arrangements. This argument could and should be conducted scientifically. But the effect of the positivist rejection of the relevance of value judgments is to make both disputants conceal value premises and seek to present their findings in the if-then terms of pure analysis. This is easy to do without any dishonesty. In this case, each disputant selects industries exhibiting the characteristic claimed. The socialist specialises in railways, the liberal

---

[1] I. Kant, *The Moral Law* (ed. and tr. Paton), Hutchinson, 1948, esp. pp. 87-90.
[2] A. J. Ayer, *Language, Truth and Logic*, 1st ed. Gollancz, 1936, pp. 158-62.

in road haulage firms. Discussion becomes hopelessly confused. Economics is a policy-directed science, and economists are people with views of their own. It does no good to suppress them.

Welfare minimalism is the attempt to separate problems of the size of the national output from problems of the distribution of that output. An economic change can be said to increase potential welfare if

(a) the gainers would still retain some gain, after compensating the losers for their losses; and

(b) before the change, the losers could not, without incurring a loss larger than that involved in the change, have bribed the gainers to desist from it.[1]

Unfortunately the hypothetical nature of the test divorces this criterion from relevance to policy. For if the losers are not in fact compensated, and if the redistribution of income involved in the change is judged un-favourable (e.g. from coalminers to loan sharks), we are still left to compare some improvement in total product with some deterioration in its distribution. And the effect on welfare remains unassessed. Welfare economics is an interesting logical structure, but almost irrelevant to the selection and testing for compatibility of criteria of economic policy.[2]

So all four alternatives fail us, and we are left to plunge into the problem of the logical status of value judgments. Economists are rightly reluctant to do this. It is not part of their training, and seems pretentious however necessary it is. No more is attempted here than the construction of a framework that relates economic criteria of policy (or planning) to the factual evidence about fulfilment of these criteria.

(b) Naturalism and bridge-words

Clearly, evaluative statements like 'Murder is wrong' are of a different logical type from factual statements like 'Ten murders were committed in Oxford in 1959'. The sort of evidence adduced to support the two statements is different in type. With the factual statement, we refer to the records, or to the details of the cases from which the records were built up. With the evaluative statement, we refer to the results or motives of

---

[1] The first suggestion is due to N. Kaldor and J. R. Hicks; the demonstration of its inadequacy in certain special cases (where both a move from A to B and a return to A from B would be recommended) and the suggestion of the second, to T. de Scitovsky; and the demonstration that, in most important cases, both are necessary but not sufficient, to I. M. D. Little (*Critique of Welfare Economics*, ch. VI, where the history of the discussion is summarised).

[2] *Ibid.*, and J. de V. Graaff, *Theoretical Welfare Economics*.

the act condemned, to the consequences of rejecting the evaluation, or to a structure of values (or a principle) in the light of which murder is wrong in itself.

For logical reasons, the factual statement and the evaluative statement cannot be supported by exactly the same evidence. The different logical structure of supporting argument explains why we can never justify purely evaluative statements from facts alone. That is why Hume denied the propriety of moving from 'is' to 'ought'. That too, is the basis of the attack made by Moore and Hare on the 'naturalistic fallacy'.[1] Hare explains this fallacy as follows: If I give a set of purely factual statements and define a moral expression in terms of these statements alone, then the identification of the two becomes tautologous. But whatever moral principles or judgments are, they are not tautologies. If, for example, I accept the utilitarian principle that the good is that which promotes the greatest happiness of the greatest number,[2] and call things good if and only if they do this, it then becomes logically absurd to use the word 'good' to commend the greatest happiness of the greatest number itself; for the principle has been defined as good, and it is absurd to commend something for conforming to a definition.

The anti-naturalist argument is forceful. But the man of common sense—and certainly the social scientist wishing to make intelligent use of evaluative statements—must protest at the extension of a perfectly valid point in *logical* theory into an axe with which to cleave the subtle network of descriptive and evaluative implications of our *language*. Almost every word contains descriptive and evaluative elements. In the most important cases, these elements are so related that the word is a bridge between fact and value. It is used to catalogue a situation and to suggest an agreed principle for judging it; to use a *bridge-word* is at once to describe and to assess.

Such bridge-words must not be confused with:

(a) The abuse by propagandists of words like 'democracy' and 'freedom'. Such terms, originally largely descriptive, are now so surrounded by connotations that, unless specially and precisely defined, they have lost all non-evaluative significance.

(b) The well-meaning but dangerous attempt to convert terms that are evaluative in ordinary discourse to descriptive, even quasi-math-

[1] R. M. Hare, *The Language of Morals*, Oxford, 1961, pp. 84-93.
[2] *Ibid.*, pp. 92-3.

ematical uses.[1] This usually leads to an automatic evaluative response in the reader, however scientific the usage intended by the author.

A real bridge-word refers to a fairly complicated and specifiable set of facts or relations, and implies an assessment of it in moral terms. Such words are central in social studies, because they suggest the key concepts around which agreed values have attached themselves to determinable facts or relations. (They do not, of course, justify values; they report that certain values are prevalent among the group using the bridge-word).

Typical is the use of 'responsible' in the phrase 'responsible government'. The word is descriptive of two facts. First the government is both willing and able to respond to situations with decisions. Second, the government is ready, when the time comes, to be held to account for such responses by the electorate. The government is responsible *for* its handling of the situation, its policy, *to* the electorate. The word 'responsible' also expresses and solicits approval for the fact that a government is responsible in both descriptive senses. Here, as usual, a bridge-word depends for its evaluative connotations on the fulfilment of a complex set of factual preconditions.

This opens the door to abuse. Another bridge-word, central in social studies, is 'choice'. This affirms the existence of both a process and an act. First, some person or set of persons is rationally considering whether to perform some action. Second, that person or group correctly believes that, after such consideration, it will pursue the course decided upon. Ratiocination without decision is armchair speculation; decision without thought is mechanical selection. Only when thought and action are linked, in the same person or group of persons, is the situation validly described by use of the word 'choice', with its association of approval of the situation described. The reader might now consider the common argument advanced by persons who approve of the current British cultural scene: that everybody is able to choose either Radio Luxembourg or the BBC Radio Three. (Is the element of rational consideration present?) On the other hand, the high valuation given to choice in many societies is not compatible with the continued tolerance of inequality

[1] T. Veblen, *Theory of the Leisure Class*, Macmillan (New York), 1899, pp. 97-101, is a defence of such usages, unconvincing in view of what happens later in the book; K. Marx, *Capital*, vol. 1 (tr. Moore and Aveling), Allen and Unwin, 1938, pp. 194-203, is an attempt to formalize mathematically the concept of 'exploitation'. Notice the choice of a definition which increases the size of 'exploitation', however.

B

leading to a poverty so severe as to remove, from the poorest, the conditions for implementing vital choices; people on National Assistance may think about moving from the slums, but can they choose to do so?

(c) 'Aim' as a bridge-word

In economic analysis, there is no alternative to clarifying the logical status of standards applied to policy evaluations. In this chapter, we try to isolate and define the major aims of economic policy, and to account for the favourable valuation attached to them. First, though, we discuss 'aim of economic policy'. 'Aim' in this sense is a typical fact-value bridge-word in the sense explained above.

Suppose a politician or historian describes national prestige as an aim of de Gaulle's policy after 1958. This implies that:

(a) The persons advocating and/or executing this policy approved of national prestige;

(b) They believed the policy would have the desired result. (Notice that people, not policies, have aims. People use policies as archers use arrows, to achieve aims, hit targets).

Unless the speaker specified that the policy was ill-chosen, he would be taken as strongly suggesting (though not logically implying) that:

(c) The policy was likely to achieve the aim desired by those pursuing it.

(d) The writer approves of the aim. 'Aim' has favourable connotations (see the damning word 'aimless'). This approval is only hinted at. The hint may easily be dispelled, explicitly ('But national prestige is a narrow and selfish goal') or implicitly ('Fascist policy has always had such aims'), by invoking stronger evaluative terms on the other side.

How does the situation change if a man describes the aims of his own present policy? Suppose de Gaulle himself says, 'My current policy aims at enhancing the national prestige of France'. The implications (a) and (b) remain; (c) and (d), however, are transformed from hints into logical implications.

I cannot consistently specify an aim of my present policy and then deny that the policy will achieve its aim. It is doubtful if I can even say that my policy is unlikely to achieve its aim (if de Gaulle said this, his real aim would be, not to raise French prestige, but to maximise the likelihood of such a rise). I could, of course, pass a historian's judgment on my past policy and say it never, in retrospect, had much chance of attaining my objectives. But it is logically mistaken to do this about my policy at the time of utterance (Cf. 'I am going for a walk from 1.00 a.m. to 2.00 a.m.; my aim is to get sunburnt; I know the sun never shines then, and that one gets sunburnt only when the sun shines').

Plainly I cannot disapprove of my own aims. A rational objective is what my reason tells me it is right for me to do. This remains true, whether that 'right' be the ultimate in personal egotism, in disinterested action, or (as always in politics) in some combination of the two, some mixture of idealism and vanity, logical pursuit of principle and logical pursuit of popularity and power. I can desire or want something I believe to be immoral; but if I aim at something, I am, to a certain extent, morally committed to it.

If I speak of 'an aim of economic policy', then the act of generalisation performs, as powerfully as the personal adoption of the aim and the policy, the task of making (c) and (d) from refutable suggestions into unqualifiable implications. To say 'Greater equality is an aim of economic policy' is to approve of greater equality, and also to claim that some economic policy can achieve this aim. This is because there is no way *not* to have an economic policy. One cannot disapprove of economic policy as such, because a decision to take no thought for the morrow, or to refrain from all State action, is as much an economic policy—with either defined aims or unforeseen results—as the decision to nationalise everything tomorrow.

So, if I say, 'It is an aim of economic policy to increase income per person', I mean that:

(a) Policymakers approve of and/or advocate such increase.

(b) They believe there are possible policies to secure it, and they select political decisions accordingly.

(c) They are right in this belief, i.e. specific policies exist, in the relevant environment, that will cause income per person to rise.

(d) I approve of this objective.

An 'aim of economic policy' is thus a bridge-concept. Descriptively, it attributes to persons an objective and also a state of mind about the relation between objective and means. Evaluatively, it agrees with both the objective and the judgment that it is attainable. To use a bridge-word is not to commit a naturalistic fallacy. It is to refer implicitly both to a general structure of values, agreed by speaker and audience, and to a complex factual situation that can be evaluated in terms of this value-structure.

It is of course possible to select an aim of someone else's policy, or of my own past policy, and disagree with it. But the act of specifying an aim of economic policy (without saying whose, or when) is evaluative as well as descriptive. 'Economic' is not sufficiently specific to act as a qualification. 'X is an aim of economic policy, but not-X is an aim of social policy' is just a mistake. Tools of policy may operate through the economic or social system, or some combination of the two. But an 'aim of economic policy' is merely shorthand for an aim of policy-makers, connected with the economic structure or direction of the nation, and/or carried out mainly by economic means.

The rest of this chapter is concerned with finding some way of ranking objectives; otherwise we may find ourselves with a number of inconsistent aims, an untenable situation. In Chapter 2, we shall select a number of aims of British economic policy since the war, define them, and try to justify them. Chapter 3 examines the extent to which, in recent years, the British economy has achieved its aims. Chapter 4 examines theoretical and statistical evidence concerning the compatibility of these aims.

2. POLICY AIMS AND THE STRUCTURE OF ECONOMIC PLANNING

(a) The nature of economic planning

Government activity, minimal or total, pragmatic or planned, has many economic consequences. The most extreme advocate of laisser-faire will scarcely oppose a publicly organised police force; this has to be paid for, whether by taxation or by borrowing.[1] Which employees are to be attracted into such jobs—what outputs are to be foregone—affects the whole structure of the economy. Moreover, the Government must pay its policemen. Both the raising and the spending of the money affect distribution of income, composition of output and size of product. Such effects were little understood until recent years, but that did not stop them happening.[2] Myrdal has described formal economic planning as the co-ordination of interventions.[3] It is hard to see what is good about

---

[1] Extreme advocates of laisser-faire usually oppose budget deficits. However, suppose the Government has to finance a given amount of expenditure. Surely the Government imposes a more permanent, and less avoidable, restraint on individual choice by taxation than by raising the same sum through borrowing?

[2] In the late 1920s, Lord Norman advocated high interest rates to pull foreign money into London, even with sterling very expensive after the 1925 revaluation. He believed that this did not raise unemployment, but nevertheless it did.

[3] G. Myrdal, *Beyond the Welfare State*, Duckworth, 1961.

refraining from formal planning, since this is required even if we wish only to avoid random, uncalculated, *ad hoc* and unco-ordinated forms of government action. The consequences of Government policy will ensue whether calculated or not. Planning always exposes consequences of policy combinations, with each other and with the expected behaviour of the private sector, that were unforeseen, are undesired, and lead to a modification of the policy package initially proposed.

The more economic aims a country has, the better the case for planning. Suppose any policy successfully directed at one aim has a fifty-fifty chance of damaging another. Then, if growth and price stability are the only aims, a policy aimed at growth has one chance in two of avoiding inconsistency. Add a third aim, and the chance drops to one in four; a fourth, to one in eight; and so on. Moreover, the more complex and detailed the network of central action, the greater the danger of internal contradiction with respect to any single aim. Thus, while people become more confident of democratic checks on governments and thus more willing to allow them to take decisions, planning becomes more important.

Planning is inevitable; but a particular plan (or form of planning, e.g. 'indicative') is judged by its success in achieving the aims of economic policy, and is designed to achieve those aims. Therefore, the problems of stipulating a set of aims for future policy, preparing an economic plan, and evaluating the past performance of an economy are parts of a single problem. We shall regard it as an issue of *maximisation under constraints*. We shall seek to maximise the rate of increase of income per head. The constraints are of three types: factor limitations (availability of different types of machines, workers and land), other aims (need to avoid excessive inflation, unemployment or troubles in the balance of payments), and overall policy limitations (such as the general wish to increase the number of persons receiving higher education as an end in itself, and hence the impossibility of expecting to increase the size of the labour force from age-groups much under 21). To grasp the logic of constrained maximisation, we shall go through a very simple exercise in linear programming; for all its simplicity, the exercise reflects the essence of the problem of centralised decision-making and of economic assessment.

(b) Constrained maximisation: an elementary example

A *production function* shows the output of a product that can be produced from any combination of inputs. Suppose that a farmer, whose land can grow wheat or barley, is faced with the following simplified production functions:

(a) Each ton of barley needs three man-hours of labour per week, and four acres of land.

(b) Each ton of wheat needs five man-hours of labour per week, and two acres of land.

These production functions both exhibit two convenient characteristics: constant returns to scale (doubling output precisely doubles cost, neither more nor less) and fixed factor proportions (whatever the scale of output, the ratio of acres to man-hours is the same). Production functions with both these features are called *linear*, for reasons that will soon be obvious. We may reasonably assume that the farmer maximises profit by maximising output in some sense, for no one farmer is likely to have much effect on price. We therefore look at the frontier of production possibilities, the *efficiency locus*—the set of all combinations of wheat output and barley output, such that it is impossible to get more of either product without some sacrifice of the other. To find this locus from the production functions, we need to know the constraints.

For simplicity, we assume only factor constraints in this example. The farmer has 80 acres of land, and, with his family, is prepared to put in 90 hours' work each week. To make it quite clear what goes on, we shall consider these two constraints separately. Figure 1 shows how the land constraint would affect the attainable outputs if there were no limit on available labour; Figure 2, how labour scarcity would operate if land were unlimited; and Figure 3 (p. 26) how land and labour shortages together limit output.

In Figure 1 we assume 80 acres of land but limitless labour supply. The line CRM illustrates a *linear constraint* due to land. It joins all the maximum combinations of outputs which the farmer's land allows him to produce. For example, suppose he decides to make 20 tons of wheat. From (b) above, each ton needs two acres of land—40 acres in all. So 40 of the 80 acres are left for barley-growing, and from (a) that will make 10 tons of barley (at R on the diagram). At M all the land is used for wheat, at C all for barley. You should check that all the maximal combinations lie on a straight line, as shown in the diagram—and find out why.

In Figure 2, land is assumed unlimited, but the line AUL illustrates the other linear constraint, caused by the weekly limit of 90 hours of labour. At U, labour-time is divided equally between wheat and barley.

Since no land limit is assumed in Figure 2, (a) tells us that 45 man-hours will produce 15 tons of barley, and (b) that the remaining 45 hours will yield 9 tons of wheat. At L, all the labour is producing barley, and at

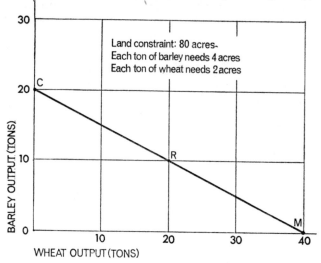

Land constraint: 80 acres.
Each ton of barley needs 4 acres
Each ton of wheat needs 2 acres

BARLEY OUTPUT (TONS)

WHEAT OUTPUT (TONS)

Figure 1

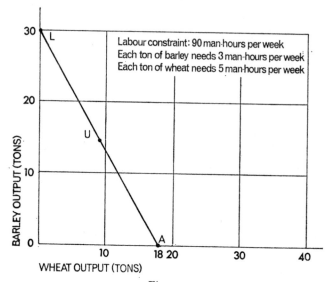

Labour constraint: 90 man-hours per week
Each ton of barley needs 3 man-hours per week
Each ton of wheat needs 5 man-hours per week

BARLEY OUTPUT (TONS)

WHEAT OUTPUT (TONS)

Figure 2

A it is concentrated entirely on wheat. Again a straight line joins the maximal combinations.

In Figure 3 we combine the labour limit of Figure 2 and the land limit of Figure 1, to obtain the full (if very simplified) picture of reality. All the combinations of wheat and barley in the shaded area OABC, in Figure 3, are *feasible*. (The combinations in BCL cannot be made for want of land, though labour is sufficient; in BAM, land is sufficient but the labour constraint is prohibitive; and beyond the 'bent line' LBM both land and labour are insufficient). But while all combinations in the shaded region are feasible, only those on the efficiency locus, the bent line ABC, are efficient. Only at such points is it impossible to

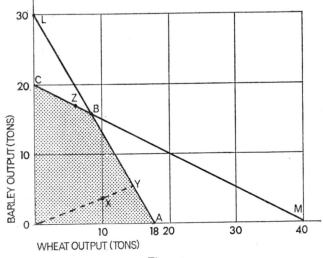

Figure 3

expand output of the products without running into factor limitations (or, indeed, to expand one output without sacrificing some of the other). For instance, production at a point like X always involves waste of factors: draw a line through O and X, and the combination of outputs at which this line cuts ABC always gives more wheat and more barley (at Y).

Indeed, with this linear efficiency locus, we can say a lot more: that A, B or C must be the best operating point for the farmer (assuming that prices are unaffected by his scale of production). The improvement from X to Y is seldom the best that the farmer can do. The slope of AYB indicates that, as the farmer shifts his chosen programme of wheat-barley combinations from Y towards A, 3 lb. of wheat are gained for each 5 lb. of barley lost. If 3 lb. of wheat fetch more than 5 lb. of barley, production at A is more profitable than at Y, *or than at any point between A and Y.* If it pays to shift south-east along YA, then it must pay to shift all the way to A. Similarly, if the plan shifts from Y towards B, 5 lb. of barley are gained for every 3 lb. of wheat lost (notice the dependence on constant-cost, fixed-proportion relationships!) so that, if the market price of 5 lb. of barley is more than that of 3 lb. of wheat, any shift from Y towards B is profitable, i.e. B is the most profitable point on BY. Similarly, unless barley is exactly twice the price of wheat, one of the two points B or C must be better than any point on BC, such as Z (Z is never better than both B and C).

To be precise: if a ton of wheat fetches at least $1\frac{2}{3}$ times as much as a ton of barley, A is best; if barley fetches at least twice as much as wheat, C is best; otherwise B is best. Can you work out exactly why?

In this simple case, profit maximisation by linear programming narrowed down the vast choice of possible outputs into a decision among three possible wheat-barley combinations; consultation of the available market prices then enabled one of these three to be picked. If the decision aimed at some other object than profit maximisation—say the maximisation of calorie value or foreign-exchange yield—then the first part of the programming procedure would be exactly the same. A, B or C is still best. Only the choice among them can be affected by the aim, or by whether the planner is the businessman or the government.[1] The more closely market prices reflect planners' valuations, the less likely is any difference between the operating points selected by private and public planning.

(c) Probabilistic planning

There are many ways in which this elementary scheme needs modification before it can be applied to economic planning. This and the next four sections review these modifications. Firstly, the western mixed economy is not a monolithic planning unit, but a network of private, public and mixed enterprises. The government, having found (on electorally approved criteria of optimality) the optimum feasible output, cannot go ahead and get it produced, just like that. It must use a complex

---

[1] See, for instance, R. Frisch, *Planning for India*, Indian Statistical Institute, 1960, pp. 45-87. If private and social optima diverge, the economy *may* settle down at the wrong optimum unless the State intervenes.

B*

battery of persuasive, incentive and compulsive instruments. The relative chances of success of such methods are discussed at many points in this book. Here two points should be made. First, if the production functions exhibit constant or decreasing returns to scale, and only then, we can prove that incompletely successful controls (pushing only part of the economy in the desired direction, or all the economy only part of the way) are better than no controls. If two products, with similar technologies, both exhibit increasing returns to scale—one much more markedly than the other—an attempt to push resources from the 'weaker' to the 'stronger' scale-economising sector is clearly beneficial if totally successful (assuming both products serve similar purposes, or can be traded abroad). But if such a policy is only partly successful the lost scale economies in the weaker sector, resulting from the transfer, may outweigh the gained scale economies in the stronger sector.[1]

Planning, to succeed under conditions of scale economies, must therefore go the whole hog. That is a powerful argument for direct State control of industries conclusively shown to demonstrate such economies. It buttresses the traditional argument that efficiency in such sectors requires monopoly, whereas the public interest requires reasonably cheap outputs.

A further result of extensive private ownership in a planning system is that good planning has to be *probabilistic*. It is possible to order private firms about, or to apply incentives and disincentives so strong as to amount to orders; but it is self-deception to think this can be done within a framework of choice, or that it will not discourage enterprise. Probabilistic planning is best illustrated by example. Suppose that all nails are produced under constant returns to scale, and that each firm in the nail industry initially produces identical amounts of two types of nail. The planners now decide that the economic programme requires 20 per cent more of one type of nail, and 20 per cent less of the other type. The probabilistic planner estimates that a given incentive will cause half the nail producers to shift 30 per cent of their capacity, a further 25 per cent to shift 20 per cent, and the rest to make no change. The central director simply orders all the producers to shift 20 per cent exactly, and the planner relying on cast-iron incentives seeks vainly for the incentive that will have that effect. In a free-choice economy, planning must include some estimate of how many producers are

---

[1] A proof is available from the author.

affected, and to what degree, by each incentive or permissive action.

(d) Many products and factors

There are not just two products and two factors. This was assumed solely for ease of explanation. But exactly the same method can be applied to many-factor, many-product situations; thus we can specify numerous different types of labour and machine, that cannot be substituted for each other. The 'hill climbing' method of finding the best solution is just as in Figure 3—if the vertex B is better than A, and only then, C may give 'higher' profit still—only now the hill is in many dimensions. If the products, or some of them, feature decreasing returns to scale, the efficiency locus is a curved hill, but can still be approximated by a series of lines similar to those of Figure 3, to any desired degree of accuracy.

The complexity of such a programming situation involves us in political, not mathematical, difficulties. The results may be both surprising and difficult to explain by common sense. Interactions through other products, using raw materials and processed outputs, may demand the restriction of output of an efficiently produced item, in order to transfer resources to something at present made inefficiently. How will an electorate face the choice between a computer and a demagogue under such circumstances?

(e) Less simple production functions

Can the concept of economic optimality be generalised to less rigid production functions than those considered on p. 24? There, no substitution between land and labour was possible; they had to be used in fixed proportions to make either product. For example, the production function for wheat in Figure 3, p. 26, if W is wheat in tons, L is labour in man-hours per week and K is land in acres, was

$$(1) \qquad W = \text{the smaller of} \begin{cases} 0 \cdot 2 L \\ 0 \cdot 5 K \end{cases}.$$

Many observed production functions, however, show some substitutability between inputs. Often they take on so-called *Cobb-Douglas* form.[1] One might observe a firm for many years and conclude

$$(2) \qquad W = 3L^{0 \cdot 75} K^{0 \cdot 25}.$$

---

[1] It has been shown in a brilliant paper that, if we 'add up' a lot of production functions for *firms* (like (1) but with different values for the coefficients in different firms then—corresponding, perhaps, to land and labour of varying quality) that we will often get a Cobb-Douglas for the wheat *industry*! H. S. Houthakker, The Pareto Distribution and the Cobb-Douglas Production Function in Activity Analysis, *Review of Economic Studies*, 1955, pp. 27–31.

Wheat output is some constant, *times* labour input to a fractional power, *times* land input to the power of (1-the power of labour). The summation of the powers to 1 corresponds to the presence of constant returns to scale. It is perfectly possible to work out the efficiency locus obtained by combining a Cobb-Douglas production function for wheat with, say, the linear relations for barley suggested on p. 24.[1]

Assumptions about linearity of production functions, then, can be relaxed—although economies of scale make for difficult programming problems. Production functions with variable proportions, or non-constant cost, produce curved (non-linear)[2] constraints, instead of straight lines like CM in Fig. 1. But the *permanence* of constraints, linear or otherwise, can hardly apply to aim and policy constraints (pp. 37–8). 20 per cent yearly inflation is more than four times as bad as 5 per cent. Usually, the more one has of any product, the smaller the value attached to an extra unit; and the same applies to any aim. As growth proceeds, so further growth becomes less important relative to other aims (though, conversely, a 1 per cent rise in income per head equals twice as much if income is twice as high to begin with). This builds non-linearity into the very planning process. If we are weighting aims against each other, their relative weighting must depend on the present level of each, and cannot therefore be constant over time (though the weighting may be an unchanging function of the levels in some way).

(f) Variable relative valuations

The index-number problem, briefly discussed on pp. 13–14 above, must now be considered with more care, since we can no longer evade the issue of how the planner is to weight various outputs. Such relative weighting is involved in all discussions of economic performance as well as (and for the same reason as) in economic programming. If we say that the national income is the same in two successive years, we never mean that it is composed of exactly the same items. There will always be less of some products and more of others. Our statement must mean that the value of outputs gained is just offset by the value of outputs lost. That

---

[1] If we graph the wheat-barley combinations as we use more and more land-and-labour, in fixed proportions, in barley (absorbing the rest in wheat, in variable proportions) we trace out a smooth efficiency locus, not the jerky one of Figure 3.

[2] So far we have assumed a linear *maximand*, i.e. that relative wheat and barley values do not change, so we maximised something like 3 (wheat output) + 2 (barley output). Section (f) considers distortions arising from this.

implies a system of relative prices of products that enables the two outputs to be compared. If there is a problem about the choice of relative prices—if both the proportions (in national product) and the relative prices of iron and apples have altered—we have an index-number problem.[1]

Suppose that national income consists of apples and pears. In 1965, twice as many apples are produced as in 1964, and half as many pears. Suppose that in 1964 as many apples as pears were grown. Has national product risen? Plainly this depends on the relative values attached to apples and pears. The only hint we have of this relative value is the price system. This is not wholly satisfactory, since

(a) one fruit may be easier to raise in price because more concentrated in orchard ownership;

(b) one fruit may be more expensive solely because it is preferred by richer buyers. Still, the price system is the best guide we have at this stage. Let us pretend that relative prices *are* relative values.

Now if relative prices are unaltered, no index-number problem can arise. If, due to inflation, absolute pear and apple prices each rise 5 per cent, relative prices are unaltered, so that we obtain the same rate of economic growth whether we evaluate apples and pears in 1964 or 1965 prices. But if absolute prices change in different proportions, relative prices also change. Of course, if the composition of output stays the same, this does not matter. Twice as many apples and twice as many pears mean twice as much fruit, whatever happens to prices. However, if both composition and relative prices change, our measure of growth depends on the base-year selected.

	Apples	*Pears*	*Total*
Output in tons 1964	100	100	—
Output in tons 1965	200	50	—
Price/ton 1964	£200	£300	—
1965	£250	£400	—
Value of 1964 output:			
At 1964 prices	£20,000	£30,000	£50,000
At 1965 prices	£25,000	£40,000	£65,000
Value of 1965 output:			
At 1964 prices	£40,000	£15,000	£55,000
At 1965 prices	£50,000	£20,000	£70,000

[1] M. Gilbert and I. Kravis, *Comparison of National Products and Price Levels for O.E.E.C. Member Countries*, O.E.E.C., 1958, pt. I.

The table on page 31 indicates the problem. We assume that pear prices have risen much faster than apple prices and that pear output has halved while apple output has doubled (a reasonable explanation might be a pear blight).

If the community's relative valuation of 1964 is accepted, apple and pear output between 1964 and 1965 rose from £50,000 to £55,000, by 10 per cent. On 1965 valuation it rose only 7·7 per cent, from £65,000 to £70,000. Both percentages are equally 'correct' measures of growth —one in terms of 1964 relative values, the other corresponding to those of 1965. (Any sort of average of 7·7 and 10, of the values of 1964 and 1965, is completely meaningless.)

Some discussions of the index-number problem stop here; but this is really where we should start. Do price movements cause output indexes to exaggerate or to understate economic growth? Do such movements offset or emphasise each other's distortions? In practice, measurement of growth (or inflation) usually takes the earlier year as the base, and measures several later years in terms of the relative prices of the base. Only one set of prices need be collected this way. It is easier than, and just as correct as, reweighting every year.[1]

In order to find out how the relative prices of two commodities will move with a change in relative output levels, we must ask this question: Was the output change the result of a movement of tastes, or of a shift in technologies? Price changes give the answer. Suppose that more apples are produced as a proportion of the number of pears. This could be initiated by

(a) a rise in apple production relative to pear production (faster cost-per-unit reduction in apple output, i.e. relative improvement in apple technology), causing a fall in apple prices relative to pear prices (as in the table); or

(b) an upward shift in the demand curve for apples, which would lead to a rise in apple prices relative to pear prices and the turning over of pear orchards to apple production.

In case (a) (change in technology), measurement in terms of the early base-year uses the high relative price for the commodity whose share in output has risen (apples in the table) and the low relative price for the commodity whose share of output has fallen (pears). It thus tends to be

---

[1] See Reichmann's discussion 'Is there an Index?' in his *Uses and Abuses of Statistics*, Pelican 1964.

a maximal estimate of economic growth: from the viewpoint of 1965 valuations, an overestimate. In case (b) (shift in tastes), the reverse is true and the early-base-year growth index is minimal, an underestimate in terms of later valuations. Notice (a) happens in our table.

Shifts in technology and tastes, then, shift the relative values (marginal costs and utilities) of outputs. They thus alter the proportions in which people wish to produce and to consume them. This generates index-number difficulties. What, in practice, is the pattern of such difficulties in a growing economy?

Firstly, growth itself—either through planning or via the market mechanism—must mean that sectors making scarce producer goods, or initially not fully exploiting scale economies, expand faster than others. Certain sectors, with relative efficiency reduced by growth owing to scale diseconomies, or making 'inferior' goods consumed less as income rises (e.g. margarine), will actually contract output. Thus technology (as well as taste) yields changes in the proportions in which things are produced. But diminishing marginal utility—the phenomenon that, the more one has of something, the less one is prepared to sacrifice to obtain even more—is bound to carry over this change in proportions into a systematic change in relative prices. If an efficient output (like battery-reared chickens) increases, while one with less scope for increases in efficiency (like free-run chickens) contracts, without a change in tastes, the relative price of the contracting product is likely to rise. Hence an index of growth based on the earlier year will tend to overstate the gain in economic welfare. Such base-year prices give the product produced in larger quantities (battery chickens) a maximal valuation, while the product whose quantity has declined (free-run chickens) receives a minimal valuation.

Secondly, achievement of the prerequisites for growth, whether through planning or the market, alters output composition and income distribution. One way to generate growth is to increase the amount of capital (machinery, plant, horsepower, schools, universities) that supports the typical worker.[1] An advanced economy is thus one in which capital is plentiful (and cheap) compared to labour, by contrast to a backward country, where, relatively, labour is plentiful (and cheap) compared to capital. As growth proceeds, therefore, goods which need much capital

---

[1] P. Sargent Florence, *Logic of British and American Industry*, 2nd ed., Routledge, 1961, p. ix. Moreover, rich countries find it easier to save.

and little labour in production (and in production of their raw materials) become cheaper relative to goods needing much labour and little capital, and above all relative to services. In growing economies, the ratio between the price of a haircut and the price of a kilowatt-hour of electricity rises; so does the ratio between the price of domestic service and the price of an electric floor polisher. This pattern tends, in particular, to raise the relative price of services. In some of these labour-intensive sectors of the economy it is difficult to raise labour-productivity. Yet wages have to go up to attract workers, since wages are rising in the productivity-increasing parts of the economy. There is considerable evidence that, as economies become very rich, they raise the share of income spent on services (especially education, civil service, white-collar workers in science and industry, etc.)[1]. An index based on an earlier year tends to understate growth in so far as tastes are changing (see pp. 32–4), especially if tastes change towards the consumption of service outputs, underpriced in the early years of cheaper labour.

(g) Multiple aims

The opposing distortions imposed upon relative values by shifts in technology and changes in tastes lead to justified suspicion of relative prices in a given year as a suitable basis for evaluating changing economic magnitudes. Such suspicion is intensified when we consider the major difficulty in applying linear programming methods to the planning of a whole economy: the existence of several economic aims in place of the firm's relatively simple maximisation problem. Even without constraints, a system cannot maximise two things at once, unless one is a very special sort of function of the other.

This problem of multiple aims is distinct from political conflict over priorities or values. Neither publicly nor secretly is any major British party against economic growth, (minimally) the avoidance of balance-of-payments difficulties, and the limitation of inflation. There is disagreement on the social aspects of aims like equality; but the inter-party dispute in Britain is much more concerned with the moral justice and

---

[1] Galbraith, op. cit., chapters 18-19; yet, in the period 1952-60, when the quest for growth was allegedly destroying U.S. 'social balance', federal and state outlays for health, education and welfare rose sharply and steadily, from 5·2 per cent of G.N.P. in 1952 to 9·6 per cent in 1960 (U.S. *Income and Output*, Dept. of Commerce, 1958; and *Survey of Current Business*, July 1962, pp. 6, 18-19; all figures net of transfers from Federal to State authorities).

political effectiveness of rival means of attaining agreed goals.[1] The problem of multiple aims comes because the aims themselves, not their proponents, are in conflict.

Sometimes there is a head-on collision: strengthen incentives to speed up efficient labour transfers for growth, and you reduce economic equality. Usually the conflict is subtler. Within a certain range, it is possible that faster economic growth reduces the danger of inflation. Nevertheless, the aims of maximising both growth and price stability conflict. The best policy to keep prices stable (never mind growth) would differ from the best policy to maximise growth (and never mind prices).

Any useful plan must take account of the multiple aims of policy and strike some balance among them—not merely by writing them all down and ignoring half of them, as is common form in countries where planning is entirely a propaganda exercise.

(h) How to aim at many targets: weighting rejected

There are two ways to deal with the problem. First, one might try to weight the objectives and adjust the maximand accordingly. For example, one might try to maximise three times the yearly percentage rise in output, *less* (or *divided by?*) twice the yearly percentage price rise. It would be quite possible to impose a minimum tolerable growth rate, and/or a maximum permissible price increase, upon such a system.

The trouble with this idea is that there is no guide to the correct set of weights of criteria. When weighting products to measure growth, we have market prices of the base-year as a first approximation (however prejudiced in favour of the products of the strong or the tastes of the rich) to relative valuations. No such approximation exists to guide weighting of aims.[2] Such weightings involve value-judgments more

---

[1] This becomes clear when one compares the underlying aims (as opposed to the rhetoric) of the 1964 and 1966 British election manifestoes. Differences about means are still profound matters of principle in many cases (cf. steel nationalisation). But the debate about social services—universal coverage, advocated by most Labour supporters, or selective concentration on need, advocated by most Conservatives—concerns application of an agreed egalitarian principle.

[2] This objection makes nonsense of the sort of 'analysis' of benefits carried out by the Buchanan Report (*Traffic in Towns*, H.M.S.O., 1963, pp. 216-8), where schemes are marked on a scale $\dfrac{\text{Environment} \times \text{Accessibility}}{100}$. Even if Environmental and Accessibility advantages are measurable, the weighting is arbitrary. $\dfrac{10(\text{Environment}) + 3(\text{Accessibility})}{100}$ would rank schemes of the same cost in a totally different and equally unjustifiable way.

obviously than (but in no basic way differently from) the acceptance of any set of prices as product-weights. But, so long as the weighting formulation is used, choices among value-judgments expressed as alternative plans are hard to give political content. If party A says, 'Growth is 1·5 times as important as equality', and party B replies, 'No, 1·3 times as important', it is going to be very difficult to have a well-informed election on the issue, especially as 'important' might mean different things, and influence Plan weighting in different ways, for the two parties.

Moreover, goals possess diminishing marginal utility as well as goods. Suppose that a party aims at both equality and growth, but is mandated to prefer growth much above equality. As it realizes its stated aims, achieving much growth but little equalisation, its supporters' valuations shift away from growth towards equality, precisely because of the relative rate of attainment of the stated goals. This effect works statically as well. Constant weights cannot reflect preference patterns if goals have diminishing marginal utility, because the relative importance given to any given aim in the maximand, at a particular moment in time, should vary inversely with the amount of success in achieving the aim up to that moment. To ask even the most sophisticated electorate to choose between governments on non-linear weighted promises is to ask too much.

The problem is not that electors are stupid, but that no guide-lines exist for decisions of such complexity. Sir Dennis Robertson rightly remarked that we would all tolerate:

(a) 1 per cent yearly inflation to get 10 per cent growth, while hardly anyone would consider

(b) 10 per cent inflation adequately compensated by 1 per cent growth. But the choice between;

(c) 3 per cent growth and 3 per cent inflation and

(d) 4 per cent growth with 5 per cent inflation is not just difficult, but impossible to make in general.[1] Most voters, probably rightly would rather rely on Government and Civil Service judgment to 'treat each such choice on its merits,' while retaining the right to 'turn the rascals out' if those merits were too often demerits.

---

[1] This choice is a value-judgment, distinct from the factual, decidable issue of the relation between growth and price stability in recent experience (see pp. 223-6 below). In the former case, most people's valuation would depend on the composition of growth and inflation in each case—who gets more, what prices rise, etc.—together with effects on other aims (e.g. exports).

(i) Aim constraints

The alternative method, which can be shown to be mathematically correspondent to the first only in perfectly linear systems,[1] relies entirely on aim constraints (p. 17). This has the advantage over weighting that reducing the crudity of our assumptions does not render choices excessively complicated. A crude aim constraint, subject to which the growth rate was to be maximised, might say that prices should not rise by over 3 per cent a year. A little less crudely, we might constrain price rises to 2 per cent yearly, *plus* one-fifth of the percentage growth rate (e.g. if the economy grows at 5 per cent, prices would not be allowed to rise by more than $2 + \frac{5}{5} = 3$ per cent). That would allow leeway if some scarce but highly growth-inducing raw material, a large component of the cost of finished goods, turned out to be very responsive in supply to the price offered.

Aim constraints make clear the value-judgments involved in many-aim choices. They are thus more helpful than a weighting formulation to considered selection among rival sets of evaluations. More important, aim constraints make *sensitivity analysis* possible; crowding all our objectives into a single complex and obscure weighted constraint does not.

Sensitivity analysis begins after we have discovered our constrained economic optimum. We can then examine the effects on our optimum of relaxing or tightening each constraint in turn. To take a simple case: suppose we have maximised the growth rate, subject to factor constraints *plus* the aim constraint that price rises are not permitted to exceed 3 per cent yearly. We then see what happens to the model of the economy when we tighten the aim constraint, first down to 2·9 per cent inflation, then down to 2·8 per cent, and so on. At each stage we see how much growth we lose in return for the added price stability. If we lose none, the 3 per cent inflation constraint was not *binding*. Then we do the same thing in the opposite direction; if the 3 per cent inflation constraint *was* binding, we relax it in turn to 3·1 per cent, 3·2 per cent, and so on.

[1] In other words, *if and only if* the whole constrained-maximisation system (aim and constraints) is linear, one can perform the following exercise. Take out the maximand and the aim constraints. Form them into a single maximand, with weights adding up to unity. (For example, instead of maximising growth subject to the constraint that prices shall not rise by over 3 per cent yearly together with the factor constraints, we maximise, with $0 < x < 1$, (x) times the yearly growth rate *plus* $(1 - x)(-r)$ where r is the rate of price increase, subject to factor constraints only). There will exist a value of x such that the same policy, including the same factor allocation, is best on both formulations of the problem. This set does not exist if the system contains non-linearities. I am grateful to Dr. S. Chakravarty for proving this to me.

Especially if the model has non-linear elements, the results of sensitivity analysis may be surprising.[1] And they may lead us to change our aim constraints. For example, if the 3 per cent inflation constraint is binding, and produces a solution where 3 per cent yearly growth is the best we can do, but 3·1 per cent inflation allows just enough price incentive to clear a crucial bottleneck and raise maximal attainable growth to 4 per cent, we should certainly want to re-examine the wisdom of the 3 per cent inflation constraint initially chosen. Conversely, if a reduction of our inflation constraint to 2 per cent yearly lowers maximum attainable growth very little—say to 2·9 per cent—we shall want to consider accepting this combination.

(j) The optimising model
This consists of:

1. Objective function, e.g., Maximise rate of growth of net national product per person over a stated planning period. Weights are needed for components of output, so that there is an index-number problem.

2. Production functions, showing what output of each product to expect from each combination of factor inputs.

3. Constraints:

(a) Factor constraints: the amounts of various sorts of labour, machinery, buildings, land, transportation, etc., available at each stage to the whole economy, or confined to some part of it; the amounts to be left for future use at the end of the plan period (*terminal stock conditions* to stop 'maximal growth' that eats the seed-corn);

(b) Aim constraints: specifications of minimum tolerable progress towards (or maximum tolerable regress from) other economic aims than that of the objective function.

(c) Policy constraints: general, not necessarily economic, restraints on methods to achieve agreed goals, e.g. a prohibition of child labour.

In the next chapter, we look at the selection of aims for British economic policy. Chapter 3 examines the recent progress of the economy towards these aims. It is too early to attempt to set up an exact programme on the lines specified, partly because we have little quantitative idea of the relations among economic aims in British experience. In Chapter 4, therefore, we use the evidence of performance presented in Chapter 3 in order to begin to fill this gap.

[1] See J. Sandee, *A Demonstration Planning Model for India*, Asia, 1960, pp. 44-8, for sensitivity analysis of assumptions and factor constraints in a linear model.

CHAPTER TWO

The Aims of
British Economic Policy

The Radcliffe Report[1] listed five aims of economic policy towards which monetary measures might usefully contribute. They are: economic growth, full employment, price stability, an adequate balance-of-payments surplus, and the building up of an adequate level of foreign currency reserves. We shall consider the meaning, measurement and justification of these aims. It will turn out that the fourth aim implies the last, which (by traditional standards of adequacy) is too strong an objective in any event. Further, there are three aims not considered by the Radcliffe Committee, probably because they are less affected by monetary policies alone: the achievement of a desirable composition of output, distribution of income, and freedom of choice in economic matters. These three aims must also be considered. The question of the composition of output leads directly into the problem of interdependence, in supply and demand, among the activities of an economy. The question of income distribution compels us to decide how, in planning over time, the needs and choices of future generations are to be assessed in comparison to those of our own.

I. THE AIM OF ECONOMIC GROWTH:
THE OBJECTIVE FUNCTION

(*a*) *Meaning and measurement*

A rate of growth is easy to understand. Four problems of definition

[1] *Report* of the Committee on the Working of the British Monetary System, Cmd. 827 of 1959, para. 68.

arise when we ask what is growing in economic growth. Is it total output, output per person, or output per man-hour that we wish to maximise? Which measure of output is the best? How do we are to deal with the index-number problem? Finally, how can the model incorporate the fact that the goal of economic activity is not production but consumption?

To maximise total output, economic power, is a normal wartime aim. To supply the front line, both output per man-hour and welfare per consumer are reduced—the first by drawing the old and the in-experienced into the labour force and by getting it to work long hours, the second by diverting factories from making consumer goods to making arms. The interaction among the three possible maximands is seen if we regard welfare as the outcome of potential participation in the work-force, actual participation, duration of work and productivity of work,[1] i.e.:

$$\frac{\text{Output}}{\text{Population}} = \frac{\text{Working age group}}{\text{Population}} \times \frac{\text{Persons seeking work}}{\text{Working age group}}$$
$$\text{('Welfare')} \qquad \text{(Age-structure)} \qquad \text{(Workforce participation)}$$

$$\times \frac{\text{Hours worked}}{\text{Persons seeking work}} \times \frac{\text{Output}}{\text{Hours worked}}$$
$$\text{(Employment duration)} \qquad \text{(Productivity)}$$

To maximise total output in the short run, the method is to expand in both directions one's concept of 'working age' and raise workforce participation and employment duration. At severe levels of unemploy-ment—if industry can be compelled to absorb the new labour—these actions are likely to increase productivity as well, since machines are used at a higher level of efficiency.[2] Near full employment, however, a conflict appears. To raise output quickly, it is necessary to use overtime, or to draw less skilled workers into the workforce. This process, while increasing output per head of population, lowers productivity. Indeed it is possible that a point will come where the marginal physical product

---

[1] This identity was used in my work for Professor Myrdal on the Twentieth Century Fund's South Asian project in 1961. It is obvious but useful.

[2] S. Fabricant, *Basic Facts about Productivity Change*, National Bureau of Economic Research, Occasional Paper No. 63 (1959), p. 14, shows that, from 1889 to 1957 in the U.S.A., output per man-hour rose in 44 of the 51 years when total output rose, but in only 7 of the 17 years when it fell.

falls to zero, output is maximised, and productivity has been lowered enough for the output losses, resulting from yet more employment, to outweigh the output-raising effects of higher labour participation. Long before this point, the increasing unpleasantness of extra labour will have started to reduce welfare in spite of the increase of output per head —a very imperfect indicator of welfare largely because of its omission of the welfare-reducing effect of long hours of work.

Moves towards the maximisation of total output, then, conflict quickly with productivity in any economy near full employment; less quickly, long workhours outweigh higher output, and economic welfare is reduced. Ultimately, machinery may be saturated, and further attempts to raise total output (or, since population is unchanged, output per head) are hopeless. Direct conflict between the maximisation of total and per-head output is very unlikely in advanced economies, since birthrates and deathrates are influenced far more by wars, social customs and class-structures than by the availability of total product. Thus no policy (within reason) towards total output will greatly affect the number of heads among which it is divided. Certainly the distribution of income affects demographic variables, especially stillbirths, within one country,[1] even when medical care is not rationed by the purse. Also, Malthus notwithstanding, wealth is associated with longer education, later marriage and fewer children.[2] But all this affects the *relative* birthrates of rich and poor within one country. There is no evidence that a country systematically changes its birthrate during (let alone because of) growth in total product.[3] It could be argued that a Government intent on maximising total output would also try to raise the number of heads through population policy, but this—at least when directed towards raising birth-rates —is long-run and uncertain in its effects, and concentrated for many years on non-producers.

To choose labour-productivity as a maximand would be to confuse

[1] R. M. Titmuss, *Birth, Poverty and Wealth*, Hamish Hamilton, 1943, pp. 30-40.

[2] True even in societies whose Governments claim to value equality very highly, like post-Stalin Russia. In 1958 Mr. Khrushchev expressed his alarm at the low proportion of proletarian children in Moscow University. Wealth leads (through less financial pressure towards early school-leaving, and the build-up of an unhurried and often cultured home environment) to greater educational opportunity, longer education, later marriage and hence fewer children. (Greater knowledge of contraceptive techniques is much less important.)

[3] The U.S. and U.S.S.R. today have rates of population increase far *higher* than India ever had prior to 1940, and far *lower* than India has had since 1955.

means and ends. There are many workers who make substantial contributions to output, but have low productivity, so that productivity would be raised but welfare lowered if they were withdrawn from the labour force. Also labour-productivity could be increased by simply closing down industries with low capital endowments. In an economy there is seldom just one scarce factor of production, and even efficiency would suffer from concentrating on the productivity of one to the exclusion of the rest.

Let us look at the causal chains set up by these two choices of maximand, total output and productivity, with the help of the equation on p. 40. We assume that growing output per head tends towards rising welfare, although, owing chiefly to the disutility of labour input, the two are not the same. It can be seen that:

(i) Maximising total output, near full employment, involves raising employment duration or participation, hence lowering productivity. Initially, the process increases output per head, but eventually it lowers welfare.

(ii) Maximising productivity, and discarding under-mechanised workers, greatly lowers both total and per-head output.

There remains the third choice: maximisation of output per head. This cannot be simply equated with welfare; but rises in output per head —if unaccompanied by rising labour-input per head, by growing inequality in the distribution of income or effort, by falling consumption per head, or by 'worsening' output composition—are probably sufficient for rising welfare. It is most sensible in the long run to take output per head as the planning maximand or objective function. Since there will be constraints on available labour, the maximisation process is almost certain to involve higher productivity; and since population is not simply determined by economic policy, total output will also rise. Thus there is least contradiction between our three possible maximands if output per head is chosen. Some 'unaccompaniments', of the type suggested, must be introduced as constraints, to ensure that welfare rises with output per head.

What sort of output per head is being maximised? First, some people's heads are bigger than others! We must allow for the differing needs of young and old. In a community with a larger proportion of children, the same consumption per person implies a higher level of satisfaction of needs and wants. This is taken care of by the device of the 'Lusk consumption unit', which weights the population according to age-structure.[1] In assessing *performance*, we shall want to use such a measure where possible. It is not likely, however, that any predictable effects of *planning* choices on age structure will be considerable in an advanced economy; however, demographically foreseen shifts in age-structure should be used to project changes in output and consumption 'per Lusk' implicit in various plans.

The concepts of output and consumption are more difficult than the notion of 'heads'. We have to decide whether to maximise product

(a) gross or net of depreciation (using up of capital in the process of production);

(b) domestic or national (national product, unlike domestic product, excludes the profits accruing to foreigners from holdings in U.K. companies, and includes Britons' profits from their interests in foreign concerns);

(c) at factor cost (deducting purchase taxes from prices paid in shops, and adding subsidies) or at market prices.

If we had decided to maximise productivity, gross domestic product (per man-hour) would be the correct measure. Since output per head is the maximand, however, net national product is to be preferred: net, because the product that merely replaces capital does not increase usable per-head output or consumption; national, because returns accruing to British workers, businessmen and Government, not output produced by them to the profit of others, is the appropriate guide to welfare; at factor cost, because (as long as we pretend prices reflect value) the total value attached to a product by society is equal to the sum it is prepared to pay for it, whether through the market or through direct subsidy to the producer,[2] and is not affected by the extent to which the Government raises revenue by indirect taxation.[3]

Are we to measure a period's growth by valuing each year's output at the relative prices of a single base-year (Laspeyres) or at those of the latest year available, so that the base changes each year (Paasche)? The longer a period, the more relative prices and the composition of output are likely to change (remember that *both* have to change to create differences in the growth measure between the two price-indices) and

---

[1] F.A.O., *Calorie Requirements*, Rome 1957, or any edition of their *Food Balance Sheets*.

[2] This is so despite the extraordinary use of market-price measures of growth in the National Plan (H.M.S.O., 1965, p. 15). Such 'growth' can be simulated by raising purchase tax, cutting farm subsidies and keeping prices stable.

[3] Since quarterly data, in constant prices, are available only for gross domestic product, we have to use this in some contexts. See Chapter 4.

hence the less meaningful is any index of growth based on a particular year. In the short run, though, such changes are seldom so large as to rule out a measure of growth, though index-numbers based on different years will always differ by one or two per cent (so that it is silly, even if statistics are perfect, to worry about year-to-year fluctuations of, say, $\frac{1}{2}$ per cent in the measured growth rate). The yearly reweighting of each year's output by the prices of the most recent year, the Paasche index, is a tedious, long and expensive job. Since it is not superior to the Laspeyres index method, in which the prices of a particular, fairly recent base-year[1] are used to measure output for a few subsequent years, the latter method is used in practice.

We have considered the index-number *problem*, but to understand the measurement of growth in constant prices of a base-year we must now look at an index-number *effect*. Growth, as we have seen, involves changing tastes (for instance, the substitution of butter for margarine as incomes rise) and changing cost conditions (for example, the steady shift in all Western countries, since 1945, out of wool and cotton into nylon and terylene textile production, because technology was improving, i.e., costs were falling, faster in the plastics sectors). It can be proved[2]

---

[1] In the U.K., the bases used for the Laspeyres index of *real output* have been 1948, 1954 and 1958. Since 1962, the *price* index has been Paasche.

[2] If a commodity is getting dearer, relative to others, solely for supply-side reasons (e.g. slower technical change, more militant trade unions), consumers will devote a smaller proportion of expenditure to that commodity. The earlier the year on which the index is based (i.e. the relative prices of which it adopts), the less will be the relative value given to each unit of such a commodity. The Laspeyres index therefore gives a lower value to goods that, for supply-side reasons, have got less important as a share of total spending than does the Paasche index; and the earlier the base of a Laspeyres index, the lower will be its valuation of such 'technically slow-growing' goods. By giving a *low* weighting to the declining and slowest-growing items a Laspeyres index *overstates* supply-side induced growth. Conversely, if a commodity is getting relatively dearer because consumers want to buy more of it (demand-side reasons—changes in tastes, incomes or income-distribution), producers will tend to divert resources towards making it, and its share of total output grows; the earlier the base-year of the index, the lower the prices in which these products, which are growing faster than others for demand-side reasons, are valued. Thus the Laspeyres index gives a lower value to those goods that, for demand-side reasons, have got more important as a share of total spending, than does the Paasche index; and the earlier the base of a Laspeyres index, the lower will be its valuation of such goods. By giving a *low* weighting to the relatively fast-growing items, a Laspeyres index *understates* demand-induced growth. Therefore, when we compare a Laspeyres and a Paasche index, we must expect the first to show faster growth than the second if relative costs (technologies, supply conditions) have been changing fast, and tastes slowly; and the second, if tastes have been changing fast relative to techniques.

that the effect of changes in tastes is to make Laspeyres index-numbers understate economic growth, while the effect of changes in cost (technology) is to make them overstate it. The effects gain strength with the length of time from the base-year. In an economy that is technologically slow-moving, but well endowed with supposedly (as opposed to genuinely) new products and instruments of consumer persuasion—and also shifting its family composition fast—the understatement effect is likely to predominate.

There is some evidence that, in the U.K., technology has been changing quickly compared to tastes. The earlier the base-year for prices, used to measure growth over a given period, the faster such growth seems to be.[1] Since recent data are seldom recalculated on earlier base-years, most ouput series are based on the last base-year available.

The earlier the base-year, the more rapid is apparent growth; most published data for output in fact use a recent base-year; therefore welfare has grown faster than the data for output per head suggest. Further, the published series involve a bogus acceleration of growth towards the end of a period, because the base-year is then earlier relative to the years being compared. However, the fact that demand and supply index-number 'distortions' offset each other permits us to use the convenient Laspeyres index with a certain amount of confidence, at least to measure short-run growth.

The maximand is thus constant-price Laspeyres national product, net of depreciation, at factor cost; it is per Lusk consumption unit, to which per-head estimation comes fairly close. But we are still speaking of maximising *output*, while it is *consumption* that promotes economic welfare.[2] If we instruct a computer programme to maximise (subject

---

[1] One has to use a fairly distant period to be sure of getting finally-revised data in each available set of prices. From 1948 to 1952, gross domestic product, at constant factor cost of 1948, rose 11·0 per cent; of 1954, 10·0 per cent; and of 1958, 9·0 per cent. (U.K., *National Income and Expenditure*, 1964, p. 14; *Annual Abstract of Statistics*, 1958, p. 256; 1959, p. 248.) It is hard to see how anything other than index-number factors, such as the Korean War, could have caused this.

[2] The line between investment as both sacrifice and future output-raiser, and consumption as neither, is easier to draw in advanced than in very poor countries; in the latter, even increases in food consumption have some output-raising features. But current outlay on education—e.g. teachers' pay—is almost unclassifiable; it has both intrinsic and instrumental value. In practice it is all classified as consumption—humanist but not very sensible.

to factor constraints alone) the growth rate of output, it will produce an answer that puts aside all output in early years for investment, so as to produce at a tremendous rate in the final year of the programme; for computers, unless told, do not know that people can starve. Conversely, if the instruction is just to maximise consumption, not merely will there be no investment in the final year of the plan, but we shall be told to consume the seed corn—to eat such capital as we can.

It is possible to set up a programme that overcomes these difficulties. The problem that consumption-maximising means ultimate capital-eating can be dealt with by specifying a very long planning horizon, or by demanding that the captial stock shall never (or not in the last year) fall below a specified minimum level. An output-maximising programme can be constrained not to permit consumption growth to fall below a given rate. In an underinvesting economy, as Britain is often claimed to be,[1] this rate should be near the minimum politically acceptable for some years. Some of these problems of balance between generations, between consumption now and investment for consumption later, will be considered when we discuss equality. Diminishing marginal utility of total income (DMU), if admitted,[2] reduces the optimal investment income ratio, and hence the growth rate of consumption; for DMU means that extra consumption is worth more earlier, when one has less, than later in the growth process. But it turns out that this is often insufficient to prevent the programme from investing an implausibly large amount in early years, for the sake of future growth;[3] we can prevent this by valuing future consumers' marginal utility of income, at each income level, lower than that of present consumers, but we need some ethical justification for this.

(b) Evaluation

Thus the chosen maximand is Laspeyres growth, over the plan period,

---

[1] This claim is denied by J. R. Sargent (*Out of Stagnation*, Fabian Society, 1963) and C. Clark (*Growthmanship*, Hobart Economic Paper, 1962) for opposite reasons; and indeed Britain is so labour-starved that the huge rise in the investment/output ratio during the late 1950s brought no acceleration of growth. But it is hard to deny that some industries—housebuilding, shipbuilding—feature under-investment; the huge dispersion in performance and investment between domestic 'best' and 'worst', and between home and overseas, industries is almost conclusive.

[2] To reject it, one has to be prepared to assert that a person's capacity for enjoyment depends upon his level of income.

[3] S. Chakravarty, in a series of lectures at M.I.T. in 1964.

of net national product per equivalent adult male, subject to constraints that consumption shall rise at not less than (say) $1\frac{1}{2}$ per cent per person per year, and that the capital stock shall not fall over the plan period. We now know what this means, and how it is measured. But do we want it?

The classical economists from Adam Smith onwards were deeply concerned with the causes of increase in 'the wealth of nations', but neo-classicists such as J. S. Mill, Alfred Marshall and A. C. Pigou, switched the focus of interest to the problem of the distribution of output between labourers, businessmen and landlords. Between the wars, economists were primarily concerned with problems of cyclical instability and chronic unemployment, and with extension of the neo-classical model. Lately, five developments have revived interest in growth.

First, Keynesian techniques have enabled those countries prepared to adopt them[1] to conquer instability and unemployment due to fluctuating or deficient demand for output. Second, poor and newly-independent economies, such as India, have begun to plan, and their dismal initial levels of economic welfare make any maximand other than growth inconceivable. Third, the cold war between capitalist countries (some democratic) and communist countries (most totalitarian) has required an accretion of economic power for military uses by both sides, and this has been compatible with rising consumer welfare only under conditions of rapid growth. Fourth, the transition from cold war to peaceful co-existence, and the growing ideological awareness of the countries of Africa and Asia, have led the U.S.A., the U.S.S.R., and their allies to indulge openly in a growth competition, with the ability to give inspiration—and aid—to (and win economic imitativeness from) neutral countries as a reward. Finally, the development of new tools of planning for growth has been accompanied by a great relaxation of dogmatic opposition to it (compare the use of the words 'planning' and 'controls' by the Conservative Party in 1951 and 1964).

So there are plenty of historical reasons why we have come to want growth. But *should* a fairly well-to-do society want growth at all? This question cannot be asked in any context other than Professor Galbraith's *The Affluent Society*.[2] This work rests on a series of dichotomies. Throughout, it suggests that, by aiming at growth, we have forgotten

---

[1] As the U.S. has not been, until very recently.

[2] J. K. Galbraith, *The Affluent Society*, Pelican, 1962. For an expansion of these criticisms of Galbraith's work, cf. M. Lipton, The Mythology of Affluence, *New Left Review*, Jan.-Feb. 1966.

about more important things—poverty, the composition of output (especially 'social balance'—basic capital and welfare services provided by the public sector), the need to prevent inflation, and so forth. Professor Galbraith is no Puritan, crying that water-closets and refrigerators imperil our immortal souls. Unfortunately, his assault on growth rests on faulty logic and on a number of factually incorrect propositions.

The logical error is the confusion between affluence (a high *level* of income per person) and growth, a rate of increase in income per person. For instance, Galbraith cites the Soviet success in launching the first orbital satellite—ahead of the U.S.A.—as indicating that purposive economic direction is more important than affluence.[1] But the striking difference between U.S. and Soviet economic performance in the five years to each side of Sputnik (1952-62) was the far faster growth of Soviet income per head. Thus the U.S. had to choose between rising living levels and growing military might, while Russia could have both. The Russian people compared their standard of living with the recent past, not with the distant and rumoured affluence of the United States. Similarly, Galbraith's complaint concerning social balance cannot be logically reconciled with his attack on growth. The public sector, in a stagnant economy, cannot grow except at the cost of private spending. In a growing economy, the share of national output at public disposal can rise, as well as personal spending per head. People will fight hard to retain the tailfins and striped toothpaste they already enjoy; economic growth enables public policy, with a minimum of social tension, to lower these follies as a share of a growing product.

Associated with this logical mistake is a failure of observation. If we rank economies by income per person and also by social balance, measured by Government non-defence spending as a proportion of GNP,[2] we see that economies that have grown to greater affluence show larger public sectors. This can be seen from studies over time in the same country, too.[3] Exactly the same applies to equality; the richer and the faster-growing an economy, the more successful in promoting equality are (i) the market forces enabling people to move from poorer to richer regions and occupations, and (ii) the income tax system, in that more wealthy and complex economies are far better able to

---

[1] Galbraith, op. cit., p. 10.

[2] See U.N., *Yearbook of National Accounts Statistics*, 1964, appendix tables.

[3] See *U.K. National Income and Expenditure*, C.S.O., passim.

support the machinery required to tax and transfer effectively.[1]

Even the most fundamental requirement for Galbraith's thesis is lacking. So far from an abnormally rapid growth of output per person, the U.S. experienced exceptionally slow growth, by the standards of her own past and of her major trade or political rivals, in the period under review by Galbraith.[2] Such growth, so far from having been purchased at the cost of inflation, was accompanied by almost complete price stability since the Korean boom, at least by contrast to Western Europe. And recent world history exemplifies fast growth and slow inflation (Japan), fast growth and fast inflation (Brazil), slow growth and fast inflation (Indonesia, and, less dramatically, the U.K.), and slow growth and slow inflation (U.S.A.).[3] The facts on 'social balance' in the U.S. are again dramatically contrary to Galbraith's speculations. From 1952 to 1960, U.S. Government social expenditures rose from 5·2 per cent of GNP to 9·6 per cent,[4] while regional inequality, both in income and in the incidence of unemployment, showed substantial declines.[5]

Much more should be said concerning Galbraith's interpretation of economic theory. Beginners in economics must be warned that the theory of wages, and the output-maximising intentions, he attributes to all or most economists are at best a controversial interpretation of a few U.S. marginalists at the turn of the century.[6]

A recent onslaught blames growth for the destruction of the environment, especially by motor vehicles.[7] These enable many people to enjoy Cornwall and Florence. Only further growth can build underground car parks to preserve such places.

Growth, in fact, is the great softener of social improvement. In a static economy, change requires severe social friction, since the losers

[1] The ratio between actual and theoretical Indian income tax yield is variously estimated from 1:2 to 1:4.

[2] Under 1 per cent per person per year, 1951-61. *U.S. Income and Output*, Dept. of Commerce, 1958; *Survey of Current Business, July 1961, May 1962*.

[3] U.N., *Monthly Digest of Statistics*, current number, for price data; *Yearbook of National Accounts Statistics*, do., for output.

[4] See p. 34, note 1.

[5] Gallaway, *American Economic Review*, 1963; and the numbers of *Survey of Current Business*, showing income by states.

[6] J. B. Clark believed that marginal-productivity theory implied a unique distribution of income between capital and labour; Marshall nor Menger did not.

[7] E. J. Mishan, *The Costs of Economic Growth*, Staples, 1967. The paradoxical title surely suggests adjusting the relative prices in which output is valued (see pp. 74-84 below), and including environmental safeguards as contraints on the "terminal capital stock" of a policy.

cannot be compensated if no rise in output is being attained. Whatever a nation's goals—more help for the poor countries of the world, stronger defences, a larger public sector, a larger share of output for under-privileged persons at home—they can be most easily achieved by providing more resources through the growth of available output per head.

Growth in output per head, increasing the ability of a society to raise welfare by supplying consumer goods, is surely amply justified as an aim. But why choose this aim as the maximand, rather than, say, the level of employment? An aim can as well be embodied in a constraint. Part of the answer lies in the traditional orientation of economic theory towards efficiency, in the Paretian sense discussed on p. 4; in a dynamic context, this means maximising the rate of growth subject to resource and other constraints. But there are better reasons for choosing growth as the maximand than tradition. It is relatively easy to quantify (compared to choice or equality, for instance) and to grasp. It is more universally accepted than any other aim. It is clear that 'more means better'. This is not true, for instance, of anti-inflationary policy, where going too far is at least as bad as not going far enough.[1] Growth is a difficult aim to achieve, so that there is much to be said for orienting policy towards it; the steps needed to maximise the balance-of-payments surplus under constraints, for instance, are far clearer than those required to grow as fast as possible.

Choice of a growth maximand leaves plenty of room for dispute on principle (how much should choice be constrained in the interest of growth?[2]) and policy effectiveness (how much would state intervention in a given field help, or hinder, growth?) and such debate is clarified, not stultified, by advance agreement on the maximand. Certainly, the very specification of a growth maximand requires special policy constraints. The permissible increase of labour-inputs is limited, perhaps even negative.[3] Productive potential for future welfare has to be balanced against present growing consumption needs.

Even subject to these limitations, growth is not a quantified version of

[1] Generally falling prices, which imply a rising real burden of debt, have seldom been historically associated with growth.

[2] P. J. D. Wiles, Growth versus Choice, *Economic Journal*, 1956.

[3] Since 1955, U.K. workers have increasingly chosen to take welfare improvements as leisure rather than as real income. Weekly hours actually worked (per manual worker in all industries) fell by 4·3 per cent from 1955 to (October) 1965. *Economic Trends*, Feb. 1966, p. 28. To raise planned labour-input even as fast as population growth, therefore, would run counter to the pattern of choice on the present structure of incentives.

increasing happiness, but it is the nearest approach to it that economics can provide. It is not a materialistic goal. It covers the increase of resources of all types, including those devoted to the better training of painters and violinists, the support of scientific research and poets, and the improvement of industrial productivity so as to increase leisure time. It is the faster-growing economies of Europe, not their involuntarily ascetic neighbours, that have most substantially lowered the working week in recent years.[1] There is a sort of blasphemy in building a Chartres while people starve. Most, though not all, of the greatest cultural achievements have taken place in periods of accelerated economic growth (Italian renaissance art, English Elizabethan drama). The artist starving in the garret is a vulgar myth, and the notion that empty bellies stimulate productiveness, cultural or scientific, is the crassest materialism of all.

2. THE FULL EMPLOYMENT CONSTRAINT

(a) Possibilities and definitions

Look again at p. 26, Figure 3. You will notice that, under certain sets of relative prices, the best output was at C, with the unemployment rate of labour measured by $\frac{CL}{LO}$. Nevertheless, in the many-factor, many-product, non-linear real economy, 'full employment' of labour is considered a reasonable aim, fully compatible with efficient use of resources. How is this paradox to be explained?

Part of the explanation lies in the word 'non-linear'. Suppose that some production functions do not use labour and capital in fixed proportions, but can absorb varying amounts of labour with the same capital. This is what marginal analysis assumes to be true for all production functions. For most, it possesses some truth even in the short run, though not so much that the linear programming formulation is a bad approximation. But in almost all cases it is possible, in the long run,[2] to adapt both capital inputs and labour inputs, so that, for the same level of total product, we concentrate on a process using less capital but employing more labour. Whether such processes are efficient depends on the relative price of capital and labour.

This considers only the supply side. As we saw on p. 6, reductions in the real wage may (since most profit incomes are saved) so lower

[1] O.E.C.D., *General Statistics*, Jan. 1965.
[2] On Marshall's definition of the long run (that period in which all factors can be varied by the entrepreneur) this is tautologous.

C

purchasing power as to reduce the incentive to produce and invest. Paradoxically, however, Governmental understanding of Keynesian economics has restored a pre-Keynesian world. Neo-classical economists wrongly believed that, with *no* control over aggregate demand, a wage cut would automatically raise the level of employment (p. 5). Monetary and fiscal policies are now used to maintain effective demand near whatever level is desired. Hence, in a quite neo-classical way, adjustments in the relative price of capital and labour affect the relative incentives to employ men and machines to produce the desired output level, within the limit of permissible unemployment of labour set by public policy.

Non-linearities assist the attainment of full employment not merely by preventing factor proportions from being fixed, but also by making complete specialisation (at a point like A in Figure 3) less likely. Neo-classical theory shows that relative product prices can determine an optimum *anywhere* on the smooth efficiency locus (corresponding to ABC of Figure 3). Moreover, if an economy makes many products, with widely differing technologies (capital/labour ratios in each unit of output) and with mild scale economies in some lines, then there are losses (in lost scale economies from the *other* sectors) from fully exploiting scale economies in a very few. It can be shown that, the more sectors featuring scale economies, and the more widely dispersed their technologies, the less likely is it that optimal output implies complete specialisation,[1] and thus unemployment due to the imperfect adaptability of labour to a specific task. Thus non-linearities *plus* many-product economies make rigid technological unemployment less likely than the simple two-product linear model suggests.

Full employment is attainable, finally, because it is not defined too tightly. Beveridge's White Paper of 1942, in which it was first proposed that the Government accept responsibility for a full-employment target, set that target at 97 per cent of the labour force; that is, he considered that for every 97 persons at work on any particular day, there should be no more than 3 looking for jobs and receiving unemployment benefit.[2]

---

[1] See above, p. 28.

[2] Beveridge, *Full Employment in a Free Society*, Allen and Unwin, 1944, p. 21. Though he regarded 3 per cent as the irreducible minimum for unemployment, he believed this was compatible with an even higher ratio of vacancies to workforce. Our measure of the level of employment, the National Institute's 'excess demand for labour', is the seasonally-adjusted difference between vacancies and registered unemployed as a percentage of the labour force. Beveridge aimed at excess demand for labour, in this sense.

In fact the British economy has done much better than that. The proportion of the workforce receiving unemployment benefit since 1945 has fluctuated around 1¾ per cent, with small cyclical variations. The figures probably understate total unemployment, owing to non-registration of those not qualified for benefit, especially married women. However, total true unemployment in Britain must have averaged under 2½ per cent of the labour force.[1]

Can we accept this as satisfying our definition of 'full employment'? Two doubts remain. First, certain areas have experienced far more severe unemployment—especially Northern Ireland, with registered levels around 7 or 8 per cent and actual levels probably nearer 10 or 11 per cent. Except in 1945-8, Government policies to encourage businesses to move plants to such areas have been rather unsuccessful.[2] Such a situation, while not shown in the national unemployment figures, imposes the requirement 'move or starve' (or at best 'move or go on National Assistance'), which is scarcely a situation that a fairly wealthy and humane society would want to term full employment. Second, other countries, notably West Germany, have experienced unemployment rates down to 0·5 per cent of the labour force without serious associated problems.[3]

The precise definition of full employment for the purposes of this constraint is therefore rather difficult. Presumably a stipulation that the national unemployment level should not rise above 2 per cent for any period of more than six months, nor the level of any major region above 3½ per cent for such a period, would be acceptable and attainable. It must be remembered that there will always be some seasonal unemployment, especially in agriculture (which, however, occupies only one in every 25 British workers);[4] and that mobility of labour, especially during economic change, means temporary frictional unemployment for job-changers.

(b) Why full employment?

Why is such a high level of employment desirable? The answer is not as obvious as it seems. If a community could produce its entire needs with

---

[1] That is, even if we assume the real female rate is as high as the registered male rate—probably too pessimistic (see p. 130 below).

[2] In the sense that regional dispersion of unemployment rates has not gone down since 1955. See pp. 132-3.

[3] O.E.C.D., *Main Economic Indicators*, Feb. 1965, pp. 14-15.

[4] U.K. *Annual Abstract of Statistics*, 1964, p. 111; 977,000 of a working population of 25,575,000, in June 1963. Unfortunately the Ministry of Labour has now stopped giving data for the industrial distribution of total working force.

no labour at all, few people would work just for fun. The main motive for working is to earn access to consumer goods and services through wages. Suppose, however, a situation where a given number of hours of work are needed to produce the national product. There are three arguments for spreading these hours of work among many persons.

(i) For efficiency, it is desirable to minimise the effort needed to produce a given output and therefore to 'spread the load' among all competent workers, because boredom and fatigue reduce output per man-hour (or increase mechanical assistance or supervision required per unit of output) towards the end of a working day.

(ii) For price stability, overtime rates should be avoided, since the rising marginal disutility of effort which brings them about also means less extra output to absorb the extra money incomes.

(iii) From the distributional point of view, the existence of many unemployed workers implies severe inequality, for either they receive compensatory payments well below current wage levels (inequality of income) or they receive benefits close to the wage in employment (inequality of effort).

To this must be added the harmful social, political, and above all personal consequences of enforced and involuntary leisure. Thus, even though the notions of a 'labour force', an 'adequate' working year, and a 'full' employment level have flexible and conventionalist elements, full employment is well justified as an aim of economic policy. In any event, most people seek income from work rather than from charity. This is an attitude that both the economist and the moralist would surely encourage.

3. PRICE STABILITY

(a) *Meaning and measurement*

This aim of economic policy is easier than most to define and understand, but more difficult to justify. It cannot mean that we wish to stabilize all prices. This would stultify the entire mechanism of economic signalling and incentive. Changes in tastes could not lead to relative-price shifts causing responsive changes in the structure of output; cost-cutting could not be passed on as price reductions leading to the transfer of buying habits towards the goods where technology had improved. (Precisely the same line of thinking refutes the suggestion that *all* wage increases should be limited to some fixed percentage given by the overall rise in labour productivity).

Price stability, then, must mean the stabilisation of the price for some fixed bundle of goods: of the *cost-of-living index*—the ratio of the price of a typical housewife's bundle of goods bought in a week (discovered from a household sample survey conducted by the Ministry of Labour) to its price in a base-year, multiplied by 100. Thus if, on a 1960 base, the cost-of-living index is 105 in 1962, that means a 5 per cent rise in the price of the 1960 bundle of goods (a Laspeyres index).[1]

Notice that the effect of measuring inflation by the price of the 'bundle' bought in an early base-year is to overstate the erosive effects of inflation upon purchasing power.[2] Some products in the 1960 bundle will rise in price faster than others, as a result of higher increases in costs or profits. As time goes by, the housewife increasingly switches her buying away from these products to those which have increased less in price; but the Laspeyres index cannot reflect this switch.

Admittedly, there is an understatement effect from the demand side. A shift in tastes causes the housewife to devote a rising share of her outlay to commodities which, because of that shift, are rising in price faster than the Laspeyres bundle. Changes in tastes thus raise the relative price of goods representing a higher share of consumption in the current year than in the base-year. However, there is a counter-effect here: reductions in unit costs, by the adoption of bigger plant, often follow in an industry to which tastes have switched, reducing the relative price-rise there. Moreover, cost-induced shifts in relative prices—causing the Laspeyres index to exaggerate the effective rise in living costs—are the very essence of recent British inflation, and changes in tastes are a far slower process.

When we speak of price stability, we usually refer to the limitation of rises in the cost-of-living index. An atcual fall, by reducing the value of stocks, might discourage production; but a rise of more than, say, 2 or $2\frac{1}{2}$ per cent a year in the cost-of-living index is held to be undesirable. Even within this index, some prices are more important than others.

---

[1] Since 1962 only, the base of the index has switched to Paasche. This may be better or worse: it probably reduces the apparent rate of increase of prices (why?). If that curbs wage claims it constitutes neat statistical counter-inflation.

[2] Unfortunately it is impossible to *prove* this from official statistics—series with base-years *outside* the period of the price increase are not relevant. But the argument seems correct theoretically. Also, *any* index of prices aggregates commodities into groups; however fine the disaggregation of commodities (i.e. however many the groups), housewives always substitute for the items rising faster in price. This, too, brings 'actual' below 'indexed' rates of inflation.

The poor spend a larger proportion of their income on food and are thus hit hardest if food prices rise. From a distributive viewpoint such rises are particularly undesirable. Price rises are also particularly undesirable in products made for export since, even if the price rise is confined to the home market, it will encourage producers to switch production and salesmen away from the export sector. Similarly, price rises of items for which imported substitutes are available are dangerous. In constructing the inflation constraint, therefore, it is wise to allow rather less leeway to the prices of food, substitutes for imports, and exportable goods, than to other prices.

(b) Why not inflate?

Why is it desirable to limit inflation? The main reasons concern the incompatibility of inflation with other aims, especially the maintenance of a satisfactory balance of payments, and will be considered when we discuss compatibility in Chapter 4. Inflation, unlike stagnation or severe inequality, need not be harmful *in itself*. If all prices—of all assets, goods and services—and all incomes rise by 5 or 10 or 100 per cent every year in all countries, it is no more than a nuisance. It must be said that during the mild ($2\frac{1}{2}$-4 per cent per year) post-1945 inflation in Britain, few of the foreseen disastrous consequences have materialized.

First, inflation has not been the father of slump. This fear is generally based on propaganda, naïveté, or the doctrine that lightning causes thunder.[1] Let us give the argument the best possible run for its depreciating money. It might be suggested that inflation, by eroding the real value of fixed interest payments, drives lenders to charge higher rates of interest, and that this in turn discourages borrowers and chokes off new investment, leading to a slump via the multiplier. But the prices of final goods, and thus the profitability of new investment, rise with the cost of borrowing. So the businessman is neither encouraged nor discouraged.

Second, inflation is alleged to carry dangers of collapse into uncontrollable hyperinflation. Germany, Rumania and China, in the interwar period, experienced situations where prices multiplied thousands of times within a few months, and the value of savings was almost wiped out. But these inflations were not caused, or even preceded, by prolonged

[1] Or on pre-Keynesian myth: what recent experience teaches us is that policy can substitute, for the old cycle, boom-highlevel stagnation with price and import rises-boom-etc.

gentle inflation.[1] Since 1945, very many countries have experienced steady inflation, some at much faster rates than Britain, but none have collapsed into hyperinflation—even in such cases as Indonesia, where annual doublings of the price level have been commonplace.[2]

Third, apart from specific redistributive effects, inflation is allegedly cruel to an ill-defined group of persons living on 'fixed incomes'. These people are of two main types. Pensioners have votes, and their incomes are thus not fixed, but raised regularly before elections; indeed their real income per head, since the war, has risen more quickly (though more jerkily) than that of the average citizen.[3] Holders of bonds (fixed-interest securities issued by Governments and firms) are not a poor group deserving special sympathy;[4] most of them bought at prices heavily discounted against dangers of inflation. If bond-buyers are allegedly scared off lending to firms by inflation risk, the proper remedy, which has indeed been adopted in most new issues, is to issue equity shares instead, and that is probably desirable on other grounds also.[5]

Fourth, inflation is supposed to have harmful distributive effects, reducing the share of labour owing to the lag of price rises behind wage rises. This argument was unsound even in the days before trade unions, for planned labour supply is determined, in the long run, by *real* wages (taking price changes into account) even in a competitive market. Nowadays trade unions see to it that the share of wages in GNP does not fall, and it certainly has not fallen during post-war inflation in Britain. It is true that weakly unionised sectors feel the initial shock of price rises, but figures compiled by *The Guardian*[6] indicate extremely

---

[1] C. Bresciani-Turroni, *The Economics of Inflation*, Allen and Unwin, 1937, pp. 28-29.

[2] U.N., *Monthly Bulletin of Statistics*, Feb. 1965, p. 152.

[3] U.K. *Annual Abstract of Statistics*, 1964, pp. 55, 295.

[4] Morgan, *Structure of Property Ownership in Great Britain*, Oxford, 1960, Table 65, shows that persons (as opposed to financial institutions, Government, companies, and charities) held a smaller proportion of fixed-interest paper than of ordinary shares in 1953-5.

[5] Bonds hardly ever carry votes. A large number of non-voting shares makes take-over, even against the wishes of most owners and without relevance to the economic case for it, much easier, and divorces owners of a company from the power to control it; if these shares are also fixed-interest, they are not even likely to want to do so.

[6] *The Guardian Wage Index*, Devons *et al.*, The Guardian, 1962; and *Statistics on Incomes, Prices, Employment and Productivity*, Dec. 1964, pp. 12, 15. From April 1960 to April 1964, average hourly earnings rose 25·5 per cent; the luckiest workers (in brewing and malting, and in lacemaking) got only 33·8 per cent;

little difference in wage increases among occupations since 1960.

Workers such as bank clerks, commercial travellers and university teachers, who for social reasons refuse to form trade unions of sufficient power, fall behind *temporarily* in the wage race. However, if workers consciously prefer status to cash it is not for society to put them 'right'. More seriously, Government policy against inflation is temptingly easy to direct at the public sector. This carries the danger of a steady drift of the best personnel out of the civil service, universities and nationalised industries. Such persons have exceptionally high international mobility. However, the competition of union-negotiated earnings in the private sector is strong enough to stop this being very important. So if inflation has regressive effects on income distribution, they are probably weak. They are counterbalanced by the important fact that most repayments of loans (especially H.P. and overdrafts) are fixed in money terms. Inflation thus relieves debtors at the expense of creditors—and that usually helps the poor and hurts the rich.

So why worry about inflation at all? Leaving aside loose and emotive arguments about effects on business confidence on the basis of accounting estimates of profit, etc. (which assume all businessmen are idiots), we are left with the really serious consequence of inflation: its effect on the balance of payments.

There are many paths through which domestic inflation worsens the foreign balance—substitution by home buyers of imports for domestic produce, discouragement of foreign buyers, diversion of home producers from exports to the more lucrative home market, and diversion of foreign producers from their market to ours being only the more obvious micro-mechanisms. These effects are considered in more detail on pp. 241–4. Here it need only be said that they constitute ample reason for seeking to limit inflation. It should, however, be emphasised that a perfectly anticipated, *worldwide* rise of x per cent per year in *all* prices, incomes and asset values (including values of bonds) would be no more than a minor nuisance.

---

the least (domestic electric appliances) 11·5 per cent and the second least (textile machine workers) 18·3 per cent. There were over 110 groups listed, but the divergence of income rises was small. This, by the way, does not prove that unions make no difference; strong unions in some sectors, by forcing up national levels, pull up earnings paid to workers in other sectors (where employers must pay more to keep their employees).

4. THE BALANCE OF PAYMENTS

(a) What do we want?

'Export or die' is one of the oldest and silliest of political slogans. 'Import or die' makes good sense for a country that produces less than all its needs domestically. But there are three ways to pay for imports: now, by current exports; from the past, out of accumulated reserves of gold and foreign exchange; or in the future, by repayment of current borrowing. The division into these three categories depends partly on the accounting period. There are many days, and several months, in which any country has a substantial excess of imports over exports, and it is not really rational to get specially worried about a deficit because it happens to accrue during the period required by the Earth to go round the Sun. If one country is prepared to run an excess of exports for a year or two, there is no reason why its trading partners should look at their temporary import surpluses with too much alarm.

Of course, the day of reckoning is bound to come, so that prolonged import surpluses are not tolerable. They involve some combination of risking enforced devaluation due to depletion of reserves, and paying heavily to borrow short-term funds. Also they mean that a country is unable, without increasing these dangers and costs, to give assistance to (or finance military outlays or productive investments in) other countries. It is for this last reason, together with the supposed need to preserve our 'banker's role', that the British Treasury, in its evidence to the Radcliffe Commission suggested that a yearly surplus in the current-account balance of payments of some £450 million was required![1]

The current *balance of trade* comprises exports, less imports, of goods ('visibles'); the current *balance of payments* adds to this 'invisible' receipts (*less* expenditures) on banking, insurance, shipping and tourist services, and also profit (and—negligible—wage) incomes earned by Britons abroad, net of those earned by foreigners here. In the U.K., a long-standing trade deficit has been less and less adequately compensated, during the period since 1955 anyway, by a shrinking invisible surplus. Since the requirements of the balance of payments are the main single cause of both slow growth and unstable prices, it is worth investigating whether we really ought to strain towards such a target as the £450m. yearly surplus desired by the Treasury.

[1] Committee on the Working of the Monetary System, op. cit., p. 20; Memoranda of Evidence, vol. 1 (H.M.S.O., 1960), p. 117.

C*

It is certainly of doubtful realism. First, it is impossible for every country to have a current balance-of-payments surplus, unless Earth has net exports to Mars. Indeed the ultra-cautious attitude of accountants to the foreign sector has caused the illusion of world imports far in excess of world exports.[1] An economy that makes year-by-year surpluses its aim inflicts corresponding deficits on others. It is therefore in danger of upsetting the entire mechanism of international payments, and risking deserved retaliation. It is against this danger that West Germany and Holland have taken steps to cut down their export surpluses.

Secondly, there is some evidence that the maintenance of a boom leads, via stock-building imports, to balance-of-payments difficulties. At really full employment, home suppliers cannot meet growing demand. Thus any programme for accelerated growth will have to wait for its balance-of-payments surplus until the imports can be used to invest in export or import-substitute industries. French and German evidence indicates that such a surplus is achieved and kept after 4-6 years of steady growth.[2]

In practice, only in a single year since the war has the U.K. managed a surplus of anything like the dimensions required by the Treasury.[3] So it is doubtful if the target can be attained without rather severely limiting the other aims. In view of the smallness of our reserves[4] and the high cost, in a world of risk and inflation, of short-term loans, deficits should be avoided as far as possible. Certainly no period of, say, three years of

---

[1] World visible imports exceed exports in most years by over 8 per cent! A small part of this is caused by measuring imports c.i.f. and exports f.o.b.—but more by pessimism, and the actual disparity is larger, since smuggled imports are concealed but smuggled exports scarcely exist. U.N., *Monthly Bulletin of Statistics*, Feb. 1965, pp. 88-9.

[2] France devalued in 1958, but subsequent steady growth has permitted (or at least not impeded) the build-up of so strong a reserve position that, by early 1965, her threat to sell dollars for gold seriously embarrassed (if no more) the U.S. government. West Germany and Holland were able to revalue by 5 per cent in 1962.

[3] In 1958 our current-account surplus reached the minimum £300m. (though not the desired £450m.) Treasury target. This was the only year it did even that. U.K., *Annual Abstract of Statistics*, 1958, p. 237; 1964, p. 239.

[4] Accumulated deficits on the balance of payments (current and long-term capital accounts) from 31.12.1958 to the end of 1964 exceeded by some 5 per cent total gold and foreign-currency reserves on the earlier date; but for an unexplained 'balancing item' the excess would have been almost 30 per cent (Table 19, p. 165 below). As Mr. Wilson told the Economic Club of New York on 14th April, 1965, we could always pay our debts by selling assets abroad to raise more reserves; a bankrupt could usually sell physical assets (bed, furniture, clothes) in the same way. In 1965 we retained some £850mn. reserves solely by the grace of our creditors. This is a strange foundation for sound banking.

deficit should be tolerated, and the programme might also be constrained to avoid deficits of more than, say, £70-80 million in any single year, on plausible assumptions about the movements of import and export prices. But is Treasury insistence upon a yearly £450 million current surplus—nearly 2 per cent of total output used solely to accumulate gold and dollars—really justified?

(b) The 'banker's role'

The justification from Britain's banker's role can no longer, in my opinion, be usefully advanced. The City of London is a great financial centre. In other words, foreigners transact business in sterling, and hold short-term assets in interest-bearing claims on flows of sterling, especially in Government and local-authority bills and bonds. This brings in a lot of foreign exchange. Most of it is not British property, since it has to be repaid when the bills, etc., mature. But a substantial sum is payment for banking services, and hence a genuine contribution to our foreign reserves.

Unfortunately, the banker's role carries great and growing dangers to Britain. Firstly, it evolved in a period (around 1870-1914) when the annual yields from British assets abroad were enormous in relation to her largest conceivable annual balance-of-trade deficit. Two wars, decolonisation, and world trade expansion mean that this is no longer the case. There is thus no longer the automatic confidence in sterling which is necessary to support a banker's role.

Second, as a direct result of this, British-owned reserves of gold and foreign exchange (many of which used to flow from overseas investments no longer in British hands) have shrunk to a far smaller proportion of liabilities than was once the case. Consequently, the British tend to treat these liabilities—foreign assets banked in London—as convenient extra permanent U.K. reserves. Hence we talk ourselves into speculative (rather than true) balance-of-payments crises when these bogus reserves are—perfectly legitimately—run down, as by the Indians in 1957.

Third, as a result of the declining contribution made by the yield from foreign investments to the British balance of payments, the slightest temporary balance-of-payments difficulties lead to speculation about devaluation. This speculation causes many foreigners, who hold sterling and sterling-yielding assets (like Consols), to sell sterling for other currencies and for gold. Such sales reduce the market demand for sterling and raise its supply. They thus make the danger of devaluation real.

Fourth, profitable banking depends on intelligent use of one's clients' money. It thus requires confidence that not too many clients will want to withdraw at once. British banks, in domestic business, usually keep cash in hand amounting to some 8 per cent of deposits—the 'cash ratio'. On the world scene, many of our foreign clients are countries (or importers) in balance-of-payments difficulties. Almost all are liable to periodic bouts of suspicion of sterling. Therefore Britain is forced to carry on her banker's role with a high cash ratio in case of a run on sterling. Thus she retains a low proportion of her clients' money for profitable investment overseas.

Fifth, in so far as foreigners acquire sterling assets, interest payments on Government and local-authority loans drain out of the U.K., instead of being mere internal transfers. Thus the 'burden' of national debt, formerly nominal and fictitious, becomes real. If foreigners use interest payments to accumulate more British bonds, compound interest renders the growth of the burden cumulative. Worse, if—for reasons of home policy alone—it is desired to raise interest rates (i.e. to lower Government bond prices),[1] foreign buyers will be drawn into the market if one's currency is international. This temporary boosting of reserves by 'hot money', volatile among international financial centres at the lure of small interest rate differentials, is expensively bought, and leads to reliance upon standby money which is really liable to sudden drainage. Further, it brings the risk of internationally competitive upward auctions of interest rates, with eventual harm to employment levels.[2]

Finally, the adoption by Britain of a banker's role makes devaluation very difficult politically. It means writing down the value of foreigners' assets in British banks; and thus any repetition of the 1949 devaluation would certainly spell the end of many clients' confidence. But devaluation is sometimes a very sensible policy. It makes exports cheaper and imports dearer, and under certain circumstances (which are not as obvious as they may appear)[3] this will improve a threatened balance of

---

[1] If the rate of interest obtainable on *new* issues goes up, the face value of old bonds must fall until they yield as high a rate as the new bonds; till then sellers for old bonds will outnumber buyers. This is why higher interest rates on new bonds attract foreign money to London even to buy old bonds.

[2] This process set up a minor recession in 1966-7.

[3] They are not exhausted by a tautology about elasticities (the Marshall-Lerner condition for 'successful' devaluation). Consider its economic meaning in terms of substitutes. How has the composition of British imports altered? Are they now more price-elastic than, say, in 1913? Despite our far higher employment levels? What of the effects of devaluation on demand for imports through changes in income distribution? Through cost-push inflation?

payments. There is a strong *prima facie* case against devaluing, as against any act which requires workers to produce more exports in order to obtain the means to buy fewer imports. But this does not make it desirable for a country to be unable to devalue if it wants to, yet constantly in danger of being forced to devalue by speculations too large to be counterbalanced by official action.[1]

(c) Overseas investment needs

It must be emphasized that the above remarks are the opinions of the author. Readers should check the argument and see if they can find arguments on the other side—and supporting statistics. However, it is my view that the banker's role argument for a current-account balance-of-payments surplus can rest only on notions of political prestige (misconceived, because over-extension is a poor basis for policy, always vulnerable to embarrassing exposure), not on any real economic justification. What, then, of the other major argument for British *current* balance-of-payments surpluses, that they permit private overseas capital investment and thus help discharge our obligations to poorer nations? Recent balance-of-payments deficits *on capital account* have been around £100m.-£250m. a year. In the long run, only current-account surpluses can make this tolerable.

By suitable selection of examples, it is possible to make 'overseas investment' sound adventurous and daring (Everest expeditions, mission hospitals) or progressive and generous (Unilever of West Africa, I.C.I. of India). However, the vast bulk of British overseas investment, to maintain which we have cut down growth with a view to financing it by a necessary surplus, is of a very different sort. The biggest single recipient is South Africa, and other major ones are Canada and Australia.[2] The proportion going to underdeveloped countries is not above one-third and has been rapidly falling.

[1] This is irrespective of whether one wants devaluation; one wants to retain the right to decide. In October 1964 it was evident that supply of sterling, in that year, would exceed demand by about 80 per cent of total British reserves (i.e. of our ability to meet those demands). Most of even these reserves were held only because our creditors kindly delayed calling in past debts. However, sterling was a major trading currency, and this meant both income and prestige for London. Whether or not you agree that the first group of considerations should have prevailed, it cannot be argued that, to sustain a bankers' role, one should surrender economic sovereignty in such a matter—and not to any properly designed international organisation, but to random creditors!

[2] A Shonfield, *British Economic Policy Since the War*, revised edition (1959), p. 133, citing A. R. Conan.

Most overseas investment is in support of established projects, and its yield has been considerably smaller than could have been obtained at home.[1] This is not because it has been managed badly, but because much of it has been in mines yielding diminishing returns, and because many Boards of Directors have a natural prejudice in favour of investing in their own concerns rather than acquiring non-controlling share interests in other people's.

Even such investments as have gone to underdeveloped economies have been largely in mines and plantations (Malayan rubber, Ceylon tea, Rhodesian copper). There they have sustained the living standards of small privileged groups, and done little to advance either the productivity or the welfare of the poor and backward agricultural subsistence labourers. These are 70-90 per cent of underdeveloped populations; they constitute the core problem of poverty in these countries. British overseas private capital still yields more on current account than it costs on capital account (pp. 182-4). But it might yield much more foreign exchange if reinvested in British export industries. It is *not* the 'cause' of our balance-of-payments problem (p. 184), but neither is it a sufficient reason for striving for a huge current surplus at the cost of growth.

(d) Export surpluses?

Neither the banker's role nor overseas investment appears to justify using 1 to 2 per cent of national income each year to building up an export surplus. Certainly we do not want a running deficit, with its high maintenance costs (interest charges from borrowing). However, we should look forward actively to (i.e. help bring about) the time when perfect, year-to-year balance in foreign payments goes the way of its cousin, the balanced yearly budget, and is seen, not as a goal, but as one of many possible tools of policy. For example, countries with inflation could run balance-of-payments deficits, counterbalanced by surpluses in those suffering from unemployment, to the advantage of both. The excess of exports over imports would create employment via the multiplier, while in the inflationary economy the net inflow of imports would create alternative sources of supply to home products, and thus press down on their prices.

[1] *Ibid.*, chapter 6, *passim*. Nevertheless until the 1965 Budget British taxation so favoured overseas investment that the *private* yield, net of tax, remained relatively attractive. Tax discrimination in favour of 'development areas' may be justified on social grounds; but South Africa is not Northern Ireland.

While monetary reform is a long-run British objective, there is no doubt that, in the world as it is, continual deficits must be avoided, and that this is a generally accepted aim of economic policy. But there is no sense in aiming at more than we need to sustain a role we cannot afford with resources we do not have. In the immediate short run, surpluses must be sought, to repay obligations incurred as a result of the monster deficit of 1964. In the long run, a balanced current account is all we should aim for. International aid—even if Britain gives far more than now—need not be in gold and dollars.

(e) Adequate reserves

Of course it is impossible for Britain honourably to discard overnight her obligations as an international banker, or to change dramatically her pattern of investments abroad. These matters require negotiations with clients and with recipient countries and firms, combined with incentives towards a more rational allocation of funds. In the interim, it is desirable to stop British monetary policy from being dictated by speculators: emotive words, but accurate ones. Speculators sell sterling because they hope to buy it back cheaply after devaluation. To destroy such expectations, the British Government cuts imports (by reducing the growth of income), and attracts short-term investment funds by raising interest rates (thus making it more expensive to borrow money for productive investment).

Much the best way to defeat the speculators is by international monetary agreements to increase total world liquidity, whether by raising the value of gold, giving credit-creating powers to the I.M.F., or other means.[1] The present arrangements, the Basle agreements, involve the grant of standby credits by central banks to any of their number suffering from temporary speculation. If many speculators buy dollars from the Bank of England, it can replenish its dollar stock by using such credits, and thus kill speculation that the stock will run out and compel devaluation. This arrangement against speculation supple-

---

[1] As *The Economist* rightly and often points out, any group of economists could swiftly produce (and argue about) several workable liquidity-raising schemes: meanwhile their disputes about the merits of Stamp, Bernstein, Triffin, *et al.*, obscure their near-unanimity that there is not enough liquidity. Meanwhile any success by the U.S.A. *or the U.K.* in cutting her deficit dangerously reduces world liquidity; and France and West Germany are of course delighted to 'support' sterling when necessary, thereby avoiding the danger of having an international reserve currency (and hence a speculatively vulnerable brake on growth) of their own.

ments access to I.M.F. loans to cover temporary balance-of-payments deficits. Such arrangements, while far better than nothing, are expensive for borrowers, and expose lenders to dangers of political blackmail. It is thus desirable for an economy to operate with reserves of gold, or acceptable foreign currencies, sufficient to tide it over temporary crises, whether caused by speculation or by lags of exports behind imports.

British reserves in the 1950s, while a small proportion of trade by comparison with pre-war years, would have been ample if they could have been thrown safely into the breach as need arose. The reserves fluctuated around £1,000 million; in 1952-63 no *current* annual balance-of-payments deficit, even if financed wholly out of reserves without borrowing, would have required over one-third of that sum, and most of the outflow would have been recouped in the following two years.[1] But the reserves could not be committed. Britain's proud dual role as international banker and trading-currency nation meant huge numbers of bondholders with sterling-yielding assets, ready to sell on a massive scale (thus raising the supply, and hence cutting the price, of future claims on sterling, and practically forcing unwanted devaluation) if British reserves were allowed to fall substantially. Thus huge, expensive international loans had to pay for deficits, instead of running-down of reserves.

The experience of recent years seems to indicate—though this is bound to be a matter of opinion, since the evidence bears rival interpretations—that the 1950's level of British reserves would be adequate, if U.K. policy were directed towards reducing the role of sterling as an international currency, the (reserve-draining) requirements of British investment in such places as South Africa, and the excessive reserve needs implied by the banker's role. Hence there is no more need to accept the building up of huger reserves as a policy aim, than to endorse the Treasury's estimate of the huge balance-of-payments surplus required to achieve it. However, accumulated deficits on current and long-term capital accounts, since 1959, far exceed total reserves at the end of that year. *In the short run* it is build-up or bankruptcy.

5 · IMPROVED COMPOSITION OF OUTPUT

(a) *The area of agreement*
It has been suggested that the disproportionate market power of the rich

---

[1] See p. 165, and *Economic Trends*, March 1965. In 1951 the deficit was £403m. on capital account; in 1964, £371m.; otherwise from £100m. to £250m.

consumer and of the monopolistic or oligopolistic producer, together with the capacity of good advertising and bad education to mould tastes, render price *mechanisms* (if not price *policies*)[1] dubiously desirable determinants of output composition in the growth process. There is general agreement among British political parties that the share of national product devoted to certain activities—especially the provision of houses, roads, schools and hospitals, and the support of education, the arts and sciences, and the care of special groups such as the mentally ill —has been too low by the standards of comparably rich countries and of our own humane sentiments.

It is also agreed by most people that too big a share of resources (as measured by national income) is devoted to demonstrably harmful products like cigarettes, to much-advertised but identical substitutes for simple and cheaper products (like 'Aspro' for Aspirin B.P.)[2], and to the numerous worthless placebos in drugs and cosmetics. By 'too big' we mean that these resources could be better used, not in the sense that a free society is entitled to *force* the abandonment of these types of outlay, but that both taxation and education should be used to *encourage* it. This is not for ascetic or puritan reasons, but because it is reasonably certain that the people so encouraged would be grateful very soon afterwards. This sort of argument is always dangerous, but far less so under an elective system of government in a sophisticated, educated society. There, an administration that (in the electorate's opinion) abuses it will soon be thrown out.

(b) Consequences of composition decisions

In order to define 'improvement' in the composition of output, we need:

(i) a moral decision regarding what types of output are to be preferred, and how they are to be weighted against each other; acceptance of the composition given by price incentives is one among many such possible decisions; but first

(ii) a logical examination of the distinction between intrinsically valued output and instrumental output, made only in order to produce other goods and services.

---

[1] This useful summary of a familiar dichotomy is due to Myrdal.

[2] *Which* is one of several publications to have proved their chemical identity. Martin Mayer, in *Madison Avenue: U.S.A.*, argues that the advertisement 'adds value' and thus enhances the worth of the product: a form of faith-healing in which the real worth of an advertisement is inversely proportional to the intrinsic merit of the product!

Steel is a totally instrumental product, made solely as an *intermediate good* between (a) coal and iron inputs and (b) outputs of steel goods like cars, scissors and refrigerators which are desired for their intrinsic worth in consumption. Ice cream is totally intrinsic—an input into nothing except indigestion. Coal is both intrinsic (final-use) if burned in a grate for warmth, and intermediate at numerous different levels of 'distance back' in the process of production; if coal is used to heat the baker's oven, it is only one stage back along the line leading to final-use bread; if it is used to make steel, which in turn makes a machine-tool for making a baking oven, the economic distance from the final product is far greater.

Before we can see the economic consequences of various moral decisions regarding the composition of output, we have to look at the implications, for the entire productive structure of instrumental goods (raw materials and intermediates) of different decisions concerning the desired structure of final-use, intrinsic goods and services for consumption. The decision that 'society wants' fewer cars and more roads means a realignment of the whole resource-structure towards making roads (and gravel), away from making cars (and digging coal and iron to make steel to make cars). The technique for analysing the economic consequences of such changes is called *input-output analysis*.

To see how this works, let us examine it in an extremely oversimplified context. The simplifying assumptions fall into two categories. Those in the first category are for explanatory purposes only, and can easily be relaxed subsequently; they do not affect the structure of input-output methods. Those in the second category do, but are reasonably close approximations to reality in the fairly short run.

In the first category are the assumptions:

(i) that our hyper-simple economy has only two sectors, 'industry' and 'primary producers';

(ii) that there is no foreign trade;

(iii) that there is no Government economic activity; and

(iv) that each sector makes just one product (or, which for analytic purposes is the same thing, that each produces outputs in fixed ratios, e.g. that primary producers always make 3 bushels of wheat for every 2 bushels of maize).

More fundamental are the assumptions in the second category—those which cannot be abandoned without totally restructuring the model, but which seem to be fairly well in accord with *short-run* experience. They are:

(v) that returns do not vary to scale—doubling all inputs exactly doubles output in each sector; and

(vi) that factors of production cannot be substituted for each other—the marginal product of coal in steel-making is zero, because labour, iron, etc., are needed in fixed ratios to the extra coal before it can increase output.[1] These assumptions of technological rigidity are reasonable if our model is to be used for short-run analysis only. If technology changes systematically and predictably, that can be incorporated; but usually, as Professor Stone has demonstrated, the economist must turn to the engineer to see how his various relations between inputs and outputs are likely to change between the various 'short runs' during which they are roughly fixed.[2] On these assumptions we can now examine our extremely simple agriculture-industry economy.

Figure 4

Sales by	Purchases by			
	Primary producers	*Manufac- turers*	*Final consumer*	*Total Sales*
Primary producers	*a* £40m.	*b* £39m.	*c* £21m.	*d* £100m.
Manufacturers	*e* £10m.	*f* £78m.	*g* £42m.	*h* £130m.
Wage-earners, profit-receivers	*i* £50m.	*j* £13m.	*k* —	*l* £63m.
Total Purchases	*d'* £100m.	*h'* £130m.	*l'* £63m.	*d+h+l* £293m.

In Figure 4, we have entered the value in £ million of each sector's purchases from each other sector. Thus primary producers buy £40m. from each other (square *a*), £10 million from manufacturers (square *e*),

---

[1] Notice that these assumptions are the same as those of linear programming. Both sorts of linear economic model have similar mathematical structures, though input-output is *descriptive* while linear programming is *optimising*.

[2] Stone, Bates and Bacharach, *A Computable Model for Economic Growth: Input-Output Tables 1954-1966*, Cambridge 1963.

and £50m. from suppliers of labour, wage-earners, and of capital, profit-takers (square *i*)—a total of £100m. (square *d'*). Squares *a* and *e* indicate the value of the raw materials entering primary production; the payments to factors of production in square *d'* correspond to the value added by them to those raw materials.

Now, unless producers are changing the level of stocks (which, to simplify, we assume not to be the case), the total value of purchases, including profits (*d'*) must be the same as total sales by primary producers in square *d*. Reading across the first row of figures, we have already seen that primary producers sell £40m. to one another (*a*); further, they sell £39m. as raw materials to manufacturers (e.g. as minerals) (*b*), and £21m. as final-use, 'intrinsic' goods to consumers (e.g. at greengrocers') (*d*). You can trace a similar pattern for industrial sales and purchases.

In Figure 4, notice that the £63m. in squares *l* and *l'* is the national product value-added by (and final incomes received by factors in) the two sectors together;[1] and that the ratios i/d' and j/h' are, in a sense, indicators of the *independence* of the sectors. Plausibly, we show the industrial sector as relying more heavily on inputs from the other sector, relative to factor inputs, than primary producers. Indeed, the ratio $l/(d + h + l)$ is a sign of how much the economy has industrialised, and mobilised sectors in each other's support. Usually, the higher the ratio, the less developed the economy.[2]

How does one use a set-up like Figure 4 to examine the implications of rival compositions of output (whether selected by planners, the price mechanism or some mixture of the two)? Suppose a planning decision is made to double the amount of agricultural products going to final consumers; what are the implications for intermediate production of raising *c* to £42 million? Figure 5 shows what happens. The rise in *c* raises total sales by primary producers, *d*, to £121m. To keep the balance, *d'*—purchases of inputs by primary producers, including profits —must also rise to £121m.

---

[1] Foreign sector and government are easily dealt with.
[2] Harvie and Kleeve, *The National Income of the Sudan*, Khartoum, 1957; and W. Leontief, in *Technology and Economic Development* 1965.

people want more primary products
    c rises to £42m.
    $d' = d = a + b + c$ rises to £121m.
primary producers' needs for all inputs rise in proportion
    a to £48·4m. (40% £121m.)
    e to £12·1m. (10% £121m.)
    l to £60·5m. (50% £121m.)
so sales by firms making primary producers' inputs rise
    $d = d'$ to £129·4m.
      (new c + new a + unchanged b)
    $h = h'$ to £132·1m.
      (new e + unchanged f and g)
so all needs for inputs rise in proportion—but less than before
    a to £51·76m. (40% new d)
    e to £12·94m. (10% new d)
    l to £64·7m. (50% new d)
    b to £39·63m. (30% new h)
    f to £79·26m. (60% new h)
    j to £13·21m. (10% new h)

so suppliers' sales rise again—but less than before
    $d = d'$ to £133·39m.
      (new a + new b + new c)
    $h = h'$ to £136·2m.
      (new e + new f + unchanged g)
so all needs for inputs rise in proportion—but less than before
    a to £53·356m. (40% new d)
    e to £13·339m. (10% new d)
    l to £66·695m. (50% new d)
    b to £40·86m. (30% new h)
    f to £81·72m. (60% new h)
    j to £13·62m. (10% new h)

so suppliers' sales rise once again, but by still less than before
    $d = d'$ to £136·236m.
      (new a + new b + new c)
    $h = h'$ to £137·059m.
      (new e = new f + unchanged g)

this requires another, still smaller rise in suppliers' inputs

a to £54·494m. (40% new d)
e to £13·636m. (10% new d)
l to £68·118m. (50% new d)
b to £41·1177m. (30% new h)
f to £82·7154m. (60% new h)
j to £13·785m. (10% new h)

many more such steps converging to Figure 6.

Now our assumptions of constant returns to scale and fixed proportions mean that this rise of £21m. must be divided among receivers of primary incomes, a, e and i, in just the same proportions as the initial £100m. produced in d' in the last diagram. That is, a rises to £48m., which is $\frac{4}{10}$ of £121m., as shown in Figure 5. This means that the *extra* output of agricultural products for final consumers requires extra inputs in the same ratios as the *initial* output. Thus, in the same way, this first round of increased demand raises e to £12·1m. and also i to £60·5m. But the table is still not in balance, for though our new d and d' are the same, the rises in inputs into agriculture needed to achieve this have set up differences between inputs and outputs in manufacturing, and between final incomes and expenditures (h and h', l and l'). In other words, more inputs are needed to make the extra inputs used by agriculture to satisfy the higher final demand.

This process is shown, for several rounds, in Figure 5. It clearly *converges*, in the sense that the changes in any component of the input-output table will get smaller and smaller at each stage.[1] For example, a, inputs of agricultural products to make more of themselves, rises first by £8·4m. to satisfy higher consumer demand; then by £3·36 to satisfy the implications of the demand for supply of raw materials to agriculture; then by just under £2·1m. to produce that supply, both agricultural and industrial; and so on. Figure 5 illustrates this process of convergence for a few rounds, and Figure 6 shows the final equilibrium implicit in the rise in consumer demand for primary products, after all adjustments have been made.

[1] This is not sufficient to guarantee convergence (the sum of $\frac{1}{2} + \frac{1}{3} + \frac{1}{4} + \frac{1}{5} + \ldots$ is not finite). Sufficient is the Hawkins-Simon condition—in effect, that the total industrial inputs, direct and indirect, for £1 of final industrial output are less than £1, and similarly with total primary inputs for final output of primary products.

Figure 6

Sales by	Purchases by			Total Sales
	Primary Producers	Manufac- turers	Final consumers	
Primary producers	*a* £56m.	*b* £42m.	*c* £42m.	*d* £140m.
Manufacturers	*e* £14m.	*f* £84m.	*g* £42m.	*h* £140m.
Wage-earners, profit-receivers	*i* £70m.	*j* £14m.	*k* —	*l* £84m.
Total Purchases	*d'* £140m.	*h'* £140m.	*l'* £84m.	*d+h+l* £364m.

Real economies, of course, are far more complex. A good input-output table has hundreds of sectors[1] and makes allowances for possible changes in input-output ratios[2]: but the principle is as shown in these diagrams. Regularly revised, accurate input-output tables are essential to economic planning, whatever the balance of controls between price-mechanism, incentives and compulsion. Yet the U.K. has had no official table since 1954.[3] The National Economic Development Council, in preparing estimates of the implications of a 4 per cent growth rate for various industries from 1962 to 1966, relied not on any consistency test, but simply on what some official in a 'typical' firm thought it might be able to produce![4] So there could be a surplus of coal, but inadequate steel owing to iron shortage.

In the context of input-output analysis, let us look again at what can be said about desired compositions of output as economic policy aims.

[1] H. Chenery and P. Clark, *Interindustry Economics*, Wiley, 1959.

[2] Stone, Bates and Bacharach, *op. cit.*

[3] The 1963 table, produced in 1966, relies too heavily on extrapolation of 1954 data to be regarded as an adequately useful, accurate or new input-output table.

[4] N.E.D.C., *Growth of the U.K. to 1966*, H.M.S.O., 1963. The extraordinary belief that you estimate growth needs by industry through sample-survey—non-random at that—into self-assessed intentions, with no consistency test, seems to have escaped criticism. But the *National Plan* to 1970 (published in 1965) at least pressed the respondents to a random sample to adjust their predicted outputs towards the consequences of the rate of growth of consumption, as these were estimated by Stone's input-output construction.

Of course, if one believes that the price mechanism produces the ideal allocation of productive efforts, one is neither willing nor able to say anything about desired output composition in a planning context. But this belief is a value-judgment, and in view of differences in consumer pressure (income distribution) and market power (degree of monopoly) one that few would accept.

(c) Towards defining 'improved composition'

To get anywhere near defining a 'shift in the composition of output that is an improvement', we have to look at specific ways in which adjustments through the price mechanism (inevitably used by non-totalitarian planning to a great extent) and possible planning steps could distort the structure of relative prices (notice that 'distort' is an evaluative word). To take price-mechanism distortions first, one might suspect:

(i) Systematic underpricing of public-sector products, leading to their undervaluation in the maximand if market prices are the weights used;

(ii) Overpricing of commodities bought mainly by the rich (and by those growing richer) relative to those bought mainly by the poor, or by those losing relative income share;

(iii) Overpricing of monopolised (or monopolising) sectors' outputs, relative to more competitively produced items (or those becoming so);

(iv) Related to all these, a maximand that values human needs too low (and expands them too slowly) *vis-à-vis* money-backed demands for less essential items, and similarly undervalues genuine demands, originating with the buyer, from those stimulated artificially from outside. (Warning: the use of 'underpricing' and 'overpricing' in (i)-(iii) is descriptive, but in (iv) 'too low', 'too slowly', 'less essential' 'undervalues', 'genuine' and 'artificially' are evaluative.)

(d) Undervaluation of public outputs

The price mechanism undervalues public-sector products, because in a time of gently rising prices (usually a concomitant of growth) public-sector prices are held back both by conventionalism (entry to a public convenience costs 1d now just as it did fifty years ago) and by public pressure against inflation. Directly, increases in prices in the public sector reflect especially adversely on the popular view of the efficiency of the Government in limiting inflation. This kept the price of coal far below its economic level for many years.[1] Indirectly, wage-pause policies can be carried out most easily in the public sector.

---

[1] I. M. D. Little, *The Price of Fuel*, Oxford, 1953, chs. 1, 5, 9.

Further, the effect of advertising is to raise the demand for products advertised relative to others. The public sector makes a relatively high proportion of things like schools and houses, which are neither easy to advertise nor produced by oligopolies, and which thus tend to go un-advertised. During the 1950s, in the U.K. as elsewhere, advertising has been a growing part of total national effort, and almost all the increase has gone towards advertising privately-made products. Comparison of the U.K. with other, rather richer countries indicates that we are no-where near the end of prospective growth in the share of effort going to advertising, and hence in the tendency to undervalue public-sector output. Professor Galbraith's discussion of 'private affluence amid public squalor', of bigger and better cars driving along deteriorating roads, and taking drivers to eat increasingly sumptuous picnics by ever more polluted streams, applies to the U.K. as forcefully as to the U.S.[1]

Perhaps most important of all, large sectors of public output (health, education) contain no profit income. In national accounting, they are valued at current cost alone. All this adds up to undervaluation, of un-known size, of public output by market prices and accounting conven-tions. We could well upvalue government output by 5 to 10 per cent in the maximand.[2]

(e) Overvaluation of demands by the rich

The second distortion of the price system, by contrast to one reflecting a more equal income distribution, is the overpricing of goods for which market pressure is more effective because they are in demand by the rich. It should be noted that the market effect of this distortion is equalising and tends to correct lopsided income distributions, but it is a highly inefficient way of doing so, since it directs a much larger share of national productive effort into making luxuries—and goods to make luxuries, goods to make those goods, etc.—than would be the case under a more equal distribution of income.

Our specification of income equalisation as a policy objective (pp. 86-102 below) will reduce the distortion. For such a distortion tends to over-value goods going to (a) the rich and (b) those getting richer faster, and under a programme of equalisation these people are different. However,

---

[1] Galbraith, *op. cit.*, pp. 206-8.

[2] Any assessment is arbitrary; one must consider a whole host of relatively stable prices, from council-house rents through postage stamps to entrance to Kew Gardens, and make some 'guesstimate'.

in constructing our maximand, we shall do well to raise the planned price-weighting given to necessities, since these from a larger part of the income of poor consumers than of the rich, and are thus underpriced.

This does not mean that the State should try to raise the *market* prices of necessities relative to luxuries. Such a policy would be regressive, since necessities bulk largest in the expenditures of the poorest. Moreover, the incentive effects of such a policy would result in the production of more necessities than a fairly rich economy wanted. The market 'underpricing' of necessities implies only that the *accounting* prices, used by planners to determine the relative importance of growth in luxuries and in necessities, should be raised for necessities. 'How much?' and 'What are necessities?' are problems of theoretical interest and difficulty, but would hardly hold up practical planning. Here, as in deciding how much to upvalue Government outputs, the decision would depend on input-output analysis, showing the amount of resources used to produce the maximal configuration of final outputs decided by the programme. If a certain choice of revaluation involved the devotion of a very high share of national productive capacities to making intermediate goods, it would presumably be rejected. One can envisage rival parties offering alternative plans in which these weights—and the implicit production levels—formed the basis of discussion.

(*f*) *Overvaluation of relatively monopolised products*
There is another topic on which disagreements on means (and cowardice in withstanding pressure groups) have camouflaged a growing political agreement on economic principle. It is the topic of action against restrictive practices (cartels, price-fixing, etc.) and *to a lesser extent* against monopolies. There is economic sense in this emphasis. There may be an excellent case for concentrating (say) all light-bulb manufacture into a single firm (and thus a single vast machine), in that scale economies (by shifting the industrial supply curve to the right) reduce prices more than enough to offset the opposite effect through monopoly profits. These can, in any case, be checked by tariff-free imports or direct Government pressure. A cartel, however, has all the drawbacks of monopoly pricing (the participants will collusively adopt the price that a monopolist could attain, if they believe that the cartel is stable—that no member will act independently—and if entry is restricted) without its advantage of scale economies derived from concentrating equipment in few plants. In other words, in industries with scale economies, near-

complete monopolies tend to correct their own distortions of the price system; their prices are higher (relative to other producers') than they would have been under perfect competition because inflated by monopoly profit, but lowered by scale economies. But cartel prices are distorted upwards without correction in this way, and—as the experience of British cement indicates—prone to lead and worsen inflation and damage the balance of payments especially in booming industries, unless regulated by the State.[1]

Intensive action against cartels, whatever its other advantages, will certainly reduce the distortions of the price system and make it a better guide to planning. In practice, most of the heavily cartelised sectors in the U.K. will probably have to expand output faster than the national growth rate. This is because they have grown up in industries with big capital costs, and thus great risks attached to price wars—and much extra security from cartel formation. Such industries (steel, cement, glass, chemicals) tend to produce investment goods. Thus U.K. cartels are producing goods that come into much heavier demand (and hence will get dearer, both in actual market prices and in shadow scarcity-prices) as a result of early planning for growth. However, accurate planning requires allowance for the initial overpricing of such goods.

(g) Overvaluation of wants relative to needs

The 'welfare ideology' permeates British thinking, in all parties, fairly thoroughly. Most people, including almost all Conservatives, think that the State should not pay huge welfare allowances to those who do not need them—e.g. old-age pensions to directors on large retirement benefits from their companies. Most people, including almost all Labour supporters, feel that the tests of *means* (not just of income, which is easier) needed to limit payments in this way are both costly and undignified.

Differences of view regarding the financing of social services cut across party lines. Beveridge's classical insurance principle, under which each employee, employer and self-employed person, and the State, pays a given sum irrespective of income, has all the inequities of a regressive poll-tax. True, it seems to show people exactly what they pay for. But

---

[1] Hence the creation of the Iron and Steel Board. Cf. also C. Schultze's analysis of 'demand-shift inflation' in the U.S. (*Recent Inflation in the U.S.*, Study Paper no. 1, prepared for the U.S. Joint Economic Committee's *Study of Employment, Growth and Price Levels*, Washington, 1959.)

the National Insurance funds are never balanced. They are subsidised from general taxation, to a different extent each year. Government accounts are, in fact if not in form, consolidated; *total* expenditure is financed by *total* income (perhaps with a surplus or a deficit). So the notion that one buys National Insurance with one's weekly stamps is a fiction.

People differ on issues like universal coverage, and on financing. They differ, too, on the desirable size of any rival private sector in health or education. Such a rival preserves choice, and provides stimulant (if scale-diseconomising) competition for the public sector's social services. Most people want this. However, it tends to subject the best obtainable health and education to rationing by price. Most people oppose that.

These differences do not affect the almost universal agreement on the *right* of every citizen, however lazy or thriftless:

(a) not to starve;

(b) not to die of exposure or curable disease;

(c) to receive an education.

Our concepts of tolerable subsistence minima have risen considerably faster than the general standard of living.[1] It is the purpose of this section to *record* our agreed ethical choices and analyse their consequences. My own feeling is that these choices reflect credit on our society, and that our refusal to extend them into more fields, especially housing and retraining for the jobless, is arrogant whip-and-carrot materialism such as few economists would support.

The agreed 'welfare ideology' suggests that needs must be placed before inessential wants, in two senses. First, if people have needs (e.g. for protein) of which they are unaware, the State should indicate those needs to them if private entrepreneurs fail to do so. Second, it is not morally acceptable for the luxury demands of some to be fulfilled, while substantial numbers of people fall below a (rapidly rising) socially tolerable minimum.

In recent years both major parties have increasingly defined this minimum by reference to the standards *normally* enjoyed by a person

---

[1] From 1953 to 1965, the single person's retirement pension, the unemployment benefit and the sickness benefit all rose from 32s. 6d. to 80s. od., i.e. by 146 per cent; average *money* income (GNP per head) meanwhile rose about 80.1 per cent. *Annual Abstract of Statistics*, 1964, pp. 1, 55, 252; 1965, p. 50; *The Times*, 11.3.1966, p. 13. Different choices of years alter details only, not result. See pp. 190, 200.

or family. More slowly, politicians are beginning to regard 'contingency redistribution', over the lifespan, as more important than redistribution among persons. True, market mechanisms (in particular insurance, and investment in insurance-linked unit trusts and bonds) exist by which a family can carry out its own contingency redistribution, and can guarantee itself a secure minimum income. The time may come when few will be so poor or ill-informed as to be unable to make such a choice. However, poor people now seldom have access to the best advice on such matters. The very contingencies which *reduce* money-earning power (maternity, sickness, the decision to give a child further education instead of letting him bring money into the home by work) in many cases actually *increase* the need for income. In any case, society is increasingly unwilling to penalise thriftlessness by insecurity in essential matters, especially if the sins of the father are being visited on the children (or the wife). All these seem to be problems of income redistribution rather than output composition; but the first implies changes in the second, owing to the implicit adjustments in the structure of demand (more bread, fewer diamonds). For all these reasons, it is a part of planning to identify inadequately fulfilled needs, and, if maximisation of output at otherwise optimal prices fails to fulfil them, to alter the accounting price-weights accordingly.

Thus planners have to stray into nutrition and psychology to discover what human needs are, into sociology to find and use measures of their fulfilment, and into philosophy to provide some sort of conceptual analysis of 'need'. On this last matter an economist is hardly competent to pronounce, but he must try to understand. 'Need', as a bridge-word, is typical of the whole discourse of 'aims' of economic policy. 'People ought to get what they need' is a value premise assumed, in a welfare ideology, by use of the word 'need'. So 'A needs X' strictly entails 'A should get X if possible' (though nothing is implied about if, and how, he should pay for it).

'A needs X' is also a statement about (a) and/or (b), *and* (c):
(a) A's constitution,
(b) The demands made of (or standards set for) A by society, and
(c) The relation between X and (a) and/or (b).
Needs in the food-shelter-clothing-sex group concern (a) and (c). (Even sex needs can be relevant to aims of economic policy if, for example, a nation faced by a labour shortage encourages selective immigration of males.) Educational needs, being relative to a society's

level, form and direction of development, involve (b) and (c). Health needs involve (a), (b) and (c).

In each case, our standard for fulfilment of need rises with, and usually faster than, the prevailing level of living. There are four reasons for this. First, increasing affluence renders really acute poverty rarer and thus more shocking. Second, if income per person rises by 10 per cent, it becomes *more than* 10 per cent easier for the State to alleviate any given shortage; taxable capacity rises by more than 10 per cent, owing to the diminishing marginal utility of income to the rich. Third, reinforcing this effect, a given growth rate generates more extra resources for relief of need at higher levels of income per head; 3 per cent of £1,000 is more than 3 per cent of £900. Above all, certain needs, especially that for education, rise faster than income as a part of the very process by which income rises. When a country gets 10 per cent richer, people want more than 10 per cent extra education; and education, like other inputs, suffers from decreasing returns, so that the hundredth rise in income per head requires much more extra outlay for skill and training than did the first rise of equal size. In England and Wales the proportion of employed males in the Registrar-General's social classes IV and V—very roughly, the unskilled—fell from 35·7 per cent at the 1931 Census to 29·2 per cent at the 1951 Census,[1] and this tendency is all the more marked from international comparisons.[2]

(h) Overvaluation of outputs consumed from habit

Price mechanisms, together with unequal income distribution, under-value needs and overvalue wants. They are also selective within the area of wants. The individual consumer's ability to maximise his utility (p. 4) is based on free and informed choice among ways of using each week's income. Freedom, however, is inhibited by habits formed by past choices. This is seldom, if ever, foreseen when such choices are made. Hence past optimisation forms habits that reduce the scope for present optimisation; and market prices, affected by such habits, overvalue the commodities which create them.

People form habits, and thus—influenced by past optimising—currently want demonstrably harmful things. Clearly these should be weighted, in the maximand, at less than their pre-tax market values. In

[1] *Census 1951, England and Wales: General Report*, General Register Office, 1958, p. 147.
[2] I.L.O., *Yearbook of Labour Statistics*, 1965, Table 2B.

cases such as cigarettes, some action may be desirable to reduce the demand that has created those market values. Where should public opinion, and the state, draw the line in this matter? Most countries prohibit the sale of opium, let alone encouragements to its use; almost nowhere are people allowed to make propaganda for homosexuality. Yet cigarette consumption, which has certainly caused more (and more painful) deaths than both these practices combined, is not only supported by legal sales, but encouraged by massive advertising amounting to over £13m. in 1963.[1]

As to sales, our attachment to choice, as a value, is such that we want (in my view rightly) to let people go to hell in their own way whenever possible, provided they are alerted to the consequences. It is impossible, however, to see any justification for permitting the *advertisement* of a commodity such as cigarettes. In the U.K., 90 per cent of all cigarette production is in the hands of two firms, one owning 40 per cent of shares in the other.[2] Advertising, therefore, cannot be principally designed to switch smokers among brands. It must, in part, aim to raise total cigarette consumption. There are implicit admissions of this by cigarette manufacturers.[3]

'People want it but it's bad for them' smacks of complacent Puritanism, or of the planner's egocentric conviction that the man in Whitehall knows best. However, neither is at issue in a case like this. There is, first, a simple moral issue: it is wrong to encourage people in a habit that, on average, shortens their lives by five years and makes death more painful and existence less full.[4] Second, there is an economic issue: Britain is chronically short of labour (see pp. 122-125 below), yet

---

[1] The 1964 rate for Press and television alone was over £15 million a year. *The Guardian*, 9th Feb., 1965, p. 3. The ban on television advertising in 1965 has switched promotion expenditure to other media, and to coupons.

[2] Imperial Tobacco, in March 1965, changed the form in which it holds Gallaher shares, but not the fact of the holding.

[3] Royal College of Physicians: Committee on Smoking and Air Pollution, submission of Tobacco Enquiry Council (Appendix I to *Smoking and Health*, R.C.P., 1962) says this effect 'is likely to have been small', but (rightly) claims credit for not advertising at under-16s, 'in boys' and girls' papers or . . . in the breaks in children's television programmes'—implicit admission that advertising raises *total* cigarette consumption, or why this self-restraint?

[4] The typical cigarette—according to a specialist on all causes of lung diseases —shortens life by six minutes! (Sir Barnett Stross, M.P., reported in *Hansard*, 7 July, 1964, Col. 201.) A man smoking 20 cigarettes a day for 36 years typically shortens his life by three years.

cigarette-induced bronchitis alone costs us some 2·4 times as many lost working days as do strikes, on a conservative estimate,[1] to say nothing of the lost man-years of the dead.

This case has been examined in some detail. That is not because the function of this book is to influence smoking habits, but because the example shows how the planner, in reweighting output, may be forced to assign prices different from either market or programming, scarcity-reflecting accounting valuations. Either set of valuations ignores the artificially stimulated, demonstrably harmful nature of certain wanted products.

(i) Overvaluation of advertised commodities

The second way in which market behaviour distorts[2] relative values is by persuasive advertising. We shall ignore the 'baldness cures'—the cases, perhaps not so rare, of deliberate dishonesty in advertising; the possibility that advertising may reduce, or increase, responsiveness to real differences in price and quality; and the undoubted fact that most advertising draws attention, in a socially useful way, to the existence of products and thus helps perfect the market. The point is simply that some uses of personal income are easier to advertise than others. It is particularly difficult to advertise either personal saving or Government taxation.

The net effect of advertising, therefore, may well be to increase total private consumption at the expense of saving. This is desirable in time of slump, but inflationary in boom.[3] It is inimical to investment finance for economic growth—an effect not compensated by its boosting of demand if the government is prepared (as it is nowadays) to maintain near-full employment over the cycle.

Furthermore, some consumer goods are more advertised than others —especially cigarettes and tobacco, detergents, alcoholic drink (especially beer), cosmetics and toothpaste, and motor vehicles and accessories.[4] It cannot be sensibly argued that such advertising is competitive only against other goods of the same type; many of the closest substitutes for advertised commodities are outside that range.

---

[1] *Common Sense About Smoking*, Penguin, 1962, ch. 3.
[2] You should question the justification of this word wherever it appears.
[3] N. Kaldor, The Economic Effects of Advertising, *Review of Economic Studies*, 1951.
[4] *The Economist*, 17 July 1965.

Rolls-Royce advertisements reduce sales of diamonds rather than of Mini-Minors; and Mini-Minor advertisements hit British Railways, motor-bicycles and even washing machines, not Rolls-Royce. Hence certain commodities will tend to gain at the expense of other products, whatever their use. The lucky—i.e. overpriced—commodities are:

(a) those advertised more successfully;

(b) those easy to advertise;

(c) those where industrial concentration plus product differentiation make a manufacturer confident that the effect of his advertising will be concentrated on the sales of his own firm (B.M.C. cars, but not Jones's apples); and

(d) products whose shape, colour or purpose eases the establishment of a favourable image.

In general, then, advertising tends to favour (raise the demand for and hence price of) products where demand rests less on self-formed consumer wants than on external pressures created by persuasion. This constitutes an *a priori* case for suggesting that heavily advertised groups of products—possibly including private consumption in general—are overvalued by the market system, and that plans should give less weight to expansion of such output than is suggested by its relative price at the start of the plan. That price reflects the greater ease, success or penetration of advertising such output, as well as relative spontaneous demand for it. These are tentative suggestions. The reader ought to question them.[1]

(j) Revaluation and relative prices

In short, then, the market mechanism, as modified by industrial concentration, income distribution, habit and advertising, tends to overprice easily-stimulated demands and to underprice necessities. Planning for growth, if it uses market prices, thus maximises the wrong thing. It will misjudge the ideal composition of growing output. During economic growth the share of the public sector, of investment goods, of the output of some necessities that are unrecognised or underadvertised, and of items made by internally competitive sectors of the economy, should rise.

Can the process of planning itself produce seriously misleading

[1] Certainly advertising causes newspapers and magazines to cost much less than they would otherwise. We pay for newspapers indirectly when we buy the goods advertised therein. The price of newspapers thus understates their values, which must be raised in estimating the 'shadow prices'—the weights of commodities in the output whose growth rate is being maximised.

D

distortions in relative prices? It can, and it should. Alteration of the relative prices of products through taxation, and of the relative cost of factors of production through payroll taxes (including employers' National Insurance contributions) and investment subsidies, are among the most familiar, powerful and, because probabilistic and noncompulsive, acceptable means of control.

The important, and usually neglected, 'Marshall effect'[1] means that planning should use taxes and subsidies to adjust relative prices *more than* is suggested by what planners judge to be market distortions. Elasticity of demand, in response to price, is much higher in the long run than in the short, since buyers take time to find substitutes (and new complements for those substitutes). Thus, to divert transport from congested roads to underused railways by altering relative prices, one should counter short-run demand inelasticities by making the ratio between prices for motorist and rail-passenger *more than* proportionate to the ratio between the costs of providing the services.[2]

The planner must be careful to distinguish price movements reflecting changes in relative scarcities (or valuations) from those reflecting the results of his own planning decisions to alter the incentive structure. Both, too, must be distinguished from changes due to shifts in income distribution or the relative degree of monopoly power among private industries.

The discussion of improved output composition departs from the usual pattern, in that no new constraints are introduced. One might do this, for instance, by demanding that sufficient proteins, protective clothes, and houses be produced. This, however, imparts a bogus specificity to a vague preference structure. It is preferably simply to reprice various components of the maximand, both to correct monopolistic disparities between relative prices and relative costs and to express value judgments. Electorates could then choose among alternative repricings. This, indeed, is what they do now, but in a twilight of logic which it is the function of this sort of discussion to try to clarify.

[1] Marshall, *Principles of Economics*, Macmillan (paper-back edition), 1961, pp. 92-3.
[2] The vague choice of words is deliberate. Economists perhaps take too much time arguing between various forms of cost-related pricing. Obviously, whatever the 'right' prices may be, the ratio between the actual price of going across Central London by car and the price of making the same journey by Underground is much too low.

An unhappy feature is that the economic system is so permeated with 'second-bestness' as regards the price structure[1] that it is impossible to say, even on an agreed view of human needs and income distribution, exactly how much relative prices for planning should differ from market prices. But we can easily identify the most seriously mispriced items, and thus the direction of improvement of output composition. We must emphasise that the planner need not always alter actual market prices in the direction of non-distortion, only that he should not be fooled by such prices into accepting a largely chance composition of output, and hence into maximising the wrong thing.

6. IMPROVED DISTRIBUTION OF INCOME

(a) The definition of equality

We have suggested that most people want a more equal distribution of something—income, wealth, happiness?—among the population of Britain. Mr Gaitskell used to say that Socialism was about equality. Conservative thought seeks to increase welfare benefits but to confine them to the neediest: itself an egalitarian move. Most people accept the need for a long-run transfer of the tax burden from income to wealth —egalitarian because wealth is distributed much less evenly than income. Almost everyone accepts publicly-financed social services, roads, etc., which the poor (and they alone) would otherwise be unable to afford for themselves. Moreover, the basic minima guaranteed by the State to the needy—old-age pensions, unemployment and sickness benefits, and National Assistance—have risen faster than the earnings of people as a whole, whatever the colour of the governing party.

Clearly the ideology and wishes of most of Britain's rulers are egalitarian. True, these aims are modified, both by the pressure of interests giving cash to political parties and by strongly held doubts: minority doubts (the possible need for a 'leisure class') and widely held doubts (harmful effects of reductions in equality on incentives and saving.) But on the desirability of equality as an end in itself, leaving aside the need for concessions to pressure groups and the consideration of side-effects, there is widespread agreement. But agreement about what?

---

[1] Meade, *Trade and Welfare*, Oxford, 1955, pp. 102-18; R. G. Lipsey and K. Lankaster, The General Theory of Second Best, *Review of Economic Studies*, 1956 pp. 11-32. If a large number of prices diverge from marginal costs of production, we may make matters worse by putting a few prices 'right'.

We might define equality as 'the same income for everyone'. But is it equality to give the same income to twin coal-miners, one working an eight-hour week, the other a forty-hour week? Most people's answers would depend on the extent to which the two men can *choose* how long they work. If the eight-hour man is much weaker, or ill, we might not wish to pay him much less. If we believed that—despite honest mental effort to bring himself to work hard—he was hereditarily lazy, we should have doubts (see p. 93). But suppose he decides to take his enjoyments as leisure rather than as income; equality of reward, for different amounts of identical effort, would make such choices impossible. If the happiness to be equalised comprises leisure as well as money income, then 'the same income for everyone' is not a sensible definition of equality.

Light is cast on the issue by the report of the Prices and Incomes Board on railwaymen's pay.[1] They accept the egalitarian principle of comparability of pay between railwaymen and other workers with similarly responsible and arduous jobs, but suggest that comparability should be 'in terms not of basic rates but of earnings'. Equal total weekly earnings together with equal hours worked produces equality of reward. But railwaymen work longer than other employees of similar skill and responsibility, to obtain comparable earnings. Equal-earnings criteria are unfair to railwaymen, who are then 'less equal'. Yet equality of hourly rates is unfair to those groups of workers who, unlike railwaymen, do not have the chance to work overtime.

So far we have looked at:

(A) equal pay for each person

(B) equal pay for each hour of comparable work.

To this we must add

(C) equal pay in respect of equal need.

Twin coalminers, each working a forty-hour week in the same mine, may differ in respect of need, in that one may have to buy food and clothes for two children aged 15, while the other has two children aged 2.[2] Marx's original concept was 'To each according to his need'; but Marx would not have wished to argue that, before reaching a society of abundance (his 'realm of freedom'), one could ignore the maxim 'To each according to his efforts'. We may agree with him in rejecting 'To each

---

[1] Prices and Incomes Board, *Pay and Conditions of British Railways Staff* (Cmd. 273 of 1966).

[2] We picked an example that cannot be settled by sliding back to (A) above! Note that (B) is roughly 'Conservative' and (C) roughly 'Socialist'.

according to his marginal value-product', which, while economically efficient, is certainly not fair (a man cannot help being born stupid or weak). Similarly unfair is 'To each according to his power' or 'To each according to society's need for his efforts'. Every economy must compromise with these inegalitarian rewards for innate ability, but they are in no sense fair.

Equality, as an agreed economic aim in Britain, is mainly about (B) and (C). This is suggested, respectively, by the emphasis on comparability in wage and salary settlements and by the rising ratio of welfare payments to average incomes. Our measurements of equality, though, are generally about (A)—slightly modified by (B) if we look at the distribution of income not among persons but among 'households', or among those odd halfway-houses between households and persons, 'tax units' from which the authorities collect both taxes on, and statistics of, incomes. Equality among persons is a good indication of equality in sense (B) and (C) above only in so far as both need and willingness to work hard are equally prevalent among poor and rich.

Need, however, is most unlikely to be distributed in a manner statistically independent of income. Nevertheless, the obvious dependence grows less as output per head grows more. Overall growth means less likelihood of certain contingencies creating acute need (deficiency diseases, leaky roofs, etc.) that are confined to people who are very poor in absolute terms. Overall growth, *via* better general health facilities, also means lower infant mortality rates for the poor and hence fewer non-working dependants per worker in the poorer families.

The very diminution of income (and of social) inequality among persons, moreover, reduces the statistical link between poverty and need. Many diseases are still much commoner among the poor than among the rich, but the differences are far less than when Professor Titmuss[1] first noted them during the 1930s.

Thus both growth and equalisation along (A) reduce the disparity between measures (A) and (C). This is an important fact to remember when comparing the equality of incomes in (say) India and Britain. The much greater poverty and inequality of *income* in India mean proportionately even greater inequality of *satisfaction of need*.

What of the second condition—that, if we are to use (A) to measure

[1] R. M. Titmuss, *Birth, Poverty and Death*, London, 1943.

equality, the 'deserts' of a rich man and a poor man should be similar? Poor men work harder and longer. If we use 'tax units' (closer to households than to persons) to measure income equality, we must remember that more poor families than rich ones contain two or three workers.

To this extent the equalisation of U.K. household income distribution reported by Lydall[1] is not 'due to' the big increase in working-class female earning, but overstated by the figures on account of this increase. That is, the poor household has improved its income faster than the rich, but it has also reduced its leisure relative to the rich. So the reduction in inequality shown by the income data is in part illusory.

Moreover, rich people usually enjoy their work more than the poor. Shaw's paradox, that sewer-cleaners ought to earn much more than university professors, is really obvious. Only supply and demand stand in the way of this ethic. Brawn is much more plentiful, relative to demand, than brain. Jobs needing brain are therefore better paid, as well as more exciting, than jobs using brawn. So income inequality is amplified by inequality of pleasure from work, as well as by inequality of leisure. It is further reinforced by inequality in ownership of property —always distributed less evenly than income.

(b) A bundle of inequalities

Much of the difficulty in economics comes from the fact that many variables change together, so that it is not practicable to isolate which change causes which effect. Usually we hide such problems by lumping a lot of variables together and treating them as a single one, hoping that the relation between them will stay the same. A notorious case is 'national income'—a bundle of thousands of goods going to millions of persons. In using it to indicate welfare, we hope that the distribution among persons and *either* commodity composition *or* relative prices (see p. 31) are not changing enough to make the indicator absurd.

Similarly, 'equality' is a bundle of facts about distribution, treated as a single fact, e.g. the Lorenz coefficient (see p. 91), which is then hopefully used to indicate the behaviour of the whole bundle. This problem has two aspects. First, equality (even in sense (a) of p. 86) has many dimensions: equality between men and women, townspeople and countryfolk, miners and railwaymen, negroes and whites, etc. Switzerland has more sex inequality than Britain, but less urban-rural inequality. Arguably one can set up a hierarchy of types of inequality by importance,

[1] H. F. Lydall, *British Income and Saving*, Oxford, 1954. See pp. 186-8 below.

i.e. by 'evasibility'. A depressed countryman can (at a cost) go to the town, but a woman can seldom become a man, so *a priori* the Swiss type of inequality is worse than the British. But there is little justification for lumping the many types together as 'distribution of income among persons'.

Secondly, even in the latter context, and even if (A), (B) and (C) above coincide, we can usually define unambiguously only that unattainable thing, complete equality. It is not, in general, possible to rank situations precisely in order of the degree of equality attained (though the Lorenz measure—p. 91—suggests it is). Suppose I have to divide £200 between identical *twins*, with identical family obligations, tastes and needs, for identical work (criteria (A), (B) and (C) above coincide). £100 each is 'most equal', and, the higher the ratio of the return of the higher-paid to that of the lower-paid, the less the equality. But suppose I have to divide £300 among identical *triplets*. £100 each represents maximum equality. But suppose I start with a pay system that gives £50 to triplet X, £100 to Y and £150 to Z. Any transfer, up to £50, from Z to X or Y, or from Y to X, increases equality; *any* transfer from Y to Z, or from X or Y to Z, reduces equality. But what if Y—'the middle class'—loses £5 to X and £5 to Z? If inequality is measured by absolute income difference, it has fallen between X and Y, risen between Y and Z, and stayed constant between X and Z. In a society with millions of income receivers, most redistributions contain two-way elements of this kind.

(c) *Measuring inequality*

Economics is an exercise in 'it can't be done, but here it is'. We by-pass, rather than solve, the above logical problem with the *Lorenz curve*. In Figure 7 we measure along the bottom of the box the *cumulative* percentage of income-receivers, starting with the worst-off. Along the side of the box we measure the cumulative percentage of income received. A completely egalitarian society would have a Lorenz curve along the 45-degree line from SW to NE of the box; the worst-off 1 per cent of people would still get 1 per cent of income, the worst-off 30 per cent would get 30 per cent, and so on. The further away the actual Lorenz curve from the 45-degree line, the greater the degree of inequality. If one economy has a Lorenz curve lying entirely SE of another, as in Figure 7, we can say without ambiguity that its incomes are more unequally distributed. If the curves cross, it might mean that the difference between the very rich and the less rich is smaller, but the

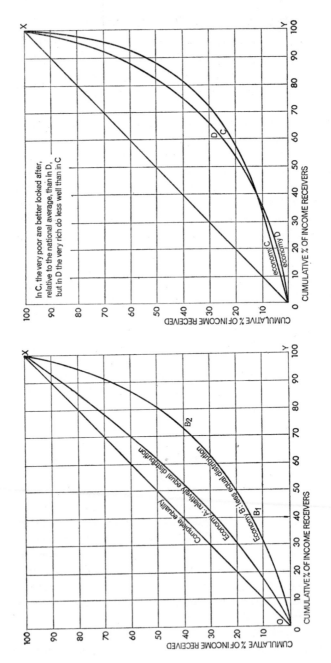

Figure 7 and Figure 8 Lorenz curves. For useful international comparisons, units must be the same (e.g. 'income receivers' must not be 'family units' in one country and 'individuals' in another; nor 'income received pre-tax in one and post-tax in another). These curves cannot allow for many vital components of income inequality, e.g. incidence of indirect taxation (beer or champagne duty?), access to bulk-purchase arrangements and consumer information, etc.

difference between the less rich and the very poor larger, in one economy than in the other (Figure 8).

Since distance from the diagonal is some measure of the inequality shown by a Lorenz curve, the degree of inequality is expressed by a *concentration coefficient*, the ratio of the area between curve and diagonal to the area of the triangle formed by diagonal and axes (OB_1B_2X/OYX in Figure 7). This is no more justified than striking an average of Laspeyres and Paasche index-numbers—less so, if anything, since some forms of inequality are much more serious than others; in particular the existence of a class of near-destitutes is far worse than huge inequality between rich and middle-income groups, bad though that may be. However, the concentration coefficient is our least bad overall indicator of income inequality.

(d) Equalisation as fairness

Let us accept the Lorenz definition of equality—and the income-independence of needs and deserts. We are now indifferent among identical changes in the coefficient, whichever the special groups that gain or lose. We assume that 'overall inequality' encompasses all forms of inter-group disparity.

Why do people advocate the more equal distribution of income among persons? Initially, from a vague sense of fairness. Why should accident of birth, parental will to make sacrifices for one's education, inherited talent or skill, or scarcities of what one makes or sells, determine one's access to commodities? There is little point in arguing about fairness itself; it is a matter of moral aesthetics rather than morality. Most people are offended by extreme inequality. But one can also ask what is fair about taking away from people living-levels to which they have become accustomed; or sequestrating the yield from assets bought on the assumption that the yield would belong to the buyer; or raising the hopes of the poor to an extent that the thinly-spread jam from the redistributed incomes of the rich is sure to disappoint.

One cannot adjudicate among emotive arguments like these. The concept of fairness presumably includes parity of treatment in virtue of specific actions; the initial actions of the *earning* rich may be more energetic than those of the poor. Also one must consider intergeneration fairness; will 'soaking the rich' for equality in this generation, by drying up the sources of finance for investment, 'unfairly' curtail the growth of income into future generations?

D*

(e) Equalisation and diminishing marginal utility

The justification of equality in sense (A), and of its correlates in other meanings of the word, has surer foundations than these, in the *utility argument* (UA). This rests on a psychological fact, diminishing marginal utility (DMU) of commodities, together with an almost undisputed valuation, the desirability of maximising total utility. So justified, the support for equality is not confined to the left. Sir Dennis Robertson, one of the most profound of modern conservative economists,[1] was a UA-egalitarian.

UA goes like this. Suppose everyone has equal capacities for, and rights to, the enjoyment of all commodities that can be purchased for money. Then, if income as a whole has DMU, absolutely equal income distribution among persons is optimal for any given level of total community income. For suppose Mr A has £1000 a year, and Mr B £500. Take away £1 from A and give it to B; B's welfare rises more than A's falls. This remains true for successive transfers from A to B until they have £750 each. On its assumptions (including measurable, interpersonally comparable utility), UA is irrefutable. Most economists would agree that UA, after all challenges to its assumptions are considered, suffices to condemn the degree of inequality in Britain today. However, side-effects of equalisation on incentives to produce, and challenges to the assumptions of UA, weaken the case for *complete* equality of incomes among persons.

(f) Assumptions: distribution of capacity for enjoyment

UA assumes that capacities for enjoyment are equal. This is not so. Often, people with especially little *capacity* to enjoy—e.g. the chronic sick—have exceptional *deserts*; but this correction does not always work. In fact, UA indicates equalisation even on a weaker assumption: that the capacity for enjoyment does not so vary with income that the rich have more capacity than the poor. DMU itself supports such an assumption: the first car means much more than the second.

Perversely, however, the appetite may grow with feeding. Acquisition of riches leads to the creation of standards which, once withdrawn, might cause intense suffering; and the satisfaction of animal needs for food permits the finer, if not sharper, pleasures of gourmetry. The rich man, by being rich, does acquire the capacity to enjoy more *things*. This,

---

[1] One of his last public utterances (a lecture to the Oxford Economic Society) was a passionately reluctant defence of equality.

indeed, is the argument for a 'leisure class' to support and develop the creative arts. But a comparison of contemporary Britain and Renaissance Italy suggests that the far bigger and wealthier leisure-class of Britain today has a deplorable record in supporting culture[1]—and an even worse one in making the fruits of this support generally available.

To attack the assumption of equal capacities is to encourage the rich to cheapen public taste, or to keep their own artistic sympathies unshared, thereby maintaining the unequal capacities that 'justify' unequal incomes. Such an attack supports both the exclusive snobbery of private art collections and the garish, mauve-lighting vulgarisation of art for profit that together seek to keep artistic appreciation from the poor. The education of the poor in the capacity to enjoy is surely a better policy than the use of their relative incapacity to justify income inequality.

In any case, if we accept the deepest assumption of UA—DMU of income—a presumption is created against the view that the rich have a higher capacity for enjoyment than the poor, especially out of *extra* income.

(g) *Distribution of the right to enjoyment*

Harder to accept is the assumption that the *right* to enjoyment is distributed independently of income (notice, again, that we can weaken the assumption of equal rights). Perhaps people are rich because they deserve to be—because they have been more persistent, intelligent, skilful or energetic. But what is it to deserve, if such traits—including application, or lack of laziness—are in large part hereditary? Is not the man born with brains excessively rewarded for his good fortune if society allots him also extra income? Admittedly these differences in reward may be needed for economic efficiency—see pp. 98-9. But there is no obvious justice in rewarding people because they are clever, or even industrious.

Moreover, even if all differences in earned income were due to differences in persistence, and if persistence were a moral trait unconnected with genetic endowment, that would not justify the main component of inequality in Britain: differences in unearned income, due largely to inherited holdings of shares, bonds, houses and land. The distribution

---

[1] The elite's concept of the relation of power to cultural responsibility is a vast, almost untouched subject. The support given to Lessing and Herder, to the eighteenth-century poet in England, or to the contemporary Swedish or Norwegian playwright by the State, show one concept of what that relation should be. *Son et lumière* and the Hilton Hotel in Park Lane reveal a different one.

of *wealth* is much more unequal in Britain than in most advanced countries, especially the U.S.A.—where differences in income are greater than in Britain, but more due to differences in earning power. Most of the difference in unearned incomes in the U.K.—where in 1951 under 2 per cent of adults held any shares, and in 1960 the top 1 per cent of all wealth was owned by 42 per cent of the population[1]—is due to the inheritance of large estates; death duties are easy to avoid, either by careful choice of property and recipient, or by exploiting the absence of a gift tax on property passed on more than five years before death.[2] Hereditary income inequality is impossible to justify on economic grounds, whether of deservingness or of incentive.

Furthermore, in Britain, personal advancement depends on hereditary distinctions more than in comparable advanced economies. The public-school system, under which great educational advantages[3] are given to children of rich parents, is both unique to the U.K. and linked to what is in effect the hereditary allocation of the best job opportunities. For example, of the Court of the Governors of the Bank of England in 1965, 5 were from Eton, 7 from other public schools and only 4 from grammar schools,[4] and the history can be repeated from almost all leading walks of life (especially management).[5] There is now some evidence that this is not due to merit, in that non-public-school entrants perform considerably better at their tasks.[6]

[1] Lydall, *British Incomes and Savings*, Oxford, 1954; J. E. Meade, *Equality, Efficiency and the Ownership of Property*, Allen and Unwin, 1964.

[2] C. A. R. Crosland, *The Future of Socialism*, Cape, 1958, *passim*.

[3] In particular a far higher staff/pupil ratio, and in the better schools sufficient endowments to staff attract the best with far higher salaries than other teachers receive.

[4] *Whitaker's Almanack, 1965*, p. 451; *Who's Who 1965*.

[5] R. H. Clements, *Managers*, pp. 174, 185. Of all 646 managers interviewed, 213 were grammar school and 159 public school. Of 182 'top managers', 54 were grammar school, 89 public school.

[6] Worswick's yearly studies of Oxford final-examination performance by grammar-school and public-school candidates, printed from time to time in the *Times Educational Supplement*, bear this out and reflect experience in other universities. The selection-bias in favour of public-school candidates happens before they apply; the share of candidates from the various types of school who are accepted is very similar (Mr Alan Montefiore, *The Times*, 13 April 1965). Those who benefit from very high staff/student ratios and hence from better teaching will start, but not necessarily finish, university life better equipped. Those who overcome home pressures to get into university will often carry their high motivation into high performance there. *Where* (Advisory Centre for Education), Jan. 1966.

Many of the top, best-paid positions in the U.K., then, are held for directly or indirectly hereditary reasons. The large part of inequality due to unearned income is mainly hereditary. There is thus probably at least as high a proportion of the undeserving among the rich as anywhere else. What is more, many of the jobs done by earners of high incomes in business and the professions, in politics and science, carry their own rewards. Coal-mining and street-cleaning carry their own punishments, from cultural deprivation to silicosis. All in all, the notion that unequal incomes reflect unequal deserts will not stand up to analysis.

The structure of earnings, as Barbara Wootton has shown, is petrified by conventional differentials;[1] it is also warped by hereditary advantage, and even if neither of these things were true, inherited brains do not mean 'deserts', nor are most inequalities the result of earnings anyhow. The assumption of 'equal right to enjoyment of earnings' is more a confession of ignorance than an ethical principle, but it avoids the arrogant and unfounded claims to moral judgment of the view that rewards equal payments. Returning to our twin coalminers (p. 86): for reasons of incentive, the harder worker must receive more, but let us not erect this into a moral principle, or pretend that it justifies the claims advanced upon the national product by the fortunate heir to a large estate.

(h) Does marginal utility of income diminish?

That it does is the most questionable assumption of UA. Before dealing with it, we must ask whether utility can be spoken of as if it were measurable and comparable among persons. Those brilliant theorists who have, with Ockham's Razor, shaved from economists the need to assume cardinal utility[2] rightly doubt if we ever can state (let alone test) propositions like 'Two apples make me $1 \cdot 8$ times as happy as one', or 'An apple means $1 \cdot 3$ times more to me than to you'. And yet . . . if the well-fed alderman gives a crust to the beggar, we *know* that the beggar's utility rises more than the alderman's falls. In practice, can't we assume that enjoyment of extra income falls as income rises? If so, we need not worry much about measurement difficulties.

But can we? If the marginal utility of consumption fell as income rose,

---

[1] B. Wootton, *Social Foundations of Wage Policy*, Allen and Unwin, 1961 (paperback edition). See also G. Routh, *Occupation and Pay in Great Britain 1906-60*, Cambridge, 1965.

[2] Hicks, *Value and Capital*, Oxford, 1938; Samuelson, *Foundations of Economic Analysis*, Harvard, 1947.

we should expect the rich to save a much higher proportion of income than the poor. Recent evidence suggests that permanent entry into a higher income bracket, such as takes place in the growth process, means adjustment to a higher expected living-standard: consequently, the ratio (hereafter PS) of personal saving to personal disposable income remains about the same (over a certain level of income below which there is hardly any saving).[1] Duesenberry suggests that my relative position in the group with which I wish to be associated determines how much I spent to maintain that position, and hence my PS.[2] Friedman suggests, with powerful statistical support, that interpersonal differences in PS are due almost entirely to the discrete or transitory nature of income rises (wage and salary increases are discrete, overtime payments are transitory), and that when a family is fully adjusted to a higher income level it adopts much the same PS ratio as before the rise.[3] All this suggests that, at U.S. income levels, consumption exhibits little DMU after full adaptation.

Yet DMU of income, if less obvious than that of apples, is still sufficiently intuitive to make us seek alternative explanations of Duesenberry's and Friedman's results. As my income rises, does something happen to make my saving 'more expensive' and my consumption cheaper? Then a tendency to substitute consumption for saving, owing to price-changes, could offset the reverse tendency arising from the diminishing marginal utility of consumption. Unfortunately this is at variance with the facts. Increased wealth means the opportunity to spread risks, to get better stock-market advice, to obtain concessions for bulk savings on loans to local authorities, and in other ways to raise one's effective rate of return; it also means ascent into an income group where consumers are less sensitive to prices and where consumer goods sometimes gain status by being expensive. Thus the changing price-ratio between savings and consumption should underpin the effects of DMU in causing richer people to have a larger PS.

Indeed, there is evidence for such a saving pattern: but it does not extend over the bulk of those affected by redistribution. Many earners —from half to two-thirds—do not save at all, over their statutory obliga-

---

[1] For a summary of the current state of theory, see R. Ferber in *American Economic Review*, Feb. 1962.

[2] J. Duesenberry, *Income, Saving and the Theory of Consumer Behaviour*, Harvard, 1957.

[3] M. Friedman, *A Theory of the Consumption Function*, NBER, 1957.

tions (to National Insurance, etc.). Most other income groups, up to the top 5 per cent of earners, have much the same PS. As incomes become very high, the PS rises once more. As for time-series, the U.K. *has* raised her PS during recent growth,[1] but most economies, and the U.K. usually, do not. Vast international differences in economic structure and levels—such as that between India and the U.K.—are reflected by differences in PS, but *within* any broad group of economies (i.e. advanced or underdeveloped) the PS bears little relation to the level of living.[2]

Thus evidence from savings behaviour for DMU of consumption, for most people and over fairly small income differences, is hard to find. As income rise, 'price-ratios' between saving and consumption move so as to make any such evidence even more tenuous (because ambiguous). Moreover, the PS excludes flat-rate social-security contributions, both from savings and from income. If we include these obligatory savings in both savings and income—as we perhaps should—the redefined PS declines as income rises, since the fixed sum made up of social-security contributions is a falling proportion of the rising income.

Can UA be rescued? First, the Friedman-Duesenberry distinction between pure consumption and pure saving is much too crude to sustain their implicit attack on so plausible a concept as DMU. A much higher proportion of the 'consumption' of the rich is concealed saving. A rich woman buys a £250 fur coat to last for sixty years; a poorer woman consumes thirty coats at £15 each in the same period. Rich families buy pictures, jewels, garages, cars, refrigerators—all termed consumption, yet all yielding future flows of benefits in return for current sacrifice. The rising ratio of such concealed saving to income, as income rises, is powerful evidence for DMU.

Second, the Friedman-Duesenberry results cast doubt on the DMU of *consumption*, not on that of *income*, including savings. To test whether income has DMU, we observe people's preferences between income and leisure as incomes rise. As hourly rates rise, overtime rates rise too; so that, as incomes rise, price-effect always leads to substitution of work for leisure. Price-effect, therefore, cannot explain the steady reduction of the actual working week during recent growth.[1] DMU of income can.

[1] Steadily, from 3·2 per cent in 1954 to 7·9 per cent in 1964. *National Income and Expenditure 1965*, pp. 4, 14.

[2] U.N., *Yearbook of National Accounts Statistics*, 1964, Appendix.

[3] Weekly hours worked in U.K. industry fell 4·3 per cent from 1955 to (October) 1965. *Economic Trends*, Feb. 1966, p. 28. In European economies (owing to faster income growth?) the fall was much faster.

Apparently the 'income package' (consumption bundle *plus* future interest flows from savings) does possess DMU, though consumption alone may not.

Another approach suggests that, *during growth*, the redistributive implications of DMU hold even for consumption provided redistribution is achieved by allotting the fruits of growth to the poor, instead of by reducing the incomes of the rich. Both the Duesenberry 'relative income' and the Friedman 'permanent income' hypotheses suggest that people acquire and maintain new, higher standards as a longrun result of income increases. Thus income reductions, in the interest of equality, might cost the rich more 'utility' than the gain to the poor. However, if we simply refrain from allotting the fruits of growth to the rich (so that neither their standard of living nor their saving/income ratio is affected), and allot them to the poor instead, we will increase total happiness more. True, the relative-income hypothesis suggests the economics of envy: that the happiness of the rich comes in part from a shared sense of superiority to the poor. But this happiness—not that such things are measurable—is set against a corresponding sense of inferiority among the poor.

(i) Size and distribution

In a command economy, the effort put into baking the cake does not depend on the equal, or unequal, size of the slices into which it is later cut. But what of an incentive economy? Will a more even distribution of the national cake (a dreary concoction in England) slow down its rate of increase by discouraging the more skilful cooks, so that, feeling that more work means only a larger distribution of their incomes to others, they fail to use their talents to the full, or leave for less egalitarian kitchens?

This case has force, but it is limited to *earned* incomes. Incomes from wealth, especially inherited wealth and even more especially inherited shares, are unrelated to one's own effort. True, a motive for such effort is to acquire wealth to pass on to one's children; but no society gives this motive unlimited tolerance, because *what is passed on is simply unearned claims on the effort of other people's children*, reducing *their* incentives.

Even for earned incomes, the argument from incentive has to be taken with plenty of salt. First, Barbara Wootton and Guy Routh have shown that relative earnings owe far more to convention than to incentive needs. This is reinforced by Fourastié's discovery that for hardly any occupation is the ratio between earnings and average national per-head income the same across national boundaries, even between countries of very similar economic structure.[1] Second, most well-paid jobs are more, not less, interesting than ill-paid ones. If the pay of a professor or a cabinet minister were less than that of a dustman, would a single university, or government, department lose its chief to the trash-cans? Third, even if we need some incentive payments (for overtime and scarce, price-elastic skills), do the huge present differentials reflect incentive requirements alone? Fourth—and most fundamental theoretically—the incentive argument cuts both ways. Ambitious men want to maintain and raise a given living standard. If they are heavily taxed at high income levels, they must work harder to do this, not less hard.

Still, the feeling remains that *some* incentives are economically necessary, and *some* special payments for hard or unpleasant work morally desirable. Thus redistribution should concentrate on wealth. The U.K. is one of the few countries without any effective taxes on gifts or capital. There are lessons to be learned from other countries. In Italy, the Rignano plan aimed to lower death duties on estates passed on in many small lots, thus preserving some freedom of choice for the testator without encouraging him to choose that other people's children shall work largely for his own. Sweden makes small annual levies on all large accumulations of land, buildings, shares and other property. Inequality of *unearned* income gains very little support from the objections to UA; and inequality of *wealth*, the source of unearned income, is worse in Britain than in other countries.

(j) Other arguments for equality

These lack the intellectual attractiveness of DMU; it is not every argument in social theory that appears to go straight from calculus to ethics. They have, however, more practical importance and fewer challengeable assumptions. These arguments are (i) the Rising Basic Minimum, (ii) the 'anabolism of wants', (iii) the reduction of social tensions, (iv) the removal of obstacles to production policy, (v) that, given our ignorance about distributive justice, equality is least likely to do harm.

(i) Social security statistics (p. 190) indicate that basic minima rise faster than per-head NNP: but why? Probably because, as progressively revealed human needs become more complex, the cost of fulfilment rises. A simple example: one of the earliest signs of growth is the reduction of

---

[1] J. Fourastié, in *Daedalus*; Wootton, *op. cit.*; Routh, *op. cit.*

infant mortality among lower income groups towards the levels of higher income groups. This is relatively cheap (eradication of rats, fleas and other disease carriers) and is a by-product of improved nutrition. But, as life expectancy grows, so the diseases needing to be treated tend to become more prolonged, difficult and expensive (although fewer, of course) so that the receipts of each diseased person tend to rise. The example of education was discussed in connection with output composition on p. 80. The whole process is closely related to (ii).

(ii) Streeten termed the process by which satisfying one demand uncovers new demands 'the anabolism of wants'.[1] This usually stimulates economic growth (by limiting the danger of choked-off demand) but can depress it (by limiting the possibility of voluntary expansion of private savings). Part of the process provides no argument for or against equality; before a man has meat he does not want horseradish sauce, but such long-run complements are not more expensive than prior wants in any systematic manner. In another way, however, the *order* in which wants are felt is determined largely by the cost of satisfying them, rather than by the nature of complementarities. A family satisfies its demands for meat before its wish for a yearly seaside holiday, largely because the smallest unit in which the second can usefully be bought is outside the family budget long after it has grown rich enough to afford useful units of the first.

The more divisible demands, then, tend to be satisfied first, and their satisfaction uncovers new demands that are less divisible and hence (usually) more expensive; and the conscience of an increasingly affluent economy reclassifies more, increasingly indivisible demands as needs. This must be added to the growing complexity and ambitiousness of anabolised wants, which, especially in the health-and-education group, become increasingly regarded as needs. (A tip for the next group of wants to be so regarded: household help, from nurseries to food blenders).

(iii) Opponents of equality (and even in this book it is necessary, and not snide, to point out how many receive large unearned incomes) often refer to the quest for it as 'the politics of envy'. But it is inequalities that create (indeed, are a necessary condition for) envy. Anybody who has seen the civil rights campaign in the U.S.A. in the early 1960s knows how much of Negro grievances stem from economic inequality—higher unemployment rates, lower income per employed person, less likelihood

[1] P. P. Streeten, Unbalanced Growth, *Oxford Economic Papers*, 1958.

of home-owning, etc.[1] It is poverty in the midst of plenty that produces social tensions and hatreds, which lower standards of morality as well as productivity. Just as the very colonisers, who emphasised settler above indigenous education, claim that the 'natives' are too uneducated for self-government, so do those whose often unearned affluence creates envy then attribute the attempt to reduce inequality to that envy.

(iv) An important reason why an economic planner must be concerned for equality is to get it out of the way. If the income distribution is far from whatever he regards as socially desirable, policies needed for allocative efficiency become socially suspect. Suppose that a large subsidy is being paid to provide rail transport to the inhabitants of a remote village with few alternative means of access. He will usually recommend fare increases in the interests of economic efficiency. If trains can be withdrawn as a result of declining demand, then resources are released to places where the free play of demand indicates they are desired more. If not, a systematic encouragement to travel to and from the village, at the cost of the taxpayer and thus of incomes that would otherwise be re-allocated to preferred lines of output, is removed. But if the villagers are much poorer than the average taxpayer, and equality is a recognised social goal, there is conflict between equity and efficiency—a conflict depressingly familiar in Britain (farm subsidies, cotton textile import quotas).

Of all income distributions that one might choose to call 'optimal', equality will minimise the number of occasions of conflict between allocative (productive) and distributive efficiency. This can be shown exactly. The nearer one has got to *any* approved income distribution, the less important will be small deviations from it caused by steps taken to increase allocative efficiency; for nearness to an ideal income distribution (like every commodity and every aim) possesses DMU. Thus the approach to any distribution selected as ideal improves the prospects of attaining allocative efficiency without serious distributional side-effects; if equality (or something near it) is selected, the improvement is all the more. So the demand of certain trade union leaders, that Government committment to income redistribution is necessary before they will accept wage restraint, has a sound theoretical basis.

(v) Suppose we must choose among income distributions in ignorance of their moral values or economic results. Two arguments for equality, different in kind from those previously discussed, now appear. First, psychologically, equality is likeliest to be chosen by anyone able to detach

[1] *Manpower Reports to the President*, U.S. Dept. of Labour, 1963, 1964.

himself from the prejudices created by his level and expectation of income. Second, arithmetically, equality is least likely to diverge violently from an extant, but totally unknown, 'optimum' income distribution.

To convince yourself of the psychological argument, suppose re-incarnation to be a proven fact. Further, suppose that your status and income are selected at random in each incarnation. If a thousand sewage-cleaners' children and a thousand barristers' children are born in the 24 hours following your death, then you have the same chance of being either—irrespective of your past or future income, status, merits, capacities or actions. Faced, near death, with the power to decide income distribution among your possible incarnations, how will you choose? Not too far from equality, I suggest; the tiny chance of an extra £100,000 on your potential annual income as an oil king will not compensate for the risk of losing £10 a year on each of 10,000 potential yearly incomes as, say, a £50-per-year Indian landless labourer.

Arithmetically, suppose there is a unique ideal distribution of income among British citizens. You know that such a distribution exists and that it fully meets all your criteria, but you have no notion of how much income each citizen receives under that distribution. Plainly, complete equality *minimises the maximum* by which the actual distribution can diverge from the unknown ideal distribution.

(k) Equality as a constraint: the intertemporal problem.
How can an equalising constraint be incorporated into our growth-maximising programme? We might express total income as a set of all the bundles of goods produced going to each member of the community, and specify that specific attributions rise at certain rates; but that would be hopelessly complicated. More simply, we might require that, after an otherwise optimum plan has been found, it should be checked for its effect on the distribution of income. Considerable distributive choice is open to us within any single plan for resource allocation. If the suspicion with regard to incentive effects (pp. 98–9) is correct, quite large redistributive changes are possible without affecting productive efficiency—especially if the economy is growing fast and becoming more pleasant to live in, so that there is little urge to emigrate even among the groups losing relatively (but not absolutely) in income. The organisation of production, including its possible planned reorientation for efficient constrained growth, has immense effects on income distribution: workers and employers in rapidly expanding industries, especially if

supply is inelastic, gain in relative income. However, what with immobilities, specificities of skills, professional loyalties, the irrelevance of
unearned income as an incentive, and the living-standard-maintaining
response to cuts in high earned incomes, considerable redistribution is
possible without much backlash upon the amount or allocation of
productive resources. Therefore, quite large moves towards an ideal
income distribution are possible without much affecting productive
efficiency.

To a great extent, therefore, we can go for maximum constrained
allocative efficiency of productive resources and tag on fiscal redistribution separately. Equality over time, however, cannot be tagged on at the
end of the plan. The less we write down the present importance of future
income simply because it *is* future—i.e., the less we *discount* future
income—the readier we are to sacrifice consumer goods now for factories
to make commodities later. Is there a case for discounting the future at
all? Ramsey, the first careful analyst of intertemporal planning and
optimal savings rates, thought not, and most economists agree.[1]

The existence of a rate of interest, even with stable prices and even
on secure loans, suggests that each individual prefers £1 now to even a
'real' guaranteed £1 later. That makes sense; he may die before 'later'
comes, and if he has £1 now he can spend it when he likes. But the risk
of the entire planned society dying before the plan period ends, while
now present (as it was not when Ramsey wrote), is presumably ignored
by planners. Moreover—even if the rate of interest is zero—*the community*, by refraining from making ice-cream in order to make steel
mills, achieves real growth, as output comes from the new plant; *the
individual* creates no goods by putting money aside instead of spending
it. Further, unborn consumers must be considered by the planner, if
not by the individual. Thus the existence of a private rate of interest—
the individual rationality of preferring jam today—does not demonstrate
the communal rationality of preferring consumption by an individual
today to consumption by one tomorrow.

However the DMU of growing per head income justifies some preference for earlier consumption. Confidence of rising living standards and
DMU—provided the typical citizen's right to, and capacity for, enjoy-

[1] F. P. Ramsey, A Mathematical Theory of Saving, *Economic Journal*, 1928.
In several recent writings Dobb has agreed, from a Socialist viewpoint, that
interest (and time-preference) are, for the planner, unjustified. But surely
uncertainty, increasing with the distance of the thing planned or predicted (and
since 8th August, 1945, extending to the future of life on earth), justifies them?

ment do not increase with time—prove that extra consumption is worth more to him now than to him or his descendants later. Since most indicators of enjoyment capacity—health, height, ability to travel, I.Q.—are secularly rising, the rate of DMU is slower as income rises *over* time, than among incomes at the *same* time.

DMU, however, means that we cannot, in planning over time, maximize total *consumption*. Given the workings of compound interest, investment produces ever higher consumption later, and maximised consumption would thus be postponed indefinitely to enable investment to take place for a glowing, growing, never attained future. The answer usually adopted in planning theory is to construct a *utility function* (UF), relating total lifetime utility (with DMU) to each year's consumption levels, and the maximisation of this UF by proper allocation of each period's resources between consumption and investment.[1] This procedure has its own drawbacks. First, almost any UF generates unpleasant paradoxes.[2] Second, there are infinitely many UF's exhibiting DMU, and no obvious empirical (or even theoretical) principle of choice. *Prima facie*, the rate of interest could help. True, the *market* rate of interest reflects the discount needed to persuade lenders to sacrifice £1 today for £1 next year; but lenders' utility is not society's. Moreover, the market rate reflects Government policy and short-run changes in lenders' and borrowers' views of economic trends as well as their UF. The *accounting* rate of interest is used as the cut-off rate below which projects are not worth while; this rate reflects capital scarcity rather than the UF.

Worst of all, even UF's with implausibly rapidly DMU tend to postpone consumption to the very end of long planning periods, because of the exponential nature of income growth. If we put aside more of

---

[1] F. P. Ramsey, loc. cit.; S. Chakravarty, M.I.T. Lectures, 1963-4.

[2] What should you be willing to pay for the right to play the following game? A coin is spun. If it falls Heads (H), I get 2d. and the game ends. If it falls Tails it is spun again. If the first H is on throw 2 I get 4d. and the game ends; if on throw 3, 8d.; on throw 4, 16d.; and on throw n, 2^n pence. If 'utility equals consumption', the game gives me half a chance of 2d., $\frac{1}{4}$ of a chance of 4d., $\frac{1}{8}$ of a chance of 8d. . . . and so on, and its value is 1d. + 1d. + 1d. . . . infinity, an absurd result. D. Bernoulli proposed the DMU function; Utility = log (consumption). Then this game is worth $\frac{1}{2}$ (log 2) + $\frac{1}{4}$ (log 4) + $\frac{1}{8}$ (log 8) . . . pence, which adds up to a (plausible) finite result. But it is easy to specify a game that does not—here, one yielding 2d. if the first H is on throw 1, 4d. on throw 2, $4 \times 4 = 16$d. on throw 3, (16 × 16)d. on throw 4, etc. In general, however fast your utility function exhibits DMU, I can always specify a pay-off that increases faster, producing the above 'St. Petersburg Paradox'.

today's income for investment instead of consumption, that means not just higher income tomorrow, but the possibility of increasing that income *by* (not just *to*) still more the day after tomorrow. To counter this destabilising effect, we need DMU at an increasing rate as income rises. But there is no reason to believe in this!

Without DMU, programmes value *consumption* in any period equally. Given steady growth from investment, they tend to postpone all consumption to the end. Even UF's with DMU—given interpersonal equality over time—push almost all *utility* to the end of the period. They still implausibly delay most consumption till then. This gets worse as the planning period is lengthened, and has been hailed by Tinbergen as a mathematical demonstration of the untenability (logical inconsistency, moral implausibility, 'instability'?) of an attractive set of moral beliefs. Are things that bad?

There are three reasons to prefer present utility to future utility, without assuming inequality between present and future individuals. Firstly, Professor Hicks points out that the idea of adding 'utilities' over time, as if each day's happiness was independent of each other day's, is artificial.[1] The utility-generating powers of any bundle of goods enjoyed today depend on the size of the bundles enjoyed previously (the standard of living). So it is realistic to suppose that an individual, or a community, prefers to see *total utility* (not just 'consumption'—*that* follows from DMU!) evenly spread (or smoothly growing) over time. That assumption removes some of the instability.

Secondly, Dr Chakravarty[2] points out that improving technology, as time goes by, cuts the working week needed to obtain any particular output; and thus lowers the marginal disutility of labour. Secularly, too, rising capital/labour ratios lower the unpleasantness and strain of labour. Technical change also increases the choice open to future generations. Thus, apart from the steady rise in NNP per head, there is a growing possibility of leisure, not expressed in the plan figures, but giving increasing advantage to future generations. So future utility streams may reasonably be discounted to allow for this.

Another consideration is uncertainty. The more distant are the fruits of a plan, the less sure is its outcome. This, perhaps, is what makes it

[1] J. R. Hicks, *Capital and Growth*, Oxford, 1965, ch. XXI; J. Tinbergen, Ordinal Utility and Impatience, *Econometrica*, 1961.

[2] In a series of lectures at Massachusetts Institute of Technology in Winter. 1963-4.

so counter-intuitive to equate the value of utility for an unknown a thousand years hence to that of utility for the planner's electors to-morrow. Removal of this odd equation of the certain and the clouded suffices to prevent the 'no consumption now' solutions to plans with long horizons.

Planners and politicians are supposed to be trustees for posterity, but seldom look much further than the voters' grandchildren. In practice, whatever optimal solutions might be, the bias is likelier to be towards neglecting the distant future than towards over-emphasising it by excessive postponement of consumption. What should theorists tell planners about such bias? If equality is right, time cannot make it wrong. But time can require more subtle definitions of equality. To accord equal weight to utility whether enjoyed now or in an uncertain, technologically luckier future, and to ignore the dependence of future utility on present enjoyment, must mean *too much* investment. We must discount the future to be fair to the present.

For a *short-run* output-maximising programme like a five-year plan— if the main need is to boost productive capacity and competitive power rather than immediate consumption—we can take care of the latter by a constraint specifying some minimum acceptable growth rate for con-sumption. Future generations can be looked after by specifying a minimum acceptable capital-stock at the end of the plan period. This is not as good as a really long-range plan, 'properly' balancing the interests of individuals in different generations. However, the latter approach is politically irrelevant, without, as yet, being theoretically fully satis-factory.

7. CHOICE

(a) Act and process

No aim of economic policy arouses stronger emotions, or more diffi-culties of definition and measurement, than choice. To strive for choice, we are told, is at once the glory and the handicap of democratic states. Such an aim makes life more full but harder to make still fuller; it maintains individual rights at the cost of progress.[1] This antithesis between growth and choice is oversimplified. Much of the choice on which we pride ourselves is not choice at all.

The dictionary does not help by telling us that choice is 'the act of

---

[1] The sharp dichotomy is based on rhetoric. How would one rank, in order of democracy or freedom, diverse systems such as those of Mexico, Yugoslavia, the Israeli *kibbutz*, Pakistan and Brazil?

choosing; preferential determination between things proposed; selection, election'.[1] 'Choice' can be properly used only of humans or human groups. Arguments about whether an animal chooses are always arguments about whether it 'really chooses' in the way a human does. A Random Number Indicator machine 'chooses' metaphorically, as a computer 'eats' input data. Human choice, when the word is used properly, is a bridge-concept, stating that two related conditions are satisfied and attaching a favourable valuation to their joint fulfilment.

These conditions are that a person or group

(A) has weighed the consequences of two or more members of a set of possible actions;

(B) has reached and can execute a decision based on preferences among the consequences assessed.

Mere ratiocination without the possibility of decision is at most hypothetical choice ('I would have advanced the left flank had I been Napoleon', or 'I vote for Party X in a constituency where it has a 25,000 minority, because I would like to choose to send its representative to Parliament if I could'.) Programmed, thoughtless or random selection is not genuine choice either. A man who knows there are two different drinks in a refrigerator, but picks one out without looking, is not choosing. Nor is a housewife who, without being aware of it, always buys the detergent with the advertising jingle she heard last night. Notice that (A) above implies that the acts to be chosen from have different consequences. The selection of one of two identical objects is not a choice. A Works Committee giving advice ignored by the manager, who anyhow imposes his own solution, is not choosing anything.

(b) Choice and central planning

Choice thus implies the union of thought and action in the same person or group. Unfortunately for simplicity, choice is seldom unambiguously increased or decreased by any Government action. Almost all such action will increase some people's choice and reduce the choice of others.

The rationing of a scarce food reduces the ability of the rich to choose large amounts of it, but by so doing inhibits the development of upward price pressures that would stop poor people from buying any at all. Nationalisation removes the right of private individuals to choose to operate in an industry as entrepreneurs, but can be used to increase the power of choice among workers and/or consumers in the management of

[1] *Shorter Oxford Dictionary.*

that industry. (It has been in Israel, Yugoslavia and Algeria.) High taxes on income are correctly attacked, by those fortunate enough to earn so much as to pay them, as 'restricting my choice to spend my income as I please'; but they can be used to finance social-security expenditures that enable all groups to choose among amenities, such as parks and water supplies, that cannot be supplied economically by the private businessman.

So, while we can get a satisfactory definition of individual choice, the presence of competing interests in a society makes it much harder to decide whether any given measure reduces or increases *the* freedom to choose. No clear measurement of the power to choose exists; certain rights (to 'life, liberty and the pursuit of happiness') are usually regarded as inviolable for each individual, no matter how much their abrogation in one case would increase freedom of choice for others, but even this is violated (by imprisonment, and even death, as penalties for crimes).

The general wish to extend choice, so long as such conflicts are avoided, means that planners in democratic countries will prefer incentive and permissive to compulsory controls, positive incentive and permissive measures to negative ones (where the distinction is meaningful), and probabilistic planning (if not too sensitive to error) to attempts to hit precise targets that involve Draconian penalties against violators. Can more be said?

The Right, and also a few old-fashioned economists, still sometimes suggest that any Government intervention *prima facie* restricts choice. It is clearly true that somebody's range of choice is altered by the intervention; otherwise there would be no point in intervening. But

(i) the change may result from giving the person information allowing him to choose in fuller knowledge of consequences,

(ii) the limitation of one person's choice may be essential to free the choice of others; laws against river pollution are needed to leave open the choice of pleasant swimming to inland populations,

(iii) present choice may be curtailed to increase future choice, e.g. by diverting resources from production for consumption to production for investment,

(iv) a person may be forced (e.g. by taxing petrol) to pay the real cost of his action, instead of choosing to inflict it on others and thus reducing their range of choice—and so on.

The Left, and a few old-fashioned economists, tend to assume that direct taxes on income always restrict choice less than indirect taxes on specific goods. This is untrue if these indirect taxes correct distortions in the price structure (of types now familiar to us); or if, given the price structure, the structure of demand is altered more fundamentally by raising money through taxes on income than through taxes on goods and services, which may well be the case. It is not even true—choices apart— that indirect tax need be more regressive than direct.[1]

There are three ways, other than selection among controls to attain a given end, in which a plan can be made more choice-enlarging.

(i) Instead of giving orders, planners can set relative prices of goods and services so that individuals (taken as a whole) choose as the planners desire; the prices desired to achieve these ends, however, may not be those wanted for other reasons.

(ii) Planning can be decentralised by finding groups of industries and firms—e.g. regions?—that supply much of one another's raw materials but few inputs to the rest of the economy, and letting each such group operate more or less independently.

(iii) Perhaps most promising for the U.K., because most adaptable to an economy with a large and flourishing privately-owned sector, is the solution attempted, in different ways, by Yugoslav workers' councils, Israeli *kibbutzim* (genuine collectively-run farms, as opposed to the Soviet parody on the idea) and, in a less thoroughgoing way, *Mitbestimmungs-recht* (joint determination) in West Germany.

In all these cases, the object is to give workers on the job increasing power to control their conditions of employment and the use made of profits. 'On the job' is important: full-time trade union leaders at the negotiating table, like full-time workers' representatives at the board of directors, cannot escape the pressure from the atmosphere that sur-rounds them to become a part of the new and higher group to which they belong. Even more important, neither method gives day-to-day choice to the man on the job. Presumably it is a value that choice is a good thing (not that it is a popular thing); the object is to stop people being told what to do by other people all the time, to get them used to taking deci-sions for themselves. This is the right and the duty enjoyed naturally by the family on its own farm, the village storekeeper, the teachers at a university or a school: in none of these cases is the conflict with final

[1] I. M. D. Little, Direct versus Indirect Taxes, *Economic Journal*, 1951, further shows that direct taxes (on income) can distort the price-structure, by indirectly subsidising goods complementary with leisure.

[2] O. Lange and F. W. Taylor, *Economic Theory and Socialism*, Minnesota, 1938.

central control insuperable. In the early stage of experiments in workers' control, there will be many mistakes; and it would be absurd to extend complete control to all workers overnight. There will have to be pilot schemes moving ahead as success is proved in the simpler tasks; the nationalised industries are the obvious places for such schemes.

Since the workplace is where most of people's waking lives is spent, and since it is there that subservience to order is most acute, no society for which choice is a value rather than a catchword can abstain from the sort of experiment here suggested. Yugoslav experience, in an environment initially far less oriented towards choice than Britain, indicates that efficiency increases with entrusted independence.[1] But of course the factory is not the only area where choice can be expanded. Parent-teacher associations; local government (including the use of town meetings on the New England pattern); local consumers' associations receiving central assistance to advise housewives in choosing among local stores; housebuilding by associations of prospective owners; control of estates by tenants' councils—all are possible loci of genuine democracy, which is the exercise of group choice, not the periodic and mechancial selection of unseen delegates.

There are obvious conflicts between central planning and the decentralisation of decisions to workers, tenants, consumers and so forth. However, the development of the habit of choice would surely be ample compensation, *even economically*, for possible divergence from planned targets. Just one example: the development, through vigorous consumers' associations (or co-operatives, as in Sweden), of motorists watching price and quality of petrol, oil, tyres and other motoring accessories with real care would do a great deal to eliminate the inefficient, and encourage the efficient, in British garaging. But efficiency is not everything. Mechanical factory work makes dehumanised attitudes all too likely. It is necessary to create units for genuine but efficient group choice, subject to central-plan pressures on behalf of society—but able to resist them.

---

[1] In 1958 I saw a group of experiments in factories at Zagreb and Ljubljana (Litostroj steam turbines) in which it was rapidly becoming clear that tax incentives enabled the Government to ensure adequate investment, so that full use of incentives to worker-controlled firms was possible. Whatever -ism one attaches to this combination of state control, private group decision and syndicalism matters little. The economic freedom of the Yugoslav factory worker is far greater than in the U.S.S.R., and almost certainly than in the U.K. His political freedom is tiny, even after the liberalisation of 1966.

CHAPTER THREE

Recent British Economic
Performance

I. THE RATE OF GROWTH OF
POTENTIAL ECONOMIC WELFARE

(a) *The British record*

Three questions must be answered before we assess the U.K.'s performance in increasing potential economic welfare since 1950. First, how has the number of persons sharing output changed? Second, has changing age-structure altered the relation between population and requirements? Third, what has happened to total output?

Table 1 shows that, during 1950-65, the U.K.'s population grew by only 7·9 per cent. Since 1958-9 the rate has accelerated, owing to rising net immigration, higher birthrates induced by earlier marriages, and, since 1962, the 'echo effect' of births to persons born during the 1945-7 'baby bulge'. Nevertheless recent population growth in the U.K. is much slower than at many times in our own past, or than in other countries now.[1]

Even slower than current U.K. population growth is the increase in total consumer requirements. Any assessment of how these relate to the age and sex of the population is arbitrary, but our conclusion, that consumer needs in the period 1950-65 rose by only 6·9 per cent as against the 7·9 per cent population rise, is not much affected by attaching

---

[1] In 1963-4 the U.K.'s rate was 0·7 per cent, and the world rate 1·9 per cent (France and W. Germany each 1·2 per cent; Italy 0·9 per cent, U.S.A. 1·4 per cent; U..N, *Monthly Bull. Stat.*, Jan. 1966). From 1801 to 1911, the U.K. rate varied from 10·9 per cent *per decade* to 18·1 per cent; from 1911 to 1951, it has varied from 4·6 per cent to 5·5 per cent (Table 1 for 1951-61; other data from Mitchell and Cole, *Abstract of British Historical Statistics*, Cambridge, 1962, p. 6).

different weights to the needs of the very young or the very old. Both groups increased faster than total population; probably these trends will continue.[1] Thus, in both recent past and near future, the growth rate of

TABLE I: POPULATION AND
CONSUMER-UNIT GROWTH, U.K. 1950-2000

	Persons	*Equivalent adult male consumers*
1950	100	100
1951	99·92	99·71
1952	100·24	100·07
1953	100·52	100·66
1954	100·89	100·72
1955	101·20	101·02
1956	101·64	101·34
1957	102·06	101·81
1958	102·48	102·20
1959	103·04	102·73
1960	103·80	103·40
1961	104·59	104·08
1962	105·62	105·33
1963	106·29	105·69
1964	107·11	106·22
1965	107·86	106·92
1970	112·20	109·93
1980	121·36	117·38
2000	147·50	141·97

Sources and Methods

In calculating Column 2,

For males: persons aged 0-4 counted as 0·3 adult males; 5-9, as 0·5; 10-14, as 0·7; 15-64, as 1; over 65, as 0·7.

Females counted as 0·875 of above proportions in each age group.

1950 data from U.K. *Annual Abstract of Statistics*, 1952, p. 8 (checked with U.N. data to 1960).

1951: *ibid.*, 1961, p. 12.

1952: *ibid.*, 1962, p. 12.

1953-60: *ibid.*, 1963, p. 12.

1960-2000: *ibid.*, 1965, p. 12, except 1965, which is Monthly Digest of Statistics, February 1966, p. 11.

[1] Such predictions are extremely volatile. As recently as October 1964, the U.K. *Annual Abstract of Statistics*, p. 13, predicted (in effect) 144·42 (col. 1) and 138·29 (col. 2) for 2000.

output per person understates that of *potential welfare* (though the same demographic trend also reduces the ratio of workers to population, and thus the ease of attainment of any desired level of output per person).

Table 2 shows the growth rate of U.K. NNP per person and per equivalent adult male (potential economic welfare, PEW). Another demographic factor, however, means that even the PEW growth data are understatements. The falling age of marriage has outweighed the

TABLE 2: GROWTH OF 'WELFARE' AND REAL NET
NATIONAL PRODUCT, U.K., 1950-1965
(1950 = 100)

	Total	*Per person*	*Per equivalent adult male*
1950	100·00	100·00	100·00
1951	102·52	102·60	102·82
1952	101·84	101·60	101·77
1953	106·60	106·05	105·90
1954	110·46	109·49	109·67
1955	113·24	111·90	112·10
1956	115·85	113·98	114·32
1957	117·83	115·45	115·74
1958	117·39	114·55	114·86
1959	121·33	117·75	118·11
1960	127·31	122·65	123·12
1961	131·77	125·99	126·60
1962	132·78	125·71	126·06
1963	138·63	130·43	131·17
1964	145·99	136·30	137·44
1965	149·06	138·20	139·41
Growth 1950-65 (percentage, compound per year)	2·7	2·2	2·3

Sources: Total and adult equivalent population from Table 1. Net national product at 1958 factor cost from *National Income and Expenditure 1965*, C.S.O., 1965, pp. 18-19 for 1950-63; *Economic Survey 1965*, H.M. Treasury, 1966, for 1964-5.

Note: In this and several following tables, no reliance should be placed on the second decimal place. It is included to enable you to make further calculations, if you wish, and to round off later.

rising proportion of the population of non-marriageable age, to produce a rise in the proportion of persons who are married—for men from 45·6 per cent in 1951 to 46·8 per cent in 1961; for women from 52·8 per cent to 53·6 per cent.[1] Whatever the effects on spiritual welfare, this must mean that any level of output brings more material satisfaction. Two cannot live as cheaply as one, but they certainly live more cheaply than twice one (in their use of living space, furniture, etc.) so even the last column of table 2 is somewhat pessimistic. No systematic correction is possible here!

From Table 2, PEW in the U.K. increased at least 2·1 per cent per year over the period 1950-65. The period was free from major depressions. But Table 2 overstates the smoothness of the growth achieved. First, a month or two of recession is swallowed up in a year's growth data. Second, annual series distribute, over several years, growth concentrated in a short period. Thus the index of industrial production did not regain its 1957 level until the end of February 1959; rose 14 per cent in the next twelve months; and then remained stationary until Spring 1962. Yet Table 2 seems to show a steady rise in PEW over the period. The rise from February 1959 makes 1959 look better than 1958; the sharp rise in January-February 1960, plus the lower levels of early 1959, make 1960 look (more dubiously) better than 1959; and 1961, a year of complete stagnation, is given a rosy glow by the yearly figures, because it maintained the level of late 1960, which was higher than that of January and February 1960.

Closer analysis, based on quarterly estimates of gross domestic product (GDP) available from 1955[2] shows the jerkiness of growth in the U.K. At one extreme, GDP per equivalent adult male consumer rose by 2 per cent in 5¼ years (mid-February 1955 to mid-May 1958, and mid-February 1960 to mid-February 1962); at the other extreme it rose by 7 per cent in February 1959-February 1960, and 4 per cent in a single quarter in 1963. This is shown in Figure 9.

Jerky growth means wasted investment—and hence wasted sacrifice of present consumption—and uncertain expectations, leading to unadventurous and insufficient investment. Timing apart, however, why worry about the long-run growth record of Table 2? Yearly growth of potential welfare at 2·1 per cent—with a static income distribution—

[1] U.K. *Annual Abstract of Statistics*, 1965, p. 14.
[2] The data are published in *Economic Trends* and the annual *Economic Survey*; ours are updated to March 1966.

First, as an economy becomes richer, so the proportion of efforts that can be directed away from satisfying immediate needs, towards making machines and factories for the future, rises. That is, the share of savings (and hence of finance for investment) in GNP rises. The U.K. devoted 15·4 per cent of GNP to gross investment in 1950-60, as against 7·7 per cent—exactly half—in 1900-13. Other countries achieved smaller expansions from a higher initial base.[1] More machines *of the same type*, especially with restricted labour supply, must bring decreasing returns to capital; but accelerated investment means speedier embodiment of technical advances in productive processes.[2] One replaces worn-out machines with the best available at any given price; therefore, for technical progress, it is *gross* investment that counts. Technical change and diminishing returns roughly balance; there is no systematic change in the amount of new investment needed for a unit of extra output over the whole period 1900-60, though most countries have experienced a marked rise in the share of output devoted to investment.

Second, the cyclical instability that dominated Western economies from the Industrial Revolution until 1939—visible in Figure 10 for 1863, 1868, 1875, 1893 and above all 1929-33—meant huge waste of productive capacity. Men and machinery stood idle for want of adequate monetary demand; Governments 'retrenched' expenditure in depressions, thereby making them worse. If, owing to depression, machinery stands idle for much of its life, greater investment *effort*, i.e. more sacrifice of current consumption, is required to generate any output level than if plant is fully used; if slumps undermine confidence, more *incentives* are needed to persuade businessmen to invest. Since 1945 there has been no major depression. The danger of inflation has caused Governments to choke off demand, and hence growth; but this has meant mainly the postponement of new investment projects. There has

[1] A. Maddison, *Economic Growth in the West*, Allen and Unwin, 1964, p. 76. By 1965 the ratio in the U.K. had risen to 21·1 per cent (H.M. Treasury, *Economic Survey for 1965*, C.S.O., 1966).

[2] Furthermore, E. Domar (Depreciation, Replacement and Growth, *Economic Journal* 1953, reprinted in *Essays in the Theory of Economic Growth*, Oxford, 1957, esp. p. 157) shows that, the faster gross investment grows, the smaller the part of it needed to make good depreciation. Depreciation is about 3 per cent of capital stock per year. If capital is thrice the yearly value of output, depreciation is 9 per cent of yearly output. If gross investment rises from 12 per cent to 15 per cent of output, net investment initially doubles, from (12 − 9) = 3 per cent to (15 − 9) = 6 per cent. The growth rate is thus doubled, from 1 per cent to 2 per cent yearly, by a rise in the rate of gross investment of only one-quarter.

means that levels of living double every 33 years. Life expectancy is rising. Continuance of these trends means that a child, born as you read these words, may expect to see the level of living rise at least fivefold in his lifetime. For an already well-to-do country like the U.K. there is nothing objectively scandalous about a record of this sort. It was achieved in face of steadily falling working hours. Moreover, the very achievement of growth not only reduces the value attached to future rises of the same amount, but also means that maintenance of the growth *rate* will increase the absolute *amount* of increase each year.

Even if you accept growth as a constrained maximand (see pp. 47-50), you may feel there is not much to worry about in the Table 2 figures, and certainly no cause to overstrain ourselves, reduce our leisure, and imperil our balance of payments in a headlong rush for faster growth. The evidence of what we *could* do, however, does not support this complacent view. It is almost impossible to assess a growth performance in isolation. We have to ask whether it is satisfactory in view of (i) the standards of our own past, (ii) the standards being set (and the economies of scale being achieved) by the growth of our competitors, and (iii) the comparative improvement made on past growth performance by the U.K. and the countries with which we would wish to compare ourselves.

(b) The standards of Britain's past

Figure 10 shows that, since 1948, growth in U.K ouput per head has almost exactly resumed the trend of 1855-98, before its interruption by stagnation (1898-1912), world wars, and abnormal slumps. In 1848-52, in England and Wales, out of every 1,000 children born, 157 died before their first birthdays; by 1917-21, 'only' 89. This meant a big rise in the proportion of adults in the population.[1] Thus PEW between 1855 and the First World War grew much more slowly than since 1948, owing to rising *per caput* needs. By historical standards the U.K.'s post-1945 growth is good. However, if we could attain only our present rate in 1855-98—when workforce was growing much faster than now[2]—can we achieve 4 per cent yearly growth now?[3] There are three reasons for believing that we can.

---

[1] D. A. Mitchell and P. Deane, *Abstract of British Historical Statistics*, Cambridge, 1962, pp. 12-13, 37.

[2] Occupied persons 1851, 9·4 millions; 1901, 16·3m.; 1951, 22·6m. (*ibid.*, pp. 60-61.) Hardly any growth is expected in 1965-75 (Beckerman, *et al. The British Economy in 1975*, Cambridge, 1965, p. 94).

[3] J. Knapp and K. Lomax, *Lloyds Bank Review*, Oct. 1964.

E

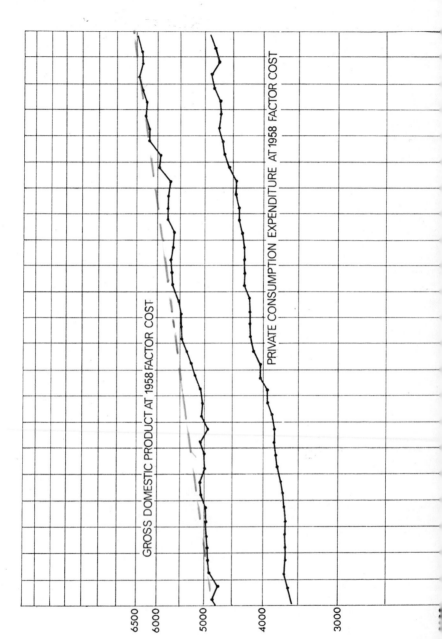

GROSS DOMESTIC PRODUCT AT 1958 FACTOR COST

PRIVATE CONSUMPTION EXPENDITURE AT 1958 FACTOR COST

R QUARTER, SEASONALLY ADJUSTED

6500

6000

5000

4000

3000

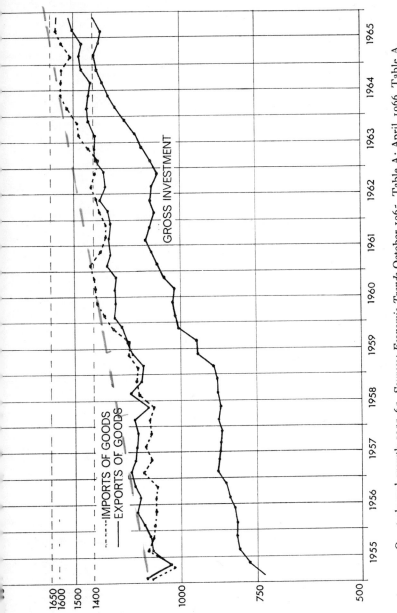

9. Quarterly real growth 1955–65. *Sources: Economic Trends* October 1965, Table A; April 1966, Table A.

TABLE 3: GROWTH OF POPULATION,
AND EQUIVALENT ADULT MALES

Period	Country	Population Growth	EAM Growth
1950-60	U.K.	103·8	103·4
	U.S.A.(a)	118·4	115·5
	Italy	108·5	107·4
1950-61	U.K.	104·6	104·1
	W. Germany(b)	110·9	110·4
1954-62	U.K.	104·7	104·6
	France	108·5	107·8

Sources and methods: An 'equivalent adult male' consumer is explained on p. 112. U.K. source: Table 2. For other countries, *Annuaire Statistique de la France*, 1956, p. 5; 1963, p. 10. Italy: *U.N. Demographic Yearbook*, 1952, p. 144; 1962, pp. 176-7. U.S.A.: *ibid.*, 1952, p. 136; 1962, pp. 162-3. W. Germany: *ibid.*, 1952, p. 143; *Statistisches Jahrbuch*, 1963 (Beilage), pp. 5-6, 10.

Notes: (a) Excluding Alaska and Hawaii for 1950 and 1960, and assuming age-structure and sex structure to be the same in those areas as elsewhere in the U.S.A.

(b) Excluding the Saar for 1950 and 1961. Allowance has been made for the fact that a considerably higher proportion of the Saar's population is male, and aged 15 to 64, than of the population of Germany as a whole.

Canada, Australia or New Zealand—all initially richer than the U.K.[1] However, our failure to use our potential as well as France, Italy and West Germany is distressing. All three have similar populations; all are reducing their working weeks at least as fast as the U.K.; all are achieving aims other than growth at least as well.

Figure 11 shows that the growth of Italy, France and West Germany cannot be explained away as post-war recovery. By 1952, output per head had easily reached (and total output far surpassed) pre-war levels, yet their rates of growth have been much the same for the periods 1947-52 and 1952-64. Moreover, the 'recovery' explanation has elements of absurdity. Would voluntary self-bombing raise Britain's growth rate? Given full-employment policies, wartime destruction of capital makes growth harder, not easier. But are recent differences between British and foreign growth performances merely continuations of historical trends?

[1] U.N. *Yearbook of National Accounts Statistics*, 1964, Tables 4A, 4B; *Lloyds Bank Review*, April 1966, p. 50.

been some waste of capacity (half-finished buildings), but not on the massive scale of pre-war slumps. Even a stop-go policy should produce faster growth than a non-policy of go-retreat.

Third, most Governments have been committed since 1945 to policies designed for growth. Total U.K. Government expenditure rose from 9 per cent of GNP in 1870-90, to 38 per cent in 1950-60.[1] Public authorities undertook 44·5 per cent of gross investment in 1965.[2] Public outlay, especially investment, is now used to promote long-run growth, though short-term policy sometimes impedes this attempt.

Therefore, for three reasons, we should expect *faster* growth since 1945 than before 1939. The investment/income ratio has risen sharply (and technical progress has offset diminishing marginal returns to capital); the new capacity thus created has been used almost to the full, instead of standing idle as in pre-war slumps; and the government, with its huge spending power, has aimed deliberately at growth. Yet British growth, while stabler than in the past, has hardly been faster. How have our main competitors fared?

(c) *The standards of Western post-war growth*

Table 3 shows that our main 'rivals' experienced faster population growth since 1950 than the U.K. Except for W.Germany, too, all showed a bigger excess of growth of *total* over *equivalent adult male* populations than the U.K. W.Germany had a faster rise in the married share of the population than the U.K.; from 1950 to 1960, the proportion of W.German men who were married rose from 48·0 per cent to 51·6 per cent, and of women from 43·6 per cent to 46·4 per cent.[3] Thus in all the European countries the rise in potential welfare exceeded the rise in NNP per head by a greater proportion than in the U.K.—in W.Germany by more than can be shown statistically.

In Tables 4 and 5 and Figures 11 and 12, the U.K.'s growth record is compared with that of some major Joneses. Plainly we have not kept up with them; since 1953, indeed, the U.K. has been surpassed in income per head by France, W.Germany, Norway and Denmark. True, U.K. income per head has grown considerably faster than in the U.S.,

---

[1] J. Verveka, The Growth of Government Expenditure in the U.K. since 1790, in A. Peacock and D. Robertson (ed.) *Public Expenditure: Appraisal and Control*, Oliver and Boyd, 1963, p. 114.
[2] *The Times*, 11 March 1966, p. 11.
[3] *Statistisches Jahrbuch*, 1963 (Beilage).

Table 6 also suggest that growth since 1870 has been overshadowed by three short-run factors: income behaviour in wars, rearmament booms offsetting potential slumps, and the depth of actual slumps.

Over the whole period 1870-1964 the U.S. performance is easily the best, because she continued growing—faster and more stably than ever —during the two great wars. In 1920, France's income per person was 17 per cent below the 1913 level; the U.K.'s 12·5 per cent lower; the U.S.'s 4·6 per cent *higher*. In 1948, the U.K. and France were still just below the 1937 level of income per head; Italy was 14 per cent below it and W. Germany 32 per cent. The U.S. was 37 per cent *above* the 1937 level!

Germany, and to a lesser extent Italy, recovered very quickly from the 1929-33 slump. The *initial* impact of their huge rearmament booms added little to welfare in terms of consumed products, so that the German rate for 1929-37—even if reliable—overstates the gain in welfare. But the huge *secondary* effects of rearmament made Hitler an unconscious Keynesian. Soldiers and aircraft workers buy food, clothes and houses with their extra income. So do farmers, tailors and bricklayers.

Figures 11–12 show that output per head fell less sharply during recessions in the U.K. than in the other four economies—especially in the world slump, 1929-33. After 1945, most economies practised Keynesian counter-cyclical techniques fairly successfully. But the U.K., having been much stabler before 1939 than other countries, had less to gain from successful stabilisation techniques. Hence, in part, her smaller improvement.

What of long-run trends? Table 6 lends no support to either the 'British national decline' or the 'long-term historical process' view of our relatively slow acceleration. In 1945-65, the U.K. has grown faster and more steadily than at any time since the 1880s (see Figure 11, p. 118)—a strange symptom of moral decay. In so far as historical processes exist beneath the responses to short-run shocks, discussed above, they suggest: ·

(a) that France, and even more Italy, are chronic slow growers (1870-1948), recently and dramatically reformed by the mobilisation of surplus agricultural workers for investment-goods and export sectors.

(b) that the U.S. is a dynamic, big-market economy that 'stole' some European growth in 1870-1913 by cutting into agricultural trade, performed badly in the 1950s owing to relatively poor assimilation of Keynesianism, and is now going ahead again.

(c) that (give a rearmament boom, take a slump) West Germany, as part of the unified German economy, performed negligibly better than the U.K. from 1870 to 1937, but has shot ahead since 1948.

TABLE 6: LONG-RUN GROWTH RECORDS

Country	*Yearly rate of growth of income per head in:*							
	1870-1913	*1913-37*	*1937-64*	*1913-29*	*1929-37*	*1948-64*	*1870-1937*	*1870-1964*
U.K.	1·6 —	0·6	1·3	—0·1	1·8	2·2	1·2	1·2+
U.S.A.	1·9	1·1	2·3	1·6	—0·0	2·0	1·7	1·9+
France	1·4+	0·3	2·5	1·7	—2·2	4·2	0·8	1·5
W. Germany	1·6+	0·8+	2·7	—0·1+	4·1	7·0	1·4—	1·7
Italy	0·7	1·1+	2·6	1·2—	1·0	5·7	0·9	1·4

Sources: As Table 4.

Notes: (i) Where a rate occurs more than once in the table, the rates are ranked by a subsequent + or — ; thus W. Germany, 1870-1913, grew very slightly faster than U.S.A., 1913-29, which in turn very slightly outstripped U.K., 1870-1913.

(ii) Especially before 1937, however, all differences in compound rates below, say, 0·2 per cent over ten years, are within the margin of measurement error.

Since 1950, most advanced English-speaking countries[1] have improved very little on their long-run trend, though they have greatly reduced the year-to-year fluctuations about that trend. The countries of Western Europe have soared ahead—in particular Italy and West Germany. And since 1960 the U.S. has outdistanced the U.K.

Why has the U.K. failed to match Western Europe's acceleration? Some candidate explanations are empirically wrong: days lost through strikes, for instance, are a far smaller proportion of total workdays in the U.K. than in Italy or France. Some are logically wrong: bad management could explain a lower level of output from any given quantity of resources, but not slower growth, though a *growing divergence* in management quality between the U.K. and Europe might logically (if not actually) explain the facts.

Differences across national frontiers in 'character', or in growth-rate

[1] Some rough estimates of annual (compound) growth rates of G.D.P. per head from 1950-60 (1960-63 in brackets): Australia 2·0 (1·9); Canada 1·2 (2·5); New Zealand 1·8 (0·8). U.N., *Yearbook of National Accounts Statistics*, 1964, Table 4A.

of the competence of workers or businessmen, can also be ruled out. They require a complex and incredible theory of historical change in such differences. What happened to the relative human natures of British and Italian workers or businessmen between 1870-1913 and 1948-1964 to account for the *change* in their relative performance?

It is more hopeful to look for economic explanations of economic change. Differences in pre-war performance can be accounted for by such means. For instance, rapid U.S. growth in 1870-1913, relative to its own past and to the growth and acceleration being achieved by other countries, can be attributed partly to the exploitation of the largest and richest new agricultural region ever brought into cultivation in such a short time, but mainly to the high price of labour and the consequent encouragement to install new capital equipment.[1] Can we explain the relative post-war performance of the U.K. and Europe in this way?

(e) A stylised explanation

The main and striking feature of post-1945 experience in N. W. Europe is the migration, on a scale without historical parallel, of agricultural workers and their families into the towns. In a mere six years (1954-60) the French agricultural labour force fell by over one million men, and the non-agricultural labour force rose by a similar amount. In West Germany between 1950 and 1963, some 3 million workers left the land, swelling the ranks of immigrants from the East into the booming towns. In Italy, between 1950 and 1960, almost two million workers moved from agriculture into the towns.[2]

France, West Germany and Italy, then, have enjoyed an annual transfer of some 1 per cent of working force from agriculture into more productive sectors of the economy. This has been achieved despite steady rises in agricultural output: the people readiest to move have come from the worst land, where the incentive to stay was smallest, and this movement has enabled agronomic skills to be concentrated on the land where their yield was the highest.

[1] H. Habbakuk, *American and British Technology in the 19th Century* (Cambridge, 1962) ch. 3.
[2] M. Lipton, Labour Resources for Economic Growth, *Aspect*, Dec. 1963. If the proportion of the 1963 work force in W. Germany employed in agriculture had been the same as in 1950, there would now be 3·1 million fewer non-agricultural (NA) workers—over one-eighth of the workforce. In Italy the whole growth of the NA workforce 1951-63 (about 3 million, from 12·4 million in 1951) came from the land; *total* workforce stagnated. I.L.O. *Yearbook of Labour Statistics*, 1964, pp. 51, 55.

The benefits of this migration are not exhausted by comparing the value of industrial and agricultural output per head and working out the static gain from a change of occupation. Indeed, this is misleading, because the factor costs of farm products, throughout the period, have been kept artificially high by tariff or subsidy in all the countries under review. The comparison therefore understates the gain in value-product per man-hour, caused by migration from agriculture to industry, that would exist if prices moved so as to reflect the relative values attached by consumers to farm and factory products. But there are more things to be considered than such a static comparison, even if it could be made in terms of correct relative prices.

First, industry enjoys economies of scale. A 10 per cent output rise may require 10 per cent more workers (and machines) but in most industries these need less than 10 per cent more foremen and directors, and much less than 10 per cent more heat, light and fuel. On the other hand, the agricultural workers who leave the land for industry do not leave land of average productivity, but tend to come from the worst land. Thus a 10 per cent cut in farmworkers, land and capital cuts output in agriculture by much less than 10 per cent.

Second, a large, steady inflow of workers to industry enables a Government to avoid certain short-run conflicts between growth and other economic objectives, The U.K. now lacks this flow of workers, because it has already flowed: fewer than 1 in 27 workers is in agriculture, as against 1 in 9 in Germany, 1 in 5 in France and 1 in 4 in Italy.[1] When there is balance-of-payments trouble in Italy (1962-63) and the government slightly deflates home demand, the new arrivals in the town find jobs in export industries instead; this directly raises export volume, and reduces upward pressure on wages, hence making exports more competitive. Germany's experience in 1967 seems similar.

When the U.K., without such a mobile labour-flow, deflates home demand, there is no such quick way of shifting workers into export industries. It is far harder to persuade settled workers to move from one job to another, than to use incentives to channel a flow already present. Deflation eventually 'works' by choking off British demand for imports, thus improving the foreign balance—but this happens because domestic incomes have been reduced.

The choice between price stability and rapid growth, too, is less acute

[1] I.L.O., *Yearbook of Labour Statistics*, 1964, pp. 51, 55; U.K. *Annual Abstr. Stat.*, 1965, p. 107.

F*

for an economy with a rapid flow of industrialising labour. At or near the full employment ceiling, Britain can coax extra output from workers with a short-run fixed supply of capital only through offering overtime rates: i.e. by paying *more* when the worker is *less* productive, thus pressing up average costs (and hence prices) in two ways. In France or Italy, employers can use migrants from agriculture at the normal wage—and benefit from their growing efficiency, as they learn new skills, to raise total output at least as fast as total cost.

This is not the only explanation of the relatively slow British growth performance, but it is the most important. As Beckerman[1] has shown, the 1950s' relatively small additions to the U.K.'s stock of capital, and supply of labour, account for only *some* of her relatively slow growth; moreover, since 1960, the U.K.'s gross investment/GNP ratio has been at European levels, and there has been little extra *total* labour in any European economies. The growth gap, however, has persisted.

Another aspect of it has been the U.K.'s continued functioning as international banker (and printer) of a world trading currency—without, since 1945, the gold and foreign-exchange reserves to take such a strain. Consider the behaviour of France in 1958, faced with a severe balance-of-payments crisis. Rather than seriously restrict domestic growth by deflating incomes and thus cutting imports, she devalued the franc by 10 per cent and thus restored a favourable reserve position rather fast. The U.K. cannot devalue without reducing the worth of other people's assets—particularly their holdings of U.K. government bonds. We lack the reserves to respond to sales of sterling by just offering foreign currency to the sellers until they cease to expect devaluation. So we borrow; and our creditors expect us to deflate.

The contrast between the handling of three balance-of-payments crises—France 1958, Italy 1962-3 and Britain 1964-5—shows the alternatives facing us. Either one is prepared to devalue, and abandon the prestige conferred by an internationally held currency, when faced with recurring substantial deficits in the current balance of payments; or one has, or gets, labour mobility between home and export sectors, so that slight deflation will produce higher exports (and not just reduce imports

[1] W. Beckerman (ed.), *The British Economy in 1975*, Cambridge, 1965, chs. 1-3. The very high correlation between investment/output ratios and growth, shown by T. P. Hill, *Economic Journal*, 1964, to hold when attention is confined to the U.S.A., U.K., France, W. Germany and Italy, is invalidated by (a) uncertainty as to which causes what, (b) the tiny number of observations on which the link is based.

by reducing employment and incomes); or one undertakes substantial home deflation (or 'pause') to cut imports. But one cannot have sustained growth, immobile labour and an international currency that may not be devalued, all at once.

2. EMPLOYMENT

(a) Standards and achievements: conventional unemployment

From 1800 to 1939, insecurity of employment was the main blot on British economic progress. In 1801, with 36 per cent of workers in agriculture and perhaps a further one-sixth providing simple services to the villages, half the population were secure from outright starvation —just as a Venezuelan peasant or an African herdsman is secure today. An ingenious peasant, with reliable rainfall and at least as many acres as family members, is always able to feed them. Their survival does not depend on fluctuations in demand for his saleable surplus, though their comfort does.

But by 1911 only 8 per cent[1] of the working force were in agriculture. From 1815 to 1939, the growing numbers in industry were subject to misunderstood and thus uncontrolled falls, large and frequent, in demand for their labour, and hence in their ability to survive decently. Substantial cuts in money-wages did not cure severe cyclical unemployment (for reasons discussed on pp. 5-6). The scanty data for 1851-1913 show that, for major unions, the yearly average proportion of members unemployed fluctuated around 5 per cent, exceeding 10 per cent in a bad slump (1858, 1879, 1886) and only in 1870-77 and 1896-1903 staying under 5 per cent for more than three years.[2] By the 1870s, most artisans could rely on the friendly-society activities of trade unions for unemployment insurance. After 1911, workers were protected by a state scheme—compulsory from 1920; but this guaranteed no more than a meagre subsistence. Until 1911, and for many long after it, primary reliance was on the grudging charity of Chadwick's workhouses, whose main objective was to render life inside less pleasant than the worst paid employment,[3] even when none was in fact obtainable.

After 1920, average unemployment rates rose sharply; not until 1939

[1] Deane and Cole, op. cit., p. 142, for 1801 and 1911.
[2] Mitchell and Deane, op. cit., pp. 64-5. In this period, such unions performed the functions of friendly societies, insuring their members against unemployment.
[3] Marriott, *England since Waterloo*, Methuen, 1950, p. 97.

did the rate fall below 10 per cent. Despite Keynes's warnings, Britain struggled by 1925 to a prestige-directed exchange rate, which made sterling so expensive that exports were rendered uncompetitive. During the world boom of 1925-29, British unemployment never fell below 10·6 per cent of the working force, because the workers in export industries, finding that high policy had cut their wages or replaced them by the dole, were forced to reduce their demands for the products (and hence the labour) of other workers in domestic-consumption industries, with depressant multiplier repercussions throughout the economy.[1]

The 1931 crisis fortunately forced Britain to devalue, making her exports competitive once more; this reduced the power of slump to worsen unemployment levels, even with the assistance of reductions in Government expenditure dictated by bankers' notions of economic wisdom. British unemployment thus rose less steeply than in most other western countries.[2] Nevertheless, at the bottom of the slump, in 1932, 22·5 per cent of British workers were involuntarily jobless. Even peak recovery in 1937 saw unemployment at 11·3 per cent. Among builders, shipwrights, port workers, iron workers, miners and fishermen, far higher levels prevailed.

This sketch suggests, first, the dreadfulness of Britain's past record on job security; second, why almost full employment since 1940 has not sufficed to erase the class-wide fear and restrictionism of the British worker, bred of a century and a half of mass insecurity ruled from ignorant, complacent prosperity; and third, what standards have to be used to judge the post-war British performance. That performance is largely admirable. In 1944, Beveridge foresaw[3] that unemployment, caused by changes of job, and by slow adaptation of industrial structure,

[1] J. M. Keynes, *The Economic Consequences of Mr Churchill*, Hogarth, 1925, pp. 5-9, 20-24. In 1929, 11 per cent of all workers were jobless in the U.K. But the percentages for major export industries were: pig-iron, 14·4; steel, 20·1; coal, 19·0; shipbuilding, 25·3; cotton textiles, 12·9; other textiles, 15·6; docks, harbours and canals, 30·3. Mitchell and Deane, op. cit., p. 67, as for other U.K. data in this paragraph.

[2] I.L.O., *Yearbook of Labour Statistics 1935-6*, Table 1 shows—for 1929-32—registered unemployed rising more than threefold in Germany to 5·6 million; over eightfold in Belgium; fourfold in Canada, sevenfold in the U.S., and just over twofold in the U.K.

[3] Beveridge, loc. cit. Notice, however, that he also expected unfilled vacancies to be some 3 per cent of workforce! He foresaw the elimination of deficient aggregate demand for labour, but overrated structural and regional imbalances between supply and demand.

TABLE 7: CRUDE UNEMPLOYMENT RATES
(Unemployed workers as percentages of labour force)

Year or Period	W. Germany	Italy	U.S.A.	U.K.
1929	9·3	—	3·2	11·0
1930	15·3	—	8·7	14·6
1931	23·3	—	15·9	21·5
1932	30·1	—	23·6	22·5
1933	26·3	—	24·9	21·3
1934	14·9	—	21·7	17·7
1935-7	6·6	—	17·1	14·0
1938-9	2·1(a)	4·1	18·1	12·5
1948-50	7·6	8·6	5·0	1·6
1951-3	8·3	9·3	3·1	1·7
1954	7·0	10·0	5·6	1·5
1955	5·1	7·6	4·4	1·2
1956	4·0	9·4	4·2	1·3
1957	3·4	8·2	4·3	1·6
1958	3·5	6·6	6·8	2·2
1959	2·4	5·6	5·5	2·3
1960	1·2	4·2	5·6	1·7
1961	0·8	3·5	6·7	1·6
1962	0·7	3·1	5·6	2·1
1963	0·8	2·5	5·7	2·6
1964	0·7	2·7	5·2	1·6
1965	0·5	3·6	4·6	1·5

Sources: U.N., *Statistical Yearbook,* 1948, Table 11; 1955, 1957, 1964, Table 10; *Monthly Bull. Stats.*, Feb. 1966, Table 8. U.K. 1929-39 from Mitchell and Cole, op. cit., p. 67.
Note: (a) 1938 only.

could seldom fall below 3 per cent of those wishing to work, so that 3 per cent was the minimum ratio of unemployed to workforce that could realistically be defined as 'full employment'. Though all political leaders accepted Government support for this ratio, few in 1944 saw it as other than a pious hope.

Yet since then the national unemployment/labour force ratio, except for brief cold spells in 1946-7 and 1962-3, never reached 3 per cent of the labour force; at 2½ per cent, Governments have trembled, and for

elections $1\frac{1}{2}$ per cent is dangerously high. Quite often, there are more unfilled vacancies in the U.K. than unemployed persons looking for them.[1]
Whatever the problems of special regions and groups, the overall situation has been transformed. Economists who complain of the discomfort
of 'excess demand for labour' or 'over-full employment'—its impedi-
ments to mobility among jobs and areas, its softening of incentives to
effort, its danger that capacity may lie idle for want of workers—should
remind themselves of the gain in human dignity for which such incon-
veniences are the price.

Different countries use different definitions of employment. Table 7
is useless for comparing rates of unemployment at a single point of time.
It does, however, show the trends; and all the countries show great
improvements. However, none (except perhaps France) has given full
employment quite so high a priority. Italy's labour force is not much
smaller than our own; in the mid-1950s, months when over 2 million
workers were jobless—10 per cent of the workforce—were common even
during rapid growth. As late as 1956, West Germany had 4 per cent
unemployment. The slump during Eisenhower's second term brought
U.S. unemployment near 7 per cent of the labour force; five years of
continuous boom have been needed to force it below 5 per cent; 4 per
cent was considered a satisfactory target until 1966.[2]

International comparisons must not be too easily assumed favourable.
U.K. data, compared to those in other countries, understate unemployment rates, by excluding (a) most pensioners, (b) some persons, such as
school leavers, seeking work for the first time, (c) many married women.
In these groups, many people do not qualify for benefit and therefore
do not register when unemployed. When we correct for the optimism of
British data, the *trends* of Table 8 are less favourable to the U.K. than
the average *levels*. German unemployment has been even lower than
ours; Italy's has fallen much faster. Their poor performance in the mid-
1950s was due largely to agricultural workers, subject to heavy seasonal
unemployment—especially on undermechanised, unirrigated land.
These have been quickest to leave for securer town jobs.

Thus the relative improvement of our rivals' employment levels is
no temporary accident. And the British experience—1958-9, 1962-3,

---

[1] See p. 246. Excess demand for labour is positive for $2\frac{1}{4}$ of the 3 years
1955/3-1958/2; for only 6 months of 1958/3-1961/2; and for only 6 months of
1961/3-1964/2.
[2] *Manpower Report of the President*, Washington, 1963, 1964.

1966-7, with deepening joblessness in each recession—is disturbingly reminiscent of the U.S. in 1953-63. But it is still true that, since 1945, job security has received higher priority, and has been more swiftly attained and more stably retained, in Britain than in comparable countries.

TABLE 8: STANDARDISED UNEMPLOYMENT RATES
(Unemployed, on U.S. definition, as percentage of labour force)

Period	W. Germany	Italy	U.S.A.	U.K.
1948-50	6·3	9·0	5·0	2·3
1952-3	6·9	9·8	3·1	2·4
1954-6	4·5	9·4	4·7	1·9
1957-9	2·6	7·1	5·5	2·9
1960-2	0·7	3·8	6·0	2·5
1963-5	0·6	3·1	5·0	2·7

Sources: A. Rees, The Dimensions of the Employment Problem, in *Proceedings of Symposium on Employment*, Amer. Bankers' Assoc., 1964, pp. 20-21, for adjustments to 1962 data 'to make them conform to (U.S.) definitions'. Above data are the estimates from U.N., *Stat. Yearbooks*, 1958, 1962, 1964, Table 9, multiplied by the ratios to U.N. 1962 data of Prof. Rees's estimates (W. Germany 0·83; Italy 1·05; U.K. 1·41).

(*b*) *Special problems and groups: conventional unemployment*
(i) *Sex.* Female unemployment is far less than male. This cannot be inferred from registrations alone, since many married women choose a form of insurance that minimises contributions, and then, having no claim on benefit, do not bother to register when unemployed. But this cannot account for the huge and widening difference in registered rates, especially not among very young age-groups where most women are unmarried (Table 9). In June 1954, despite non-registration, the rate of female registered unemployment (0·98 per cent of civil labour force) exceeded the male rate (0·94 per cent). In June 1959 the percentages were 1·79 (men), 1·30 (women); by the end of 1964, 1·57 (men), 0·98 (women).[1]

Partly the growing gap is traceable to a growing share of married women (and hence non-registrants) in the female workforce,[2] but this

---

[1] U.K. *Ann. Abst. Stat.*, 1964, Sec. V; *Min. Lab. Gaz.*, *passim.*
[2] From 66·8 per cent in 1952 to 69·9 per cent in 1960: Beckerman, op. cit., p. 85.

trend is far too slow to explain the matter fully. Moreover, the number of unfilled vacancies reported for men is usually about the same as for women, though the male labour force is almost twice the female. These differences reflect real characteristics of the labour market, not just statistical quirks. Demand for female labour, relative to supply, has outstripped that for male labour. The proportion of women in the civil labour force grew slowly but steadily, from 33·5 per cent (June 1954) to 34·9 per cent (December 1964)—in response to improving relative earnings. By the end of 1964, 91 jobs were on offer to women for every 100 for men—though women represented under 35 per cent of the labour force and barely one-quarter of registered unemployed.[1]

(ii) *Age*. We cannot use Table 9 to assess employment prospects for

TABLE 9: REGISTERED WHOLLY UNEMPLOYED
BY AGE AND SEX, JUNE 1964
(As percentages of labour force for each age-sex group)

Age-group	Male	Female	Age-group	Male	Female
Under 18	(1·81)	(1·16)			
18-19	1·50	1·06			
20-24	1·26	1·42	Under 20	(1·67)	(1·12)
25-29	1·27	1·29	20-39	1·31	1·11
30-34	1·34	0·91	40-59	1·41	0·79
35-39	1·37	0·67	60-64	4·45	(0·17)
40-44	1·27	0·62	Over 64	(0·54)	
45-49	1·27	0·72			
50-54	1·36	0·82			
55-59	1·75	1·04	All ages	1·60	0·92
60-64	4·45	}(0·18)			
Over 64	(0·54)				

Source: Min. Lab. Gaz., Aug. 1964, p. 343, for July analysis of wholly unemployed (excluding some 5,300 unemployed casuals, and temporarily stopped) by age and sex; each group is multiplied by the national ratio for wholly unemployed in June to July (1·017 men, 1·011 women: *ibid.*, July 1964, p. 292; Aug. 1964, p. 340). These June estimates are then expressed as percentages of June labour force (excluding armed forces and some 38,000 persons new to the labour force or jobless for 12 months or more) as analysed into groups by age and sex groups (*ibid.*, June 1965, p. 253).

[1] *Income, Prices, Employment and Production*, Min. of Labour, March 1965; *Ann. Abst. Stat.*, 1962.

very young or very old persons; pensioners and school-leavers rarely qualify for benefit and thus rarely register when unemployed. Levels and trends are best assessed by seeing what happens to male job prospects as age advances from 49 to 64. Even in high boom (June 1964), 4½ per cent of men aged 60-64—three times the national rate—could not get jobs. For over-65s, the true rate may be even higher—though the earnings rule, by which pension rights are forfeited if one earns too much, discourages labour supply.

At the young end, there is also some sign of reluctance to employ. This is a less serious source of wasted labour than the high rates among over-55s. Activity rates—ratios of workers and work-seekers (excluding employers and self-employed) to total population—for U.K. males over 64 were only 18 per cent, as against 88 per cent for men aged 40-64. Partly this is voluntary retirement; it also reflects withdrawal from the workforce by men who know that jobs are not available. This is shown by the unusually low activity rates for men over 64 in depressed regions (11·4 in Wales, 12·3 in Northern Ireland)[1]. For women, only 9·8 per cent of over-60s are employees: the fact that this ratio has risen every year (from 7·3 per cent in 1954), the substantial regional variations, and plain common sense confirm suspicions of substantial concealed unemployment here too.

Prejudice against older work-seekers inflicts more hardship than crude unemployment data, even adjusted for activity rates, reflect. Confining ourselves to the reliable data—men aged 20-64—we find the pattern shown in Table 10.

To minimise the risk of prolonged unemployment, one is too old at 25. If, on 13 July 1964, you had asked a reliably registered unemployed person (a male aged 20-64) how long he had been jobless, the time would rise with age. If he were 20-24, probably he would have been jobless for under 5 weeks; only 1 out of 5 such men would have been workless for over 3 months. If he were 60-64, there is only 1 chance in 8 that he was unemployed for under 5 weeks; 3 out of 4 such men were victims of hard-core unemployment (3 months or more).

[1] *Abstract of Regional Statistics*, 1965, p. 11. The Midland rate was 22·1 per cent and the London-South-East rate 21·0 per cent. This is not all regional differences in rates of withdrawal from workforce due to differences in demand for labour; both N.W. and S.W. are near the national unemployment rate, yet the first features very high, the second very low, activity rates. Self-employed persons, such as small farmers, numerous in the S.W., do not count as active *employees*.

This does mean that the disparity between the *numbers* of unemployment victims, relative to age-groups, is less than Table 9 had suggested. True, in mid-1964, men aged 60-64 had over thrice the unemployment risk of men aged 20-24; but a given unemployment rate affects far fewer persons in the older age-group than in the younger age-group, just

TABLE 10: DURATION OF UNEMPLOYMENT
BY AGE, MEN, 13 JULY 1964

(Percentages of registered wholly unemployed in each age-group)

Weeks	Age								
	20-25	25-30	30-35	35-40	40-45	45-50	50-55	55-60	60-65
Under 5	56·1	47·0	40·8	32·9	31·6	27·8	22·7	18·0	12·6
5 to 13	19·9	20·5	17·5	19·5	17·8	16·3	15·2	13·8	12·0
Over 13	24·0	32·5	41·7	47·6	50·6	55·9	62·1	68·2	75·4

Source: Min. Lab. Gaz., Aug. 1964, p. 343.

because the older stay jobless longer. But this is a somewhat heartless approach to the data. People unemployed for 5 weeks or less are usually just changing jobs; those jobless for over 3 months really suffer, and this burden of suffering, as Table 10 shows, falls more heavily on the old than Table 9 suggests.

(iii) *Region*

TABLE 11: REGIONAL UNEMPLOYMENT RATES, 1954-1965

(Registered unemployed as percentage of regional labour force)

Region	Year											
	1954	1955	1956	1957	1958	1959	1960	1961	1962	1963	1964	1965
London, S.E.	1·0	0·7	0·8	1·0	1·3	1·2	0·9	1·0	1·3	1·5	1·0	0·9
East, South	1·2	0·9	1·0	1·3	1·6	1·5	1·2	1·1	1·4	1·8	1·1	1·0
South-West	1·5	1·1	1·3	1·8	2·2	2·1	1·7	1·4	1·7	2·2	1·5	1·6
Midlands, Yks, Lincs.	0·7	0·6	0·8	1·0	1·7	1·6	1·7	1·1	1·7	2·0	1·1	1·0
North-West	1·5	1·4	1·3	1·6	2·7	2·8	1·9	1·6	2·6	3·1	2·1	1·6
North	2·3	1·8	1·5	1·7	2·4	3·3	2·9	2·5	3·8	5·0	3·4	2·6
Scotland	2·8	2·4	2·4	2·6	3·8	4·4	3·7	3·2	3·8	4·8	3·7	3·0
Wales	2·4	1·8	2·0	2·6	3·8	3·8	2·7	2·6	3·1	3·7	2·6	2·6
N. Ireland	7·0	6·8	6·4	7·3	9·3	7·8	6·7	7·5	7·5	7·9	6·6	6·1
United Kingdom	1·5	1·2	1·3	1·6	2·2	2·3	1·7	1·6	2·1	2·6	1·8	1·5

Source: Abst. Rgnl. Stat., 1965, p. 9; *Stats. of Incomes*, Mar. 1966, p. 87.

London, the Midlands and the South-East are consistently better than average; the North, Wales, Scotland and Northern Ireland, consistently worse. There has been little change in regional dispersion over the period; Northern Ireland and the Midlands have come slightly closer to the national average, while Scotland, London and the South-East have become 'more unequal'. The North, always somewhat depressed, is slightly recovering from the extremely unequalising movements of 1963.

Table 11 refutes the popular belief that recession is specially severe in areas of high unemployment. The unemployment rate appears to depend on region as much in good years as in bad.

Like age, residence as an influence on prospects of employment is far greater than registration data suggest.

TABLE 12: DURATION OF UNEMPLOYMENT,
MEN AGED 20-39, BY REGION, JULY 1964

(Wholly unemployed for each duration: percentage of unemployed in each region)

Weeks	Region								
	London S.E.	E. and S.	S.W.	Midlands	Yorks. Lincs.	N.W.	North	Scot-land	Wales
Under 5	56·6	58·1	54·9	52·0	51·2	40·5	33·9	34·0	44·7
5 to 13	20·9	18·9	18·1	19·4	18·7	19·5	18·6	19·7	20·8
13 to 52	18·1	17·3	19·5	19·1	20·0	25·9	26·8	28·2	22·5
Over 52	4·5	5·8	7·4	9·7	10·1	14·2	20·7	18·2	12·4

Source: Min. Lab. Gaz., Aug. 1964, p. 343.

As for the old, so for the mislocated; it is not that one is much likelier to be jobless at any moment, so much as that, having become jobless, one has a much longer, harder search for new work. The pattern of activity rates again reveals that even Table 12 is only the tip of the iceberg. There is no reason to believe that the activity rate, the ratio of employees to the total workforce, is more affected by self-employed and employers in one non-farming region than in another. Yet, for the group yielding most reliable employment data, and least affected by health or education as diversions from the workforce—men aged 25-44—1964 activity rates ranged from 90 per cent in the booming Midlands, East and South to 87·2 per cent in Scotland, 86·1 per cent in the North of

England and 82·3 per cent in Wales. Ability and will to get a job vary much more among regions, as among age-groups, than the crude registration data indicate.[1]

These regional disparities are hard to explain. Demography is not the answer. The age and sex structure of depressed regions are not specially unfavourable to job prospects.[2] Nor, surprisingly, is industrial structure the problem; if each main industry of poorer regions enjoyed the same employment levels as it did in the richer ones, the disparities of Table 11 would vanish.[3] Possibly the structure of this analysis is too crude; to speak of industries in regions, as Holmans well understands, is to obscure the effects of closures of firms in black-spot towns.[4] This, however, makes the problem of persistent disparities among locations more puzzling; if workers need only move for short distances within a region to improve employment prospects, why does the market fail to restore equilibrium? Lack of appropriate employment prospects in insufficiently diversified nearby towns, and absence of *general* skills in the workforce of poorer regions, suggests themselves: and we shall see (p. 209) that indeed the depressed regions feature very low opportunities for sixth-form education, concentration on general apprenticeships, and underdiversified industrial opportunities. This is distinct from the hypothesis that depressed regions have unlucky industries with income-inelastic demand; that is refuted by Holmans's evidence, by the existence of export markets, and above all by the failure of regional disparities to get worse as income continues to grow.

(iv) *Job.* In December 1964, there were 20 male applicants for every 10

[1] *Ibid.*, p. 11.

[2] Unemployed at June 1964, are analysed by age and sex in *Min. Lab. Gaz.*, July 1964, and the July labour force by age, sex and region in *ibid.*, June 1965. Applying the *Monthly Dig. Stat.*, Oct. 1964, July/June unemployment-level ratios to the June 1964 data, national July unemployment-rate estimates are obtained for each age-sex group. These are then applied to each region's labour force. It emerges that, if each region suffered only the national unemployment rate in each age-sex group, its overall unemployment rate would be close to the U.K. level. Therefore the statement in the text is proved.

[3] A. E. Holmans, in T. Wilson, ed., *Papers on Regional Development*, Blackwells, 1966.

[4] On 14.2.66, with the national rate at 1·4 per cent, the only big town over 4 per cent was Blackpool (4·6)—combining regional and winter seaside recession. Several smaller blackspots had over 1,000 workless ('Highlands and Islands' 7 per cent; Kirkcaldy 5·5; Ardrossan, Workington, Merthyr Tydfil each 5; etc.). In almost every case a specific, undiversified recession industry is clear. *Min. Lab. Gaz.* Mar. 1966, pp. 136-7.

vacancies for men. But there were 83 unemployed general labourers, other labourers and factory hands for every 10 places, and for clerks not qualified as bookkeepers or cashiers the ratio was 62:10. Yet in engineering and allied trades there were only 4 jobless for every 10 vacancies; in the chronic excess-demand sectors linked to housebuilding, such ratios extended well down the ladder of skills (7:10 for general building workers, 2:10 in woodworking).

For women—whose overall job position was better, though not as good as the $7\frac{1}{2}$:10 national ratio of unemployed to vacancies suggested (p. 129)—similar disparities existed.[1] For 'factory hands, charwomen, cleaners and miscellaneous unskilled working women' the ratio was 18:10; for lady engineers, 3:10.

In September 1965, the overall job situation was tighter.[2] Table 13 shows registered wholly unemployed and unfilled vacancies, relative to labour force, for males in main industries at that time. Four types of employment situation prevailed.

(A) Some industries—construction, shipbuilding, national government—feature, among reliable registrations (men over 18), both unemployment and unfilled vacancies well above the national average. This suggests either very poor matching of skills to needs or very high labour turnover.

(B) Where both rates are well below the national average—paper, printing and publishing, textiles, perhaps agriculture (though self-employment here demands special statistical caution)—one may infer very low mobility of labour in and out, owing to highly specific skills and/or restrictive practices in the training-periods of apprentices (by employers wanting cheap labour or unions wanting restricted entry).

(C) Sectors like catering and hotels—unskilled, employing many temporary workers from overseas—are plainly exceptions to the general situation of excess demand.

(D) Electrical engineering and metal manufacture (skills) and vehicles (boom) exhibit it especially strongly.

Wide dispersions in rate, among industries—even between largely unskilled industries—suggest an immobile and/or insufficiently informed labour market.

---

[1] *Statistics on Incomes*, Min. of Labour, Mar. 1965, Sec. E.
[2] This month is chosen for detailed analysis because almost wholly free from seasonal variations (U.N., E.C.E., *Economic Survey of Europe in 1964*, ch. II). Data from Min. of Labour, *ibid*, Dec. 1965.

TABLE 13: GREAT BRITAIN: EMPLOYMENT OPPORTUNITIES
IN SOME MAJOR INDUSTRIES, SEPT. 1965

| Industry | Thousands | | As percentages of total male labour force | | | |
| | Labour force | Male labour force | Male wholly unemployed | | Male unfilled vacancies | |
			Under 18	18 and over	Under 18	18 and over
Agriculture, etc.	875	765	0·08	0·91	0·26	0·22
Coal mining	548	531	0·03	0·97	0·24	0·88
Food, drink, tobacco	829	476	0·08	1·21	0·27	0·52
Chemicals, etc.	512	367	0·02	1·17	0·21	0·73
Metal manuf.	630	553	0·03	0·75	0·34	1·00
Engineering, elec. gds.	2269	1660	0·03	0·63	0·38	1·52
Shipbuilding, etc.	210	199	0·03	2·47	0·16	1·53
Vehicles	876	757	0·01	0·58	0·16	1·13
Other metal goods	589	391	0·10	0·89	0·86	1·33
Textiles	768	368	0·05	0·99	0·51	0·64
Clothing, footwear	543	150	0·08	0·77	0·93	0·90
Bricks, cement, glass, pottery	358	278	00·8	1·09	0·36	0·75
Timber, furniture	311	252	0·15	0·89	0·68	1·04
Paper, printing, publishing	642	422	0·04	0·52	0·33	0·41
Construction	1750	1668	0·11	2·36	0·25	1·15
Gas, elec., water	412	359	0·56	—	0·19	0·33
Tpt., commcn.	1673	1408	0·32	1·17	0·12	1·15
Distribution	3466	1746	x·13	1·13	0·73	0·57
Financial, professional, scientific services	3186	1287	0·09	0·75	0·31	0·76
Catering, hotels, etc.	696	269	0·10	2·89	0·11	0·25
Miscell. services	1697	834	0·12	1·43	0·51	1·19
National govt.	519	338	0·04	1·73	0·21	1·31
Local govt.	764	564	—	1·52	0·18	0·74
TOTAL (All Industries)	24896	16178	0·13	1·30	0·35	0·91

General note: In June 1965, workers under 18 were about 5·4 per cent of the U.K. labour force (*Min. Lab. Gazette*, June 1965, p.253); these data, however, excludes employers and self-employed, *in*cluded in the above data. 'Labour force' in this table also includes *wholly* unemployed, but *not* armed forces.
Source: Statistics of Incomes . . ., Min. of Labour, Dec. 1965, Tables E1, E12.

(v) *Skin colour.* In Table 13, the two sectors with very high proportions of coloured workers—catering, transport and communications—have ratios of unemployed to vacancies well above average. Careful analysis suggests that, in 1961-62, coloured unemployment was about 10 per cent —over five times the national rate.[1] The rate for Pakistanis was about 20 per cent, for West Indians about 10 per cent and for Indians and Africans about 6 per cent.

Part of this is due to the recent arrival of much of the coloured workforce; by now this should be outweighed by mobility in search of jobs (owing to lack of local roots). Coloured workers congregate in London and Birmingham, where excess demand, even for unskilled labour, is chronic and high. It is silly to deny that most of these discrepancies are due to sheer prejudice by unions and employers. Not only do we legislatively exclude those people who, with their high mobility and workforce/ population (and hence supply/demand) ratio, are our chief industrial need; when they settle where they are most useful, we fail to employ them.

(c) *New types of unemployment*

The solution of social and economic problems is like the sinking of a lake to reveal progressively lower hills. During mass unemployment of the conventional type, few people worry about either wasteful use of labour (for more efficiency is as likely to raise unemployment as output)[2] or *voluntary* withdrawal from the labour force due to illness, pregnancy, education, retirement or reduced hours (such withdrawals are distributionally desirable when jobs are hard to find). Yet these two— unemployment on the job and voluntary joblessness—are now serious reducers of labour input in Britain. Regional policy apart, little can be done to cut conventional unemployment, most of which, in the rich regions, now means job-changing. Our concerns, therefore, must shift away from 'thirties thinking'—from preventing joblessness induced by deficient aggregate demand, towards removing artificial limits on labour *supply*.

1. *Unemployment on the job.* A spread big among enterprises (or plants) in output per man-hour, with no compensating spread in output per unit of any other scarce input, suggests labour waste. The public

---

[1] R. B. Davison, Immigration and Unemployment in the U.K. 1955-62, *Brit. Jnl. Ind. Relns.*, Feb. 1963, p. 57. His book *Black British* (1966) shows that the discrepancy is declining, but still exists.

[2] See, for instance, T. de Scitovsky, *Welfare and Competition*, Allen and Unwin, 1952, p. 9.

relations experts of the labour-waster seek ways, often spurious, to convince shareholders, economists or 'little Neddies' that the statistics do not mean what they seem to say; by pleading the difficult environment of the poorer performer, they merely expose the failure of factors of production to shift to richer pastures.

In large building firms, output per worker is over 50 per cent above the level of the smallest, with little apparent difference, over the years, in investment per unit of output. Part of the difference may stem from types of work (large enterprises do less repair work), but most of it persists when small sub-groups of building firms, doing similar work, are classified by size. Critical variables are the supervision, mobility of stocks (e.g. of bricks), pre-planning, specialisation and sub-contracting. Largely owing to indivisibilities, these pay only big firms on big sites.[1]

Even more statistical caution is needed to infer British inefficiency from international comparisons. In Table 14, it would be folly to compare French and U.K. rail systems, because France supplies a population close to the U.K.'s but occupying twice her area, so that, with similar track length, longer (and hence, per kilometre, less labour-using) hauls predominate. But West Germany and the U.K. are almost

TABLE 14: 'PRODUCTIVITY' IN RAILWAYS, 1964

Country	Passenger Kms. carried (mn.)	Ton-kms. carried (mn.)	Workers (thou)	Km. af track operated	Traffic units per worker (thous.)	'Labour advantage' over U.K. (thous.)
				end of year		
France	37,810	65,260	360·2	81,830	286·2	189
W. Germany	37,195	62,731	448·5	69,371	222·0	129
U.K.	31,984	28,100	399·0	70,940	150·6	—

Source: Ann. Bull. Transport Stats. for Europe, U.N., 1965.

Notes: A 'traffic unit' is either a ton-km. or a passenger-km. The last column shows how many workers the U.K. could release, at her 1964 operating level, if each worker handled as many 'traffic units' as his counterpart in the country in that row. Double tracks are counted twice in Col. 5.

twins in area, population and track length. So it is not fanciful to conclude, from the above table, that unemployment on the job in British

[1] D.S.I.R., *Productivity in Housebuilding: Second Report*, 1952; N.E.D.C., *The Construction Industry*, 1963; Board of Trade. *Census of Production 1958*, Pt. 128.

Railways in 1964 cost the U.K. some 130,000 workers, i.e. about half as much as total registered male unemployment!

But different countries have different problems, and different statistical methods. Our suspicions require much more evidence. Our unique (and expensive) manned level-crossing system; union opposition to labour-saving innovations such as liner trains; the many porters at a typical London terminus where only 1 per cent even of long-distance passengers want them; 'a small country station like Normansbridge in the Southern Region . . . typical of thousands . . . (where) 80 man-hours are provided (daily) to service a place with only six hours of productive work'[1]; the reluctance of the unions to discuss such things— all this provides the evidence abundantly. Confidence in a regionally and industrially localised policy of retraining and resettlement is needed before we can reasonably expect railway unions to co-operate in removing this scandal.

A major cause of unemployment on the job is hoarding of labour. It is a stabiliser of a sort; workers are retained when demand slackens, because they will be needed when recovery comes. But sensibly designed schemes of full-pay retraining would serve the same purpose better. Such schemes, swollen in recessions, would reflate—but also, unlike hoarding, increase the economy's flexibility, via job changes, in response to variations in relative tastes and production costs.

2. *Voluntary joblessness I: illness and injury.* The age-structure of the workforce is increasingly weighted towards older men, who suffer most from chronic and recurrent disease, especially bronchitis. Possibly smoking does not cause this; in any event, hardly any non-smokers get it. The benefits of high demand for labour include jobs for old men who would once have been classified as unemployable. The benefits of medical improvement include the ability to cure (and cut work-loss from) germ-borne disease. The benefits of cigarettes include a bronchitic loss of workdays conservatively estimated, in 1964, at 2·4 times that caused by strikes.[2]

Not quite an illness, but a physical condition causing withdrawal from workforce, is pregnancy. Its effect depends on the activity rates for married women of childbearing age. The share of married women aged 15-59 in the total workforce was 19·3 per cent in 1952 and 21·4 per cent

[1] R. Shervington (a British Railways Regional Traffic Manager) in *British Transport Review*, Aug. 1962.

[2] H. Cole, in *Common Sense about Smoking* (ed. Jeger), Penguin, 1965, pp. 64-5.

in 1960, and will probably reach 29·3 per cent by 1975:[1] on this is imposed a substantial rise in the birthrate, and in the tendency of women to have children in hospital and convalesce afterwards.

Bad working conditions, through disease and injury, themselves cause much loss of work. On 31 October, 1963, 189,000 workers were receiving benefits for 'permanent industrial injury'. These are classified by the percentage of disability: counting, say, 20 per cent disablement as $\frac{1}{5}$ of a man-year, and estimating a man-year as 260 days,[2] this means 14·4 million workdays lost through industrial disablement yearly. From June 1963 to May 1964, another 20·9 million workdays were lost in industrial accidents and 1·0 million from temporary industrial disease. Thus 36·3 million workdays are lost yearly through industrial carelessness; in 1960-5 the average lost in strikes was 3·1 million.[3] Moreover, as the strike situation has improved since 1958-9, the losses from unsafe working conditions have mounted. In 1964 the Chief Inspector for Factories reported a 'substantial and most disquieting rise in the number of reportable accidents'.[4] People are too busy watching television interviews with strikers to be much disquieted.

Road accidents are another major cause of voluntary unemployment. Deaths—whether the 7,952 road deaths in 1965 or the 2,096 deaths from industrial accidents in 1963—reduce demand *pari passu* with supply,[5] and are thus humanly tragic but productively irrelevant. However, Reynolds has calculated that temporary incapacity, caused by road accidents in 1952, cost Britain 510,000 weeks of work during the first six months of hospital confinement alone.[6] The 1965 rate of non-fatal road accidents was almost twice as high;[7] with a $5\frac{1}{4}$ day week the corres-

---

[1] W. Beckerman, op. cit., p. 94.

[2] $5\frac{1}{4}$-day week, 2 weeks' paid holiday, 6 days' public holidays, rounded off. *Annual Report of Ministry of Pensions and Nat. Ins.*, 1964, p. 146.

[3] *Ibid.*, p. 132, 148; *Monthly Dig. Stat.*, March 1966, p. 27.

[4] Apparently 31·5 per cent, only partly explained by improved registration. *Annual Report of the Chief Inspector of Factories for 1964*, Min. of Labour, 1965, p. 43. Between 1962-3 and 1963-4, days lost from *industrial accidents* rose by over 10 per cent (Min. of Pensions, loc. cit., p. 132; *Annual Report 1963*, p. 124). In 1963 the work-loss from standing disability owing to industrial injury—counting X per cent disablement as the loss of X per cent of a working year—was 16·1 per cent above the 1959 level (Min. of Pensions, *Annual Reports*, 1960, p. 140; 1964, p. 146).

[5] *Ibid.*, 1964, p. 148; Ministry of Transport Press Notice of 17.3.1966.

[6] Reynolds, The Cost of Road Accidents, *Jnl. Roy. Stat. Soc. (A)*, 1956, p. 398.

[7] Min. of Transport, loc. cit. (389,985 injuries in 1965); *Ann. Abst. Stat. 1962* (203,306 in 1952). The ratio of serious to slight injuries stayed at about 1 to 3.

ponding estimate of lost working time for 1965 is 5·1 million days—double the loss from strikes.

By the standards of our past, these appalling figures seem satisfactory. From pre-war days, we have roughly halved the death-rate from industrial accidents;[1] road deaths have risen less fast than vehicle-miles. Moreover, European countries have worse safety records—both on the road and in the factory.[2] *Absolutely*, however, the contempt for life, evidenced both by our safety performance and by our lack of concern for it, is uncivilized and brutal. Certainly it is the most tragic, painful and needless of all reducers of labour-input in Britain.

3. *Voluntary joblessness II: industrial disputes.* In 1961-5, average yearly loss from strikes was 3·2 million workdays, as against 2·0 million in 1935-9, when labour force was 70 per cent of 1961-5 levels.[3] Thus almost complete security of employment has raised the chance that the average worker will be on strike, on a typical day, by barely 12 per cent. For 1960-5, this risk, for the U.K., was ten times more than in West Germany, almost the same as in France, four times *less* than in Italy, and half the U.S. risk.[4]

Compared with the causes of lost working time in the last section, this is a non-problem. But a day's strike does cause more indirect loss of work than the typical day in bed from illness or accident, because all the workers in an industry usually strike together—causing unemployment among workers who supply them with tools and raw materials, and among those who need their products to work with. Especially in an industry like vehicle-making, where processes follow a set time-sequence, a small strike can have big secondary results for employment. However, the experience of U.S. managers in Britain suggests that labour relations depend on the quality of management.[5] Anyhow, prolonged discussion of labour wastage due to strikes, combined with toleration of far worse causes of waste—licence fees for vans so low as to encourage congestion, advertisement of cigarettes—is either gross lack of balance or ingenious concealment of vested interest. Restrictive labour practices, impeding mobility into labour-starved occupations—medi-

---

[1] *Ann. Abst. Stat. 1935-46*, p. 38; *1965*, p. 58.
[2] I.L.O., *Yearbook of Lab. Stats. 1964*, Table 27.
[3] *Ann. Abst. Stat. 1935-46*, pp. 35-40, 105; *1965*, pp. 125-8; *Monthly Dig. Stat.*, Mar. 1966, p. 25.
[4] I.L.O., loc. cit., Table 28.
[5] J. Dunning, *American Investment in British Manufacturing* (1958), p. 262.

cine, dock labour, printing, primary schoolteaching—are much more significant than strikes, if we insist on concentrating on this area.

Moreover, the reduction in hours actually worked from 1955 to 1965 is 1·7 hours per week—3·8 per cent of total labour input in 1965. This amount[1] is not waste, like strike, accident or involuntary unemployment; it represents a decision to take the rewards of higher productivity as leisure rather than income. Yet, if we suffer from real labour shortage, we could have raised labour input in 1965 twice as much by restoring the 1955 working week, as by totally abolishing every one of the troubles in the following table:

TABLE 15: SOME MAIN REDUCERS OF LABOUR INPUT
(Millions of lost workdays per year: 5¼-day week, 260-day year, assumed worked)

Cause of withdrawal from work	Million workdays lost	
	1958-9	*1964-5*
Temporary disablement through industrial accident	18·7	20·9
Temporary disablement through industrial disease	1·1	1·0
Permanent disability through industrial disease or injury	12·4	14·4
Road accidents: temporary disablement (under six months)	4·1	5·1
Cigarette-induced bronchitis	?	5·4
Industrial disputes	4·4	2·6
Registered unemployment	152·0	116·1

Sources: See text. Temporary disablement data 1958-9 and 1963-4; permanent disability 1959 and 1963.

(*d*) *Unemployment: a stylised explanation*
Three linked aspects of post-war registered unemployment need explaining: the lower rates, the cut in fluctuations about average rates, and the persistence of depressed and inefficient regions, age-groups and occupations, relatively high both in level and duration of unemployment, and in propensity to withdraw from the workforce altogether.

[1] Min. of Labour, *Statistics on Incomes*, March 1966, p. 66.

(i) *Lower unemployment.* Pre-war British unemployment featured men, machines and managers idle in the same places. It was not caused by their seeking wrong jobs in wrong places; aggregate demand for goods and services, and hence for the labour to produce them, was less than aggregate supply. Keynesian theory and Beveridgean practical analysis committed all parties to maintaining enough aggregate demand to end large-scale unemployment after 1945. Early scepticism about this possibility owed much to pre-war experience, but more to failure to grasp the enormous power of the State to raise and maintain aggregate demand. Public authorities, through housebuilding, defence and nationalisation, have fulfilled Keynes's dream, 'the socialisation of investment'[1]—central responsibility for the volume of total investment outlay. If private investment plans did not suffice to maintain full employment, public plans filled the gap.

Superficially, any demand is part of the aggregate and stimulates employment (assuming all groups have similar marginal propensities to consume) to much the same extent. Two types of income, however, are *hyper-reflationary*. Some incomes are paid before anyone can supply the output bought with such incomes. True, investment goods ultimately make consumer goods and exports ultimately provide foreign exchange to buy imports, but workers in export and investment sectors use incomes to buy consumer goods *first*. Even more stimulant is income corresponding to extra output that would not, but for public action, be demanded or produced at all; most incomes paid to persons in the armed and social services fall into this category.[2]

On p. 144, we compare these 'hyper-reflationary', ultra-employment-generating incomes in 1938 and 1960-4, as shares of GNP. Such outlays may have produced insufficient growth for our need, or greed; they have eliminated the part of unemployment caused by deficient aggregate demand.

Apart from the huge rise in the reflationary impact upon the economy, the propensity to consume (and hence the multiplier operating on that impact) has been boosted by income redistribution from rich savers to poor spenders. Even before tax, the share of income from employment

---

[1] J. M. Keynes, *General Theory of Employment, Interest and Money* (Macmillan, 1936), p. 378.

[2] Blue Streaks, aircraft carriers (and Concords?) are our 'pyramids', 'masses for the dead', digging holes and filling them up again. Hole-diggers are paid cash, used to buy genuine commodities—and employ their makers. *Ibid.*, pp. 129-30.

TABLE 16: EMPLOYMENT-GENERATING OUTLAYS IN THE U.K.

Type of outlay	Value as percentage of GNP (current prices)	
	1938	1960-4
Gross domestic investment	12·7	18·7
Net income inflow from abroad	− 1·2	+ 0·1
Current outlay of public authorities	14·9	18·7
Stock investment (domestic)	—	1·3
Total 'hyper-reflation'	26·4	38·8

Source: National Income and Expenditure, C.S.O., 1965, pp. 2-3.

Note: 'Net income inflow from abroad' is net property income received, *plus* exports *less* imports of goods and services.

in personal income rose from 59·5 per cent in 1938 to 71·4 per cent in 1960-4. Tax redistribution amplified this. Thus, despite a big real rise in personal disposable income per head, the proportion consumed hardly fell at all.[1]

(ii) *Smaller fluctuations.* If 'socialisation of investment' is also to explain these, it must be combined with another pseudo-Marxian prediction, 'the euthanasia of the rentier'.[2] It is true that public investment has been counter-cyclical. When slump threatened, ex-owners of industries now nationalized (especially coal, electricity, gas and local authority building) would cut investment in response to the threat and thus bring it about. Now the Government uses such sectors to reflate. Private investment fell from 11·4 per cent of GNP in 1961 to 10·2 per cent in 1963. But public investment rose from 7·4 per cent to 8·0 per cent, public consumption from 18·5 per cent to 18·9 per cent, and net income inflow from abroad by enough to fill the gap.[3] The share of hyper-reflationary outlays in GNP was maintained; similarly in 1965-7.

But private investment was also far less sensitive to downturns in demand, for four reasons. First, Government incentives to private investment, however imperfect, were adjusted. This prevented a fall-

[1] From 94·4 per cent to 92·3 per cent. *Nat. Income*, 1965, pp. 4, 8.

[2] J. M. Keynes, *General Theory*, p. 376.

[3] *Nat. Income*, 1965, pp. 3, 63. Income inflow can be substantial (on the Table 16 definition) even in a bad year for the balance of payments, if the trouble is on long-term capital account.

back in the ratio of private investment to GNP in 1957-8 and moderated its rise in high boom. Second, compared to the pre-1939 era, private investment decisions are less influenced by dividend-hungry, easily worried small shareholders, and more by professional directors[1] and institutional shareholders (like insurance companies) with long views. Third, boards of directors realize that governments cannot afford, and know how to avoid, deep recessions; small declines produce optimistic anticipations of centrally stimulated recovery. Finally, generally tight labour makes businessmen eager to snap up scarce investment workers (especially skilled ones, and builders; see pp. 134-6) as available, even in mild recession. Hence, since 1954, investment has fluctuated less, cyclically, than consumption—astonishing all with memories of the accelerator![2]

(iii) *Immobility: the limits of Keynesianism.* The employment black spots—poor mobility, industrial injuries, depressed areas, unemployment on the job—remain because they are not amenable to the general Keynesian cures for general excess or deficient demand. Assume immobile factors, and regions specialising in product groups, so that (for instance) Tyneside and Reading produce goods that are poor substitutes in consumption and highly specific to the machinery making them. Then an excess of vacancies in Reading (or for young workers or in biscuit-making) can coexist with a deficiency in Tyneside (or for over-55s or charwomen). Keynesian general expansion of demand may worsen the inflation without curing the unemployment.

Even projects specially aimed at 'deflated' jobs or regions (e.g. the 1962-3 Tyneside ship orders) have disappointed; so have differential investment allowances, designed to pull new firms into depressed industries and regions. This is because, despite the deceptively calculable and stable *overall* multiplier, initial outlays do not spread themselves smoothly about the economy. Newly employed workers in the heavy Northern industries, centred upon defence and exports, spend extra incomes on food from the South and durables from the Midlands. There, no extra workers are available—so the new demand pulls up prices.

[1] Since 1954, the share of additions to gross assets of quoted companies (before allowing for depreciation) financed from ploughed-back profits has been around 80 per cent. *Econ. Trends*, Feb. 1966, p. xiv.

[2] Partly this is due to the secular uptrend since 1950 in U.K. gross investment/output ratios. The new stability is far less marked in manufacturing investment.

To plan in such situations, one needs data showing how income from *each type* of new employment, in *each region*, will be divided among the products of each main form of employment in each region. The lack of an array of information of this type (of a so-called *matrix multiplier*) means that incomes policy has to assume all rises in money incomes equally inflationary. It is the biggest drawback in British economic statistics that such information is absent. Regional policy must assess whether depressed regions need diversified activity, rather than more investment whose secondary effects they cannot contain.

So much for the needs of employment planning. Since 1950, however, most regional changes in employment have been influenced at least as much by the market as by planning. So the problem remains: why didn't more businessmen move North where the workers were? Why didn't more workers move South where the jobs were? Why did the neoclassical model fail to ensure that each factor commanded the same reward in each area or job? To some extent such movements happened. Workers migrating South caused *industrial* capital, in North and South, to work nearer optimal levels—but required new *social* investment (schools, houses, etc.). Whatever the net effect upon regional differences in the rate of return to capital, there was no sign until 1965 of any fall in regional disparities in earnings—or unemployment rates.[1] Not all this can be traced to the relative 'unskilledness' or job-specificity of workers in depressed areas; immobility, as reflected by substantial, persistent regional inequality—among persons rich enough to afford to move, informed enough to know how and where, and sufficiently aware of their incomes to want affluence—remains puzzling. So do persistent differences in levels of efficiency, and in rates of profit, between, and even within, industries.

In building and retailing, with output per man-hour twice as high in the giants as in the smallest concerns despite the similarity in output per unit of capital, a wave of amalgamations might be expected. Unless protection increased sharply, one would expect slower but substantial factor redistribution out of sectors like cotton textiles and aircraft production, where our international performance is poor and declining,

---

[1] *Abstract of Regional Statistics*, 1965, p. 11; *Westminster Bank Review*, Feb. 1966. E. G. West, *Lloyds Bank Review*, April 1966, rightly says that migration from poor to rich areas increases *personal* equality, even if the very poorest, by staying behind, worsen regional inequality; but we are not worried about inequality between pieces of land, rather about the allocative inefficiency of which it gives evidence.

towards sectors where we do well and are getting even better, such as vehicles, fibres, glass and tiles. Ensuing trade adjustments would follow.

These trends exist; but by international standards they are sluggish. Consider shipbuilding. From 1956 to 1964 output fell steadily, in all by 36·4 per cent. A wonderful chance to concentrate jobs in yards with efficient labour, freeing ill-paid workers for shortage sectors; and yet employment declined 33·7 percent, less than ouput, so that, during this massive competitive squeeze on inefficient yards, productivity actually fell![1] French shipbuilders—businessmen and workers—share this preference for traditional identity over profitable change; but the French Government has used its powers, both as a buyer of ships and as controller of credit, to force amalgamations.

Structural unemployment—mismatching of labour supply, by region and occupation, to demand—while some regions have labour shortages, implies severe immobility. So do persistent severe inefficiencies, while boom sectors cry out for the workers thus wasted. This cannot be cured by Keynesian remedies alone—though public commitment to them, and consequent Union willingness to believe that full employment is assured, and change therefore not too painful, must exist before cure is possible.

Most suggested cures—higher redundancy compensation, retraining, adult technical education, resettlement allowances, regional diversification (e.g. a 'Brasilia' in Yorkshire)—rightly focus on the want of skill and training that (see pp. 209) cause structural labour waste. Such cures are sensible but inflationary, creating incomes (primarily for the redundant) without, or at best before, output. Unless consequent price rises, falls in exports and rises in imports are deemed tolerable, spending, *private or public*, must be cut elsewhere—preferably in over-strained regions or industries.

Britain lacks the natural factor-mobilising advandages of her main industrial competitors. In early industrialisation the workforce erodes fast townwards, forming an artificial mobility at the margin even among industries (pp. 122-3). Immigration to West Germany, exchanges among E.E.C. countries, and relatively fast population growth in the U.S. have been further *flow* substitutes for mobility of labour *stock*. The U.S. has substantially cut regional disparities in job prospects.[2] In West Europe

---

[1] *Ann. Abst. Stat.*, 1961, pp. 106, 133; 1965, pp. 111, 134.

[2] L. Gallaway, Labour Mobility, Resource Allocation and Structural Unemployment, *Amer. Econ. Rev.*, 1963, p. 708; Table 4 shows that 1950 and 1960 had the same national unemployment rate, but regional variations fell.

F

the areas worst hit by unemployment—underdeveloped, seasonal, one-crop agricultures—have exported most labour townwards, similarly equalising regional employment levels.

In the U.K., with only 4 per cent of workers in agriculture, slow population growth, and now artificial immigration controls, no such substitutes for stock mobility exist. Local roots are strong, and—because Britain industrialised so early—there is much social capital in areas developed around traditional industries. This must be duplicated to a higher standard, at great real cost, after migration. Making the duplicates worsens labour shortage in receiver regions. Hence Needleman[1] argues for moving capital to labour, not the other way round. In any case the British problem is not that factor stocks are unusually immobile by world standards, but that, given our inability to substitute stock for flow mobility in industry, a *more* mobile stock of industrial factors is needed to achieve the *same* rate of improvement of resource utilisation as that of France or Germany.

Why, then, have not managers and workers in Britain responded more to financial incentives towards job and regional mobility? Terrible managers, lazy workers, 'restrictive practices on both sides of industry' really will not do. Such racism is not scientific. A man is no better or worse, livelier or lazier because of accidents of birthplace. (This is not to deny that migrants between societies, classes or nations are usually lively, successful people.[2]) Are the restrictive practices of dockers worse in Britain than in the U.S.? of farmers, than in France? of doctors, than in Belgium?

To explain immobility, need we really look beyond incentives? If labour is wasted, it may be too cheap to be worth the effort to economise; if investment is too low, machinery may be too dear. Our newly-uncovered forms of worklessness persist because we have not followed out the consequences of eliminating the older types. Between the wars, a rising ratio of wages to capital costs had unforeseeable effects (pp.5-6). Once the Government limits the possible variations in effective demand, this ratio again determines the capital/labour ratio—just as in a neo-classical system, where employment levels are supposed to depend directly on wage rates.

[1] L. Needleman, What are we to do about the regional problem? *Lloyds Bank Review*, Jan. 1965.

[2] The Chinese in Malaya, Thailand and the Philippines; the Greeks in Egypt and the Sudan; the Huguenots all over Europe. People with drive move far—and do well. The Chinese are not especially successful in China.

Judging by employment levels, U.K. labour is as scarce, relative to capital, as anywhere in the world. Yet the price-ratio of the most labour-intensive purchases—a haircut, an hour's domestic service—to the most capital-intensive—a ton of steel, a computer—in London is closer to Rome or even Madrid than to Washington or Stockholm. While British labour is cheap relative to machinery, it will be wasted within regions and industries and immobile among them. The incentive to economise, to take the time and patience to plan a new use of factors, will just stay too small. It is in this context that a payroll tax, together with incentives (subsidies) to investment, makes sense—though it does not necessarily make less sense for some industries than for others.

In this environment, too, it may be folly to deplore trade union militancy. Certainly it would be unwise to pursue an incomes policy that kept down the rise in labour-costs without cheapening machinery or factory building. That would make the ratio of wage rates to capital costs, which is already too low to provide proper incentives to reduce unemployment on the job and regional immobility, lower still.

3. PRICE STABILITY

(a) What has happened

Earlier observers would have been astonished by any of three commonplaces of British post-war economic life: steady, almost cycle-free growth, almost full employment and smooth, slow, lasting inflation. The three features of Britain's—and in part the world's—Great Inflation[1] that are least like the past are its duration, its measured refusal to erupt into hyperinflation, and its irreversibility—the new-found ratchet relationship by which prices move up, but not down, with aggregate demand.

Except in 1943 (when prices fell 0·8 per cent), Britain's cost of living had risen each year since 1934, i.e. for 34 years. From 1661 to 1933, even five consecutive years of rising prices were rare—ten, unknown.[2] Since then, allowing for seasonal factors, there have been few *months* of falling prices.[3] And inflation has advanced on a broad front, as well as

---

[1] A. J. Brown, *The Great Inflation, 1939-51*, Oxford, 1955; J. R. Hicks, *Essays in World Economics*, Oxford, 1959, pp. 121-57; U.N., *Monthly Bulls. Stat.*
[2] Mitchell and Deane, op. cit., pp. 464-78; *U.K. Ann. Abst. Stat. 1939-46*, p. 252; *1953*, p. 295; *1959*, p. 293; *1965*, p. 319.
[3] U.K. *Ann. Abst. Stat., seriatim.*

for a long distance; no major group of commodities has fallen in price.

Yet, despite the long, sustained inflation, in all sectors and even in recessions, confidence in the currency has remained. Certainly economic calculations affecting currency holding have responded to the acceptance of inflation as a way of life, especially by a big mark-up of interest rates;[1] but this has stemmed, not speeded, any incipient flight from cash (hyperinflation). The price series from 1661 suggest that short periods of very fast inflation used to be common in both war and peace. In 1913-20 living costs rose over 2½ times—much of this in peacetime.[2] Right through the nineteenth century, a bad harvest would mean a short, sharp, general price rise, with some flight from cash—both soon reversed. It was once thought that a flight from cash, on a big scale, must also result from gradual erosion of purchasing power. Yet, since 1945, 3 to 4 per cent yearly inflation has persisted with no sign of acceleration.

Though short, sharp price rises were once common, equally common falls prevented any secular price uptrend. In 1913 prices were probably lower than in 1661 (if this comparison makes much sense).[3] Yet in 1661-1913 prices had often risen by over 10 per cent in a single year.[4] The Korean War produced an 11 per cent rise in 1951: otherwise the rise never exceeded 5 per cent in any of the 34 years of solid inflation 1933-67.[5]

(b) The structure of inflation

To discover who suffers in inflation, we must ask what goods and services rise fastest in price, who buys them, and whose incomes lag behind. The sectoral trends in Table 17 also suggest a good deal about causation.

Prima facie, one would expect growth to equalise income distribution through changes in relative prices. As people get richer, demands for (and hence prices of) the simple needs of the poor fall relatively. For

---

[1] In 1946-7, before constant inflation was expected, the Government could fairly compensate for shares in nationalized industries with bonds yielding 3 per cent. Since then the rate of interest has more than doubled.

[2] Mitchell and Deane, op. cit., p. 478.

[3] *Ibid.*, pp. 468-78. The structure of consumption altered enormously.

[4] In 1694, 1706, 1709, 1710, 1711, 1757, 1783, 1800, 1801, 1808, 1812, 1853, 1854 and 1872. *Ibid.*, pp. 468-72.

[5] U.K., *Ann. Abst. Stat.*, loc. cit.

TABLE 17: THE STRUCTURE OF U.K. INFLATION, 1947-66

Sector	17.6.47–18.1.66	17.6.47–15.1.52	15.1.52–17.1.56	17.1.56–16.1.62	16.1.62–18.1.66	17.6.47–17.1.56	17.1.56–18.1.66
All cons.	205·3	132·0	115·8	117·5	114·3	152·9	134·3
Food	234·8	149·7	125·4	110·7	113·0	187·7	125·5
(Bread, flour)	—	—	121	127	114	—	144·8
(Nonalc. drinks)	—	—	151	98	105	—	102·9
Alcohol	144·1	108·5	103·1	108·2	119·0	(111·9)	128·8
Tobacco	166·6	108·5	102·9		120·8	(111·6)	149·3
Housing	213·7	104·2	117·9	140·6	123·7	122·9	173·9
Fuel, light	279·5	140·1	127·6	130·6	119·7	178·8	156·3
Household durab.	150·4	136·1	102·5	102·1	105·6	139·5	107·8
Clothing, footwear	168·4	148·1	98·7	106·6	108·1	146·2	115·2
(Children's clothes)	—	—	99·0	107	106	—	113·4
Transport, vehicles	—	—	127	126·7	109·1	—	138·2
(Motoring, cyc.)	—	—	—	106	102	—	128·5
(Fares, etc.)	—	—	—	143	125	—	178·8
Miscell. goods	207·2	137·1	106·6	128·2	110·6	146·1	141·8
(Books, papers)	—	—	105·1	150	128	—	192·0
(Medical, toiletry)	—	—	105·0	126	102	—	128·5
(Stnry, sports, toys)	—	—	105·8	110	109	—	119·9
Services	223·9	123·9	119·1	130·1	116·6	147·6	151·7
(Post, telgphs)	—	—	—	154	114	—	152·8
(Entertainments)	—	—	116	132	114	—	150·5
(Home help, hrdrsg.)	—	—	115	128	119	—	152·3
Imports	—	—	—	92·8	107·2	—	99·5
Exports	—	—	—	106·9	107·8	—	115·2

Sources: Mon. Dig. Stat., Dec. 1954, p. 122; Sep. 1956, p. 123; Feb. 1963; Feb. 1966, p. 134. Exports, imports: from 17.1.56, Nat. Inst. Econ. Review, *passim.*

Note: Before 17.1.56, 'housing' was only 'rent and rates' and 'non-alcoholic drinks' were an index of tea and sugar prices. 'Transport and vehicles' was a 'travel' price index. Home help includes laundry; toiletry, soap and matches.

some goods (e.g. margarine) demand falls absolutely.[1] Yet from January 1952 to January 1964, the 'pensioner's price index' rose about 60 per cent, as against 48 per cent for 'average' households.[2] Plainly dynamic and policy factors have outweighed static and *a priori* ones. Policy permitted a big rise in rents after 1956-7, towards market levels, after a freeze dating from well before the Second World War. Dynamic factors brought economies of scale and new production techniques—and much fiercer foreign competition—to vehicles and consumer durables, and thus stabilized a large part of the price-index of richer persons. But even

[1] Whether A is 'inferior' depends (like whether it is a 'substitute' for B) on given *levels* of income and relative price. In India margarine is a luxury (income-elasticity of demand exceeds 1), in the U.K. an inferior good, and in Greece probably neither.

[2] J. Hughes and K. Alexander, *A Plan for Incomes*, Fabian Research Series No. 247, 1965, p. 7.

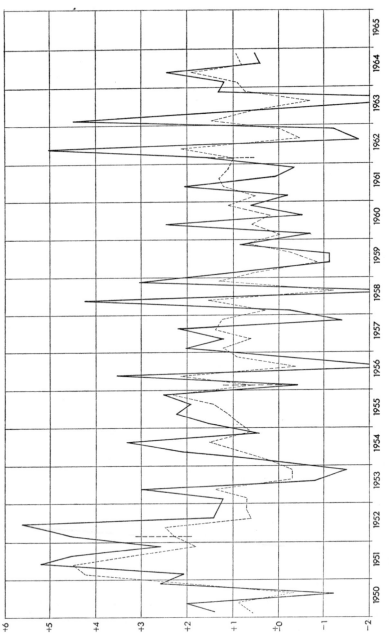

Figure 13 Fluctuations in the cost of living and in the price of food 1950–64 (Source: UK Monthly Digest of Statistics, latest available estimates; 3-month averages). Almost always, when prices rise universally fast (dotted line), food prices (solid line) are rising a good deal faster (see text).

more important has been the failure of the prices of foodstuffs, especially of those bought substantially by pensioners (bread, tea), to fall relative to others.

'Engel's law' certainly works cross-sectionally: at any period the poor spend a far bigger share of income on food than the rich. But the translation of the cross-section into a time-series is slow. From 1900 to 1955 the share of U.K. consumer outlay on food actually rose,[1] and from 1947 to 1965 it fell only slightly (34·8 per cent in Jan. 1947, 29·8 per cent in Jan. 1966).[2] Food prices have not been restrained by a prolonged fall in demand; nor has the fall been steady—demand for food rose substantially as rationing came to an end. Despite Government action, the food price rises have done much to cause inflation to bear hard on the very poor.

The *destabilising* effects of food prices on the living levels of pensioners—whose incomes rise in discrete jumps—are even more serious. As Fig. 13 shows, of the 37 quarters since the start of 1950 when the cost of living rose over 0·7 per cent, food prices were rising faster still (and hence destabilising) in 29. And in the 17 quarters of really fast inflation—1·4 per cent or more—food prices were rising even faster in 16. However much food prices may be determined at wholesale level by subsidy and import-cost, they seem extremely responsive at retail level to small market movements. Indeed, in the nineteenth century—when food could seldom be refrigerated or rapidly imported, and when food consumption (from lower incomes) and production (from a less industrialised structure of output) played a more dominant role than today—harvest variations were naturally the main cause of shifts in the supply-demand balance and hence in relative prices.

Today, however, this is no longer so natural. Only 4 per cent of British output is agricultural—and less than 30 per cent of consumption consists of food. Moreover, short-run fluctuations in farm prices are not allowed to work as signals to farmers to switch land use, in response to changing tastes or costs; a humanitarian democracy has found the consequent fluctuations in farm incomes intolerable. It is thus paradoxical that, in the very sector where prices have the least incentive role for producers, they are the most serious destabilisers at retail level. True,

---

[1] Mitchell and Deane, op. cit., pp. 370-72. True both in current prices (from 32 per cent to 34 per cent) and in 1938 prices (27 per cent to 31 per cent).

[2] *Mon. Dig. Stat.* Feb. 1966, p. 134: *Ann. Ab. St.*, 1938-48, p. 267; *Min. Lab. Gaz.*, March 1966. Current prices are used.

in the long run, money incomes of pensioners outstrip prices—and even money-wages (see pp. 190,200); but, by convention alone, pensioners cannot copy the quickfire nature of wage-settlements. So the inegalitarian effect of the fluctuations is very harmful. Moreover, roughly half our food is imported; home price fluctuations place unforeseen strains on demand for imported substitutes.

Apart from the harmful and pointless role of changes in food prices— causing inflation, damaging the balance of payments and reducing equality—what can be said of the sectoral trends of Table 17? The big real growth in demand for consumer durables is linked to their relatively slow price increase—only 50 per cent from 1947 to 1966, less than half as fast as prices as a whole.[1] Since quality also increased, even this understates the relative price fall.

Between 1956 and 1966, house prices rose at well over twice the rate of living costs as a whole, in response to the decontrol of 1956-7. This points up the role, in sequential inflation, of sectors like building, where inefficient (undercapitalized, small-scale, irresponsive) concerns show low price-elasticity of supply and hence sluggish, or even perverse, response to market incentives. The Rent Act enabled small builders to turn from repair to new work, since it lowered the risk of bankruptcy by raising profit margins on such work. So the demand curve for housing, steadily rising due to higher incomes and earlier marriages, faced a supply curve rendered less price-elastic by the Rent Act.

Look at Table 17, and ask yourself how far these changes in relative prices were either planned or socially approved. Except for alcohol and tobacco, most were the result of market mechanisms, not price policies. Mr Callaghan's defence of the selective tax on service employment shows that this has not changed; the aim is to make similar tax burdens apply to services as to goods, reducing the distortion from the market mechanism, rather than to subsidise approved (or penalise disapproved) consumption. Even alcohol and tobacco have got cheaper since 1947, relative to food, clothes and houses. Is this reliance on the market desirable?

If one believes in the value of choice, there is a strong case for it, under the following conditions:

(i) That supplies and resources are elastic in response to prices and incomes, because they are easily and swiftly transferable when market signals are received;

[1] Sources as for Table 17.

(ii) That such signals come from well-informed consumers, not from responders to television jingles;

(iii) That the distribution of economic signalling power (income) among buyers is such as to produce a socially tolerable balance between the pressure of effective demand for needs and that for wants;

(iv) That economic power among producers (degree of monopoly) is sufficiently small, or restrained, to rule out collusive price increases in response to higher demand;

(v) That the climate of economic expectations is not conditioned to inflation—that consumers are not deterred from bothering to shop around by the belief that increases in the price of a product will be followed by similar rises in prices of substitutes or by wage rises; analogously, that producers do not automatically pass on higher costs.

All this amounts to generally high price-elasticities, both of demand and of supply. This means well-informed, price-conscious and mobile consumers—and producers efficient and flexible enough to *want* to transfer quickly into more profitable activities when relative prices change. Readers should assess for themselves how far such conditions have prevailed in post-war Britain.

(c) International comparisons

Both for full employment and for price inflation, there is no historical parallel to Britain's post-war performance. But, while our employment performance is somewhat better than most of our rivals', that cannot be said of price stability.

Table 18 shows the performance of the advanced industrial West since 1949. The first four years saw two big inflationary shocks: the effect of devaluation on import prices and the Korean War. Devaluation did not affect the U.S.—and, even for the U.K., was a smaller shock than is often alleged; but we must remember, in making comparisons of inflation, that the U.K. felt both shocks with special severity. She was at full employment right from the start of the post-war period, and hence less able to shift home resources to those sectors where import prices had risen.

The post-Korean chance to recover from inflation—1953-7—was taken much less successfully by the U.K. than by her rivals. In 1957-61, only France—with Algerian expenditures and two devaluations—out-inflated us. Since 1962 our relative performance improved slightly, largely because our earlier inflation had made it easier for other nations to sell

E*

TABLE 18: PRICE RISES IN BIG WESTERN
INDUSTRIAL COUNTRIES

Country	Percentage rise in retail price index						
	1949-53	*1953-7*	*1957-61*	*1961-65*	*1849-57*	*1957-65*	*1949-65*
W. Germany	1·0	6·5	7·1	11·4	7·6	9·4	28·5
France (Paris)	42·9	6·1	31·0	16·5	51·6	52·6	131·3
Italy	14·9	10·2	7·2	24·0	26·7	33·0	68·5
U.S.A.	12·4	4·3	6·2	5·8	17·2	12·4	31·7
U.K.	26·6	15·5	8·2	14·3	46·2	23·7	80·8

Sources: U.N., *Monthly Bull. Stat.*, Feb. 1966, Table 60; *Stat. Yearbooks*, 1957, Table 161; 1962, Table 161; 1964, Table 169; O.E.C.D., *Gen. Stats.*, March 1966, p. 74. The Paris series is linked at 1962 to the new all-France index.

us cheap goods, so that import surpluses relieved the pressure of money upon commodities in the home market.

Our performance since 1949 is poor by any standards. We cannot deceive ourselves that our rivals achieved price stability by slower growth (except for the U.S. before 1961). Only in the early years of Marshall Aid did unrequited imports help to stabilise prices in Europe. During the whole period, our old friend, the outflow of labour from agriculture, helped keep down European and U.S. prices. Scale economies without overtime were made possible in secondary and tertiary sectors by the newly available workers. These economies allowed wages to rise, while the unit labour cost of production rose far more slowly. But this 'reserve army of labour'—without unemployment—is not the whole story. Rapid economic growth allows wage demands to be met without inflation. In democracies, such demands are met—anyhow— and responsive price rises follow if growth is slow.

(d) Inflation in the U.K.: a stylised explanation

Inflation is a *self-sustaining* process of price rises. To explain any in-flationary sequence we must identify first the push that starts the process, and second the mechanism that passes on such pushes from one sector to another. A useful hint is given by Ragnar Frisch's explanation of nineteenth-century trade cycles. The economy, he argued, tended to damp down any cycle-causing shock; outside shocks (wars, etc.) came often enough to conceal the damping process, and the illusion of a stable cycle was created for most of the century.[1] Models presenting economies as systems generating smooth cycles (or inflations) of constant amplitudes (or rates) are unrealistic, and rely on special, often unplausible values for particular parameters.[2] A very wide range of such values, many plausible, could account for the behaviour of economies on the assumption of damping of random shocks from outside. Some of them square with empirical tests of values of multiplier and accelerator. And the whole account squares with common sense—or with instant-historical casual empiricism. Thus the deep post-1931 recession looks like a severe outside shock (the 1929 and 1931 financial crises) imposed on the otherwise damped downswing after the post-war boom.

Why should we seek to explain cycles and inflations in similar terms? First, it is no good to account for inflation in terms of a transmission system only. A rise of 1 per cent in the cost of living produces a rise of only 0·5 per cent in wages,[3] so a single, unrepeated shock would soon die out, unless a 1 per cent wage rise produces a rise of over 2 per cent in the cost of living. Second, post-war Western governments aimed to replace cyclical instability of employment by politically more tolerable inflationary instability. Crudely, when aggregate demand hits the ceiling of potential supply, price rises, accompanying still-rising money incomes, have replaced the cyclical downturns of 1815-1938.

If inflation is a damped system with outside shocks, what are the shocks? There are two senses of 'outside shock'. The Korean War, totally outside (uncaused by) Britain's economic system, is a typical shock of *Type I*. Inside the U.K. economic system, but a *Type II* shock for the wage-price spiral within that system, are changes in structure altering the behaviour of a sector near the top of the boom. A typical shock of Type II is a cut in the supply of mobile labour (seasonal falls in school leaving, immigration control, ageing population), which worsens the total inflationary effect of any Type I shock. Since 1945 these Type I shocks have been, first, the relase of pent-up demand after the war;

---

[1] R. Frisch, Propagation Problems and Impulse Problems in Dynamic Economics, in *Essays in Honour of Gustav Cassel*, London, 1933; R. Matthews, *The Trade Cycle*, Cambridge, 1959, pp. 29-30.

[2] P. Samuelson, Interactions between the Multiplier and the Principle of Acceleration, *Rev. Ec. Stud.*, 1938. Such constant-amplitude cycles are just as unplausible as the 'knife-edge' cobweb cycle, neither tending towards nor moving away from equilibrium—and for the same reason.

[3] A. Hagger, *Theory of Inflation*, Melbourne, 1965.

second, devaluation in 1949; third, the Korean War. Since 1952 it is hard to see any big ones. Most of our trading partners were inflating more slowly than we were, and therefore our imports were getting cheaper relative both to domestic prices and to our exports.[1] Apart from the poor labour mobility (pp. 122-4), was the effect of the three early Type I outside shocks on the British economy unusually large and prolonged?

It is obvious how suddenly released, largely involuntary war savings, after 1945, constituted an inflationary shock or impetus into the economic system. Money had not been spent because goods and services were not available, due to miliary requirements *plus* rationing. But there is no apparent reason why the after-effects should last longer in the U.K. than elsewhere.

The effect of the 1949 devaluation is more complicated. Devaluation raises the price of imported raw materials, shifting up costs and hence prices; it also directly raises the price of consumer imports, leading to wage claims. On the side of costs, therefore, the effects are purely inflationary.

The demand side is less simple. If the imported goods can also be made in British factories (like cars), rising import prices will divert home demand towards these factories. This produces some increase in the price of their output, especially if resources for production are immobile, or (as at full employment) already overstrained, so that real output cannot easily respond to higher monetary demand. So, in so far as Britain makes substitutes for her imports, devaluation is inflationary on the side of demand as well—the more so as she nears full employment.

However, via imports in price-inelastic demand (such as raw materials and foodstuffs), devaluation has demand-disinflationary effects. The amount of cash going abroad to pay for such imports rises as a result of devaluation. Our inability to make substitutes means that we cut quantity bought by a smaller proportion than the rise in price—i.e., roughly, we raise total spending on such imports. So there is a leak of monetary demand outside the domestic economy.[2]

So, on the cost side, devaluation is always an inflationary push into

---

[1] See pp. 156 and 170-4. Notice 'faster inflation than trading partner's = 'improving terms of trade' ➤ (on normal assumptions—price-elastic demand for traded goods) 'worsening trade balance'.

[2] Export effects are analogous. Assume price-elastic demand. Then devaluation, *via* lower export prices, raises total exports. Near full employment, this reduces goods supply at home, and is thus demand-inflationary.

the system; on the demand side, it is net inflationary only in so far as we produce substitutes for most of our imports, so that monetary demand is diverted towards home products (themselves price-inelastic near full-employment) rather than leaking abroad to pay for essential imports. An increasing proportion of British imports are manufactured products from advanced countries; fewer and fewer are unsubstitutable primary products.[1] Therefore, over time, the inflationary demand-side impact of the 1949 devaluation has gained in importance in bidding up domestic prices of U.K. goods competitive with imports from the U.S.

Devaluation, while its *long-run* effects were much more than is generally believed because of the above trend, was not as large an *immediate* inflationary input into the system as is often argued. In 1948, 17·3 per cent of our gross national expenditure went on imports, and in 1950 the percentage was 20·0. Most import prices were unaffected by the devaluation of sterling, since this was followed by most of the non-dollar world. Thus the move from the $4 rate to the $2·80 rate in 1949 constituted a primary rise in the price of our gross domestic expenditure of under 4 per cent.[2] Though the secondary and long-run effects of devaluation are considerable, this arithmetic does suggest that the main explanation of inflation lies in the transmission system and Type II shocks, rather than in so distant a Type I shock as the devaluation of 1949.

Devaluation unlocked the system of intersectoral price-wage transmission of inflation, by making it impossible for the Chancellor, Sir Stafford Cripps, and the T.U.C. to hold the wage freeze policy of 1948-9, which had produced extraordinary price stability despite the inability of supply to expand *pari passu* with potential demand. Upon this situation the Korean War came as a further severe inflationary push. World stockpiling of raw materials, in anticipation of extension of the war, bid up the price of British imports by 42 per cent between August 1950 and June 1951, and between September 1950 and June 1952 retail prices rose by over 22 per cent.[3]

---

[1] 1956-64: imports of food, beverages, tobacco and basic materials rose by some 10 per cent in volume. Manufactured imports more than doubled. *Ann. Abst. Stats.*, 1965, p. 215.

[2] 'The actual (devaluation), weighted by trade, was only 18 per cent' (P. Ady, in Worswick and Ady, *The British Economy 1945-50*, p. 149). If all this were passed on in higher prices of final goods, then—as imports were under 20 per cent of GDP—that would mean a price rise of less than 20 per cent of 18 per cent, i.e. about 3½ per cent.

[3] U.K., *Mon. Dig. Stats.*, Dec. 1952, p. v.

Since 1953, however, it is unconvincing to blame Type I pushes for British inflation. If, because of devaluation and the Korean War, imports were for a time a big cost-push input into domestic inflation, then for many years afterwards they represented a brake upon the rise in domestic costs.[1] Perhaps the delayed impact of Government monetary policy was destabilising, but those who have suggested this[2] refer more to the effect of intended measures of disinflation (to deepen the recession eighteen months later) than to any external shocks from reflationary measures to subsequent price levels. Useful explanations of British inflation must concentrate on its transmission from one sector of the economy to another.

Not long ago, there was much argument about whether certain inflations were caused by cost-push or by demand-pull. Even at the time, the meaningfulness of the debate was suspect, partly because the same evidence was adduced by both sides.[3] The *initial shock*, starting the process of cumulative price rises, can be clearly on one side (the release of pent-up demand by dishoarding after 1945) or the other (the cost-push effects of devaluation, *via* import prices and the new militancy of the unions, in 1949). But as regards the *transmission mechanism*, which turns an initial impulse into a self-sustaining inflation, the distinction makes no sense. Why not?

Most firms' costs are mainly wages. When these costs rise, most of the rise is spent on things made by other firms, pulling up their prices through higher demand. In other words, one man's cost-push is another man's demand-pull. An initial impetus from import costs will cause profit-maximising firms using imports, and utility-maximising workers buying imports, to raise the minimal market prices they will accept for any given amount of their services. Given a policy of full employment, and the fact that higher import prices divert demand and thus makes the production of substitutes for imports more profitable, employment is likely to contract little, if at all, in this process; but higher wages, at the same level of employment, mean more demand for goods and services. This in turn raises prices via demand-pull, leading to new

[1] See Table 17 above.
[2] I. M. D. Little, in Worswick and Ady, *The British Economy in the 1950s*, introductory chapter.
[3] Cf. the use of the drift of earnings above negotiated wage rates by F. W. Paish (*Studies in an Inflationary Economy*, Macmillan, 1961, pp. 107-8) and T. Balogh (Productivity and Inflation, *Ox. Ec. Pap.*, 1958, pp. 229-30) to reach opposite conclusions.

wage claims; the cost-push generated by such claims pushes up the firm's supply curve, raising prices further; and so on. Similarly, an initial demand-pull rise in prices (due, say, to a decision to spend accumulated hoards of cash) will mean that workers require more money (to maintain real rewards) for performing the same services as before; a cost-push price increase ensues, assisted by demand-pull as workers spend their higher wages on one another's products ... and so on. In this interlocked mechanism the separation of cost-push and demand-pull is unhelpful in theory and impossible in practice.

Several cumulative (but probably, in view of the non-increasing *rate* of inflation, damped) processes are at work. The price-wage spiral is described above. The wage-wage spiral features comparability claims and leapfrogging. In the price-price spiral, an increase in the price of a commodity, especially by a recognised price leader, sets off imitative rises in the prices of substitutes, but (because of the inelasticity of most forms of consumer demand induced by the pattern of continual small rises in prices and incomes—by the time one has 'shopped around' to find a steady price, that price too, or one's income, has gone up) few corresponding falls in the prices of complements. Perhaps too, there is a 'wage-profit spiral',[1] in which trade union leaders mop up high profits through larger, harder-fought and more sympathetically received wage claims, while entrepreneurs restore profit/wage ratios by price rises.

These spirals interact to form inflation. Their effect on the Government—for all its complaints—is to make it chief culprit. To meet its needs, even if these are constant in real terms, it must (unless willing to incur the political unpopularity of higher taxes) print or borrow money. Since the second method finances Government spending out of money that would, in the main, otherwise have been saved, both methods are Type II inflationary shocks, raising monetary demand above the supply of goods and services.

Modern governments understand these dangers, but in the U.K. substantial fiscal correctives can be applied only once a year, at budget time. Emergency and election budgets are seldom properly considered substitutes! The introduction of the regulator (power to vary indirect taxes up to 10 per cent, either way, between any pair of Budgets) in Mr Maudling's 1962 Budget imparted some overdue flexibility, but not much. Monetary policy, too, cuts both ways. To make borrowing dearer

[1] Denied in Kahn, Haberler, *et al.*, *The Problem of Rising Prices* (O.E.C.D. 1956) but the heart of A. J. Brown's model (op. cit.).

may discourage some investment (and consumer H.P.) demand.[1] It may, however, lead to price rises directly when local authorities raise rents and rates to recoup higher costs of needed capital works, and indirectly if firms feel able to pass on higher interest rates as price rises. Constant, for Governments, is the temptation—often the need—to finance desirable, long-approved items of real expenditure by inflationary means, duly sanctioned by Supplementary Estimates.

This book is mainly concerned with describing, not recommending; but, if transmission mechanisms have played more part than outside shocks in inflation since 1953 the way to cope with inflation suggests itself: break the links.

(a) Higher wages would not lead to higher demand if workers were encouraged to save their extra incomes.

(b) Higher wages would raise costs less if, instead of being simply passed on to consumers, they caused some labour to be replaced by capital. Two major components in British economic stagnation—inadequate investment and hoarded, immobile labour—arise because machines are too expensive relatively to workers. This will scarcely be corrected by wage restraint.

(c) The price-wage link would be broken if consumers, when a price rose, looked round harder for substitutes, and were better informed about them. An environment where products are sold by the same firm, in the same place, at different prices[2] does not encourage the price-consciousness needed before careful buying rather than wage-claiming becomes the normal reaction to a price rise.

(d) Spirals involving the Government can be avoided if fixed-price contracts replace cost-plus arrangements. A higher initial cost may be incurred, but it is seen (and can be financed) before it happens, without later *ad hoc* expedients that become part of an established inflationary sequence, and speed it.

4. THE BALANCE OF PAYMENTS

(a) Four propositions
These may help to keep your bearings in the welter of statistics and trend-spotting that inevitably follows.

---

[1] Not much. A. C. L. Day, *Outline of Monetary Economics*, Oxford 1957, pp. 82-4.
[2] 'Square Deal Surf' (unadvertised, no free gifts) and ordinary Surf, among detergents; Phillips' 'Square Deal' and ordinary fluoride toothpaste; and 'Jet' and 'Conoco' petrol are among many examples.

1. *Post-war British visible trade performance has been excellent.* In 1963, real output was 66 per cent above 1938; yet export volume was 131 per cent higher, and import volume only 38 per cent.[1] The terms of trade, indicating the volume of imports we could buy with £1 worth of exports, were almost the same in 1955-65 as in 1938. It is thus real redirection of output towards exports, and real economising in imports, not lucky price movements, which are responsible for the following fact: whereas in 1938 goods exports paid for only 64 per cent of goods imports, the share was over 95 per cent in 1955-65. Since 1959, however, things have got worse.

2. *The current-account balance of payments has performed poorly for other reasons.* In 1955-65, the average yearly surplus was only £10 millions, as against the £300-450m. allegedly needed to finance capital-account transactions (pp. 60-61). In 1938, net private invisibles and net income from overseas assets exceeded Government current spending overseas by enough to pay for 27·3 per cent of U.K. goods imports; in 1955-65 this excess covered only 4·5 per cent of the cost of goods imports.

3. *Long-term capital account is not to blame for the poor performance on current and capital accounts together.* Net private outlays on capital account have two causes: the purchase of overseas assets by U.K. citizens and the sale of U.K. assets by foreigners. Both reflect lack of confidence in (i) the future exchange value of the currency yield of British assets, and (ii) the ability of the U.K. to keep that yield growing. Confidence in (i) and (ii) depends on the current account. In other words, private capital account is the creature of current account. *Government capital outflows*—aid or export credits—reflect policies, or moral values. The U.K. is not so poor that we restrict home investment to raise our current consumption; it is not clear why we should follow a different policy abroad, at least in the long term.

4. *Improvement in the current balance, to finance our desired capital-account deficits, must come mainly from cuts in goods imports, or further rises in visible exports, which can be achieved only by raising output per £ of cost faster than our competitors.* Impressionistic suggestions that our

[1] Table 19, and *The British Economy: Key Statistics 1900-1964*, The Times, 1965, pp. 4-5, 14-15, 53. The two estimates for 1938 GDP (at 1958 factor cost) are averaged (they are within 1 per cent of each other).

[2] 'Net' in this section always means '*less* corresponding negative transactions'. For example, 'net income for overseas assets' means 'British income from overseas assets, *less* overseas income from assets held in the U.K.'

export performance or our rising import bill stems substantially from non-cost factors (commodity composition of trade, misdirected exports, poor selling and servicing) are not supported by the evidence. The trends under (2) above, however, are irreversible, desirable or both. Arguments like 'Balance-of-payments deficit = £X; Government spending abroad = £Y; Y = X; so cut Y' are absurd: firstly because lots of other negative items also add up to £Y, secondly because X could also be cut by raising the positive items, thirdly because the real issue is what *can* be cut or raised, and finally because a value-judgment is either evaded or concealed.

(b) The evidence, 1955-65: visible trade

(i) *Statistical note.* Table 19 is simpler than it looks. Col. 14 shows the net outflow (−) or inflow (+) of foreign exchange from all transactions in a year. Col. 13 is the sum, occasionally huge, of all untraced transactions. It is on col. 12 that policy can operate. Col. 12 is the sum of current and capital balances.

Col. 8, the current balance, shows the excess of imports of goods and services over exports. It comprises the balance of traded goods (col. 4), the private service balance (col. 6—mainly banking and insurance, but also transport of goods and persons, tourism, etc.) and the Government service balance (col. 7—since 1955, mainly military spending east of Suez and in Germany).

Col. 11, the capital balance, comprises (a) col. 9—purchases (net of sales) by Britons of overseas shares, bonds, factories, docks, etc. (a minus item), and comparable net purchases by foreigners here (a plus item); past col. 9 pluses yield present col. 5 minuses and *vice versa*; and (b) col. 10—long-term loans, grants and subscriptions by the U.K. to foreign governments and international organizations—and their similar loans to the U.K. (Marshall Aid in 1948-51) and repayments (+).

(ii) *Trade: explanations and trends.* Cols. 2 to 4 show, especially in conjunction with earlier post-war years, (a) occasional years—1955, 1960, 1964—dreadful by the standards of post-war needs, though still financing far more of imports by exports than during the 1930s; (b) a distinct worsening of the trade balance since 1959. In each of the stock-building booms in net imports, 1955, 1960 and 1964, the deterioration in the trade balance was bigger and lasted longer.

British visible trade in 1959-65, while far closer to surplus than before

TABLE 19: BALANCE OF PAYMENTS: MAIN ITEMS (million £, at current prices)

Col. 1 Year	2 Imports (f.o.b.)	3 Exports (f.o.b.)	4 (3+2) Balance of trade	5 Net private property income	6 Net private service incomes	7 Current govt. balance	8 (4+5+6+7) Current A/c Balance of Payments	9 Net private foreign investment	10 Net Govt. house subscriptions (cap. a/c)	11 (9+10) Long-term Capital A/c Balance of Payments	12 (8+11) Apparent total balance of payments	13 Balancing item	14 (12+13) Actual Balance of Payments
1938	−835	+533	−302	+175	+69	−16	−74			*Not known*			
1955	−3386	+3073	−313	+173	+122	−139	−157	−60	−62	−122	−279	+123	−156
1956	−3324	+3377	+53	+227	+101	−172	+209	−119	−68	−187	+22	+41	+63
1957	−3538	+3366	−29	+245	+147	−147	+216	−172	+66	−106	+110	+97	+207
1958	−3375	+3407	+32	+290	+232	−224	+330	−142	−50	−193	+137	+78	+215
1959	−3638	+3522	−116	+263	+218	−233	+132	−127	−124	−251	−119	−15	−134
1960	−4137	+3733	−404	+238	+179	−286	−273	−83	−102	−185	−458	+300	−158
1961	−4041	+3892	−149	+252	+221	−338	−14	+122	−45	+77	+63	−24	+39
1962	−4092	+3994	−98	+324	+229	−362	+93	+11	−104	−93	0	+89	+89
1963	−4336	+4287	−79	+387	+179	−382	+105	−57	−105	−162	−57	−68	−125
1964	−5006	+4471	−535	+406	+157	−434	−406	−247	−116	−363	−769	+22	−747
1965	−5044	+4779	−265	+454	+129	−454	−136	−137	−81	−218	−354	+105	−249

Sources: Ann. Abst. Stats., 1965, Table 274; Economic Trends, June 1966. Latest source always used. For 1938,

Notes: Col. 6 includes net private transfers (see table 24, note (b))—usually under ±£25m. Col. 14 represents increase (+) or decrease (−) in the U.K.'s 'reserves less liabilities' as a result of all foreign transactions in the year. All purchases of goods, services, or assets are − in Cols. 1–12; all sales, +.

the war, is not nearly close enough given other present needs for foreign exchange, and far less close than in 1950-58. Three sorts of explanation have been advanced: complementarian, structuralist, and output/cost-rationalist.

Complementarians claim that we are bad at providing complements to our exports: that British after-sales service (car repair, etc.), export credit facilities, sales pressure, etc., are poor compared with our rivals. Unfortunately most of the evidence is bar-room gossip. At best it is confined to certain goods in limited markets, selectively[1] compared with particular rivals. Overall indicators of complementary spending by all exporters in a single market, let alone in all markets, are lacking. Nor is it obvious that the rate of return on, say, a British advertising agency or car-repair shop in Timbuctu is such that it represents the best form of overseas investment. Oddly enough, complementarians are usually hostile to British investment overseas, which they dismiss as wasteful.

(c) Structuralism

Structuralists must be treated more respectfully. Their propositions are scientific—i.e. comprehensible, consistent and refutable. They claim that we have failed to raise exports[2] fast enough because they have been unluckily directed towards slowly growing markets, and/or composed of income-inelastic, obsolescent or otherwise unlucky products. Unless this is the fatalism of the Beatles' song 'I'm a loser', it means that British resources are exceptionally immobile—otherwise they would rapidly transfer to luckier products and markets. Especially for labour, there is much evidence of this sort of rigidity; but it cannot be blamed for any inadequacies in British export performance.

For it is just not true that our exports are hopelessly tied to static markets. True, an unusually large part of our trade, now as in 1950, is with relatively slow-growing regions (the Commonwealth in particular). But this part has shrunk fast, and fastest with the slowest-growing. In

---

[1] If that: J. R. Parkinson, *Scot. Jnl. Pol. Econ.*, Feb. 1966, p. 10, cites N. Stacey's demonstration that, for U.K. manufacturing firms, the ratio of advertising to sales was only 0·5 per cent overseas as against 1·4 per cent in the home market. Without any indication of the pay-off from overseas advertising (which costs foreign exchange), or of other countries' ratios, such a demonstration proves nothing.

[2] Similar explanations, as coherent and testable but wrong for similar reasons, are advanced for imports. See the excellent discussion by M. Fg. Scott in Worswick and Ady, *The British Economy in the 1950s*, Oxford, 1962, ch. 4.

the short period 1956-63, the U.K.'s exports to Australia fell from 7·6 per cent to 5·8 per cent of her total exports; to India and Pakistan, from 6·4 to 4·4; to New Zealand, from 4·0 to 2·8; and to Canada, from 5·7 to 4·2. Equally dramatic was the expansion in export share to fast growers; W. Germany from 2·9 per cent to 5·2 per cent, France from 2·8 to 4·4, Italy from 1·9 to 3·0.[1]

What of commodity composition? Rigidity here is a more plausible explanation of slow export expansion, since it is genuinely difficult to shift resources to make new exports, but not to switch the same export from a slow-growing to a fast-growing market (assuming the relative degree of protection stays about the same). Again, however, there have been rapid shifts in structure. From 1956 to 1963, the share of chemicals in U.K. exports rose from 7·8 per cent to 9·0 per cent. From 1956 to 1964, the number of motor cars and chassis exported more than doubled (from 336,000 to 679,000), while total export volume rose only 21·7 per cent.[2] Import structure, too, has been flexible.

The structuralist argument is not as limited as the foregoing discussion (amplified in papers by Black and Major)[3] suggests. First, the strength of any structuralist argument varies, almost without limit of strength or weakness, with the fineness of structure. The smaller our regions, the greater the apparent disparity in regional unemployment levels; the finer our export structure (the more sectors into which it is divided for analysis), the easier it is to find potentially expanding sub-sectors where we have lagged, or stagnant ones where we have mistakenly persisted.[4]

Second, most structural analysis is too short-run. Both the commodity and national composition of trade show less variety in composition of markets when viewed historically. Table 20 shows how unwise are such aggregations as 'Commonwealth trade', or magnification into trends of short-run movements in trade with particular countries or groups. In

---

[1] *Annual Abstract of Statistics (U.K.)*, 1965, p. 220. N.E.D.C., *Export Trends* (1963), shows that U.K. exports rose 13·6 per cent from 1957 to 1961, but would have risen only 23·3 per cent if the U.K. had maintained her 1957 share in each national market—as against a 28·4 per cent expansion in 'world exports'. To attribute the (28·4-23·3) = 5·1 per cent lag to 'geography', as if our export direction was structurally fixed, is a mistake. Parkinson, loc. cit., pp. 8-9.

[2] *Ibid.*, pp. 215, 217-8, 233.

[3] J. Black in Worswick and Ady, op. cit., ch. 3; R. L. Major in Beckerman, op cit., ch. 5.

[4] T. Barna has produced just such a 'strengthening' of the structuralist case— useful for his own search for particular weaknesses, but not a proof of the case, *The Times*, 3 April 1963.

TABLE 20: NATIONAL STRUCTURE OF BRITISH VISIBLE TRADE
Share in U.K.:

Country	Imports			Domestically Produced Exports			Exports and Re-exports		
	1913	*1938*	*1963*	*1913*	*1938*	*1963*	*1913*	*1938*	*1963*
Australia	5·0	7·8	4·3	6·5	8·1	5·8	6·0	7·3	5·6
India and Pakistan	6·3	6·1	3·5	13·4	7·2	4·4	11·3	6·4	4·3
New Zealand	2·6	5·1	4·3	2·1	4·1	2·8	1·9	3·7	2·7
South Africa	—	—	2·4	—	—	4·8	—	—	4·7
Canada	4·1	2·8	7·7	4·8	4·7	4·4	4·7	4·5	4·4
Eire	—	2·5	3·2	—	4·3	3·6	—	4·9	3·8
Argentina	5·5	4·2	1·6	4·3	4·1	0·6	3·7	3·7	0·6
France	6·0	2·6	3·2	5·5	3·2	4·4	6·4	4·4	4·6
Germany (a)	10·5	3·5	4·3	7·7	4·6	5·2	9·5	5·1	5·7
Netherlands	3·1	3·2	4·9	2·9	2·8	4·1	3·2	2·8	4·1
U.S.A.	18·4	12·8	10·4	5·6	6·7	8·3	9·4	11·7	8·6
Russia— U.S.S.R.	5·2	0·1	3·2	3·4	2·0	1·4	4·4	3·0	1·5

Sources: Mitchell and Deane, *Abstr. Brit. Hist. Stats.*, Cambridge, 1963, pp. 284, and 'Overseas Trade, Table 12'; *Ann. Abst. Stats.*, 1965, sec. IX; for 1963 re-exports, *Board of Trade Jnl.*, Jan. 1966, Table 12.

Note: (a) Excludes E. Germany for 1963; trade with this area was less than 1 per cent of trade with W. Germany.

General note: Re-exports of imported items were 17·3 per cent of 'exports and re-exports' in 1913, 6·7 per cent in 1938 and 3·6 per cent in 1963.

most cases, trade shares fell between 1938 and 1963 with those countries with whom they rose from 1913 to 1938, and *vice versa*. Certainly tariff and quota changes—favourable to the Commonwealth in the early 1930s, and to Europe after 1945—played their part; and so did the relative slowing-down of U.S. and Commonwealth growth after 1945. But a nation's trade direction is determined largely by what it needs to buy, and has to sell.

Changes in this are looked at historically in Tables 21 and 22. The export breakdown, in particular, demonstrates revolutionary structural change in 1938-63, compared with slow change (except for textiles) in 1900-38. Changes in export and import shares by value, as shown in these tables, comprise price and quantity changes. The price-ratios of non-manufactures to manufactures were similar in 1900 and 1913, fell considerably (if jerkily) from 1913 to 1938, but were again similar in 1938 and 1963. Thus the last two rows of each table represent mainly structural (volume) shifts—and huge ones. In particular, vehicle and machinery exports rose enormously.

TABLE 21: COMMODITY STRUCTURE OF IMPORTS

Year	Total Imports as percentage of:		Percentage share in imports by value of:				
	GNP at factor cost (current prices)	GDP at factor cost (1958 prices)	Food, drink, tobacco	Basic materials	Fuels	Manufacturers:	
						Un-processed	Processed
1900	28·3	23·6	42·1	31·7	1·3	23·7	0·6
1913	32·1	28·1	37·8	35·4	1·6	18·5	6·4
1929	27·5	29·4	43·6	27·6	3·7	16·9	6·7
1938	17·8	25·9	46·5	26·1	5·2	14·2	7·1
1963	18·0	24·5	34·9	20·6	11·7	19·1	13·5

Source: The British Economy: Key Statistics 1900-1964, L.C.E.S. and *The Times*, 1965, pp. 14-15.

Note: Data are not comparable with other import tables in this book owing to differences in coverage.

TABLE 22: COMMODITY STRUCTURE OF EXPORTS

Year	Total exports as percentage of:			Percentage share in exports by value of:			
	GNP at factor cost (current prices)	GDP at factor cost (1958 prices)	Non-manu-factures	Chemicals	Textiles	Metals, metal mnfctrs.	Mchnry. transpt. eqpt.
1900	15·8	26·5	20·2	4·8	36.4	14·4	10·3
1913	21·9	38·1	19·8	5·1	34·7	13·7	11·8
1929	16·4	28·7	19·2	4·5	26·2	12·2	9·1
1938	9·1	18·4	21·2	5·3	19·7	12·1	14·6
1963	15·3	23·7	14·2	9·0	6·2	11·3	44·3

Source and Note: As above table.

Thus we see that the labour immobilities (pp. 122-5) have not prevented big shifts in long-run export structure, though they *have* stopped domestic deflation from producing big short-run rises in the share of output devoted to exports. But Tables 21 and 22 must be considered

N̄ a ꞇ͞erri̅ble definiꞇs?

together. S. B. Linder[1] has shown that, as a country becomes more affluent, its trade consists increasingly of the sort of commodities it makes itself. Notice the steady rise in imports of processed manufactures, from 0·6 per cent of all imports in 1900 to 13·5 per cent in 1963. Over any but a myopic time-span, this rise is paralleled by the last column of Table 22, and indeed the 'league tables', showing a catastrophic decline in Britain's share of world exports of manufactures, are ludicrous.

Firstly, the U.K. has rightly contracted the share of efforts devoted to technologically simpler manufactures, especially traditional textiles. Secondly, new manufacturing countries have taken up this share, and have also broken into the industrial goods market; indeed, Major[2] proves that, the bigger the Japanese share in a national or commodity market, the bigger is the U.K.'s loss of market share. Last and foremost, the U.K.'s import needs between the 1930s and the 1960s have risen more slowly than her total output, much more slowly than world trade, and very much more slowly than world trade in manufactures. Exports exist to finance imports, not as an end in themselves. In view of this welcome long-term sluggishness in imports, it is natural and right that the U.K.'s share of world exports of manufactures should have declined.

(d) Output, prices and trade

Structuralists conclude too much from special markets, particular ratios, and general unease about export performance. Output/cost rationalists concentrate on a single ratio, but one of more general significance. They make a simple claim: that British exports have risen too slowly, and imports too fast, because of price factors. The U.K.'s ratio of total cost to total volume, both of exports and of home output relative to imports, has consistently outpaced her main rivals. Many people run away from this explanation, regarding its implications as necessarily restrictionist or deflationary. However, (a) one can lower costs by egalitarian, mild deflation—lower salaries and directors' fees— as well as by lower wages; and, more important, (b) one can raise the output/cost ratio as effectively by fast growth in production as by lower costs. The more successful exporters (W. Germany, France, Japan) have raised money wages somewhat faster than the U.K.—but real output much faster.

[1] S. B. Linder, *An Essay on Trade and Transformation*, Stockholm, 1962.
[2] In Beckerman, op. cit., p. 168.

Much evidence suggests that output/cost ratios are the main determinants of trade trends.[1] We examine two types of evidence: time-series of the British past and cross-sections of recent national performances. We concentrate on quantum/*price* ratios; presumably a buyer is interested in the price of imports relative to home commodities, not in the share of price which is cost as opposed to profit.

Table 23 shows price and volume trends for 1958-64,[2] for exports, imports and gross domestic product, in all 17 advanced industrial economies for which data are available. The dominating factor was the improving trade balance of the U.S. This caused a worsening balance for almost all other nations. Imports outpaced exports even for countries like Japan, W. Germany, France and Italy, with fast growth and relatively sound balances. Britain suffered worst. Why?

Table 23 shows that, for almost all industrial nations, trade volume has grown much faster than output volume, while prices of traded goods, owing to greater competition, have risen much more slowly than retail prices as a whole. These trends are also found in long-run analysis of U.K. data (pp. 172-4). We are led to suspect a causal sequence.

To make this more precise, we set up hypotheses and carry out simple tests. For most imports, a single country's demand will be small relative to world demand, and will thus be effect rather than cause of price. The relevant price must allow for changes in the prices of non-imported goods, since the domestic consumer chooses between these goods and imports. Our hypothesis is therefore: the smaller the rate of increase in import prices relative to overall retail prices $\left(\text{Table 23, } \dfrac{\text{Col. 3}}{\text{Col. 7}}\right)$, the greater the rate of growth of import volume relative to real GDP $\left(\dfrac{\text{Col. 2}}{\text{Col. 6}}\right)$. The simple correlation coefficient $r = -0.725$, significant at 0.5 per cent for the 16 countries. Since $r^2 > 0.5$, variance of relative import prices is linked to over half the variance in relative import volume.

For exports the hypothesis is simpler. Unlike domestic buyers of imports, export buyers are not interested in the quantum or price of a

---

[1] J. Black, in Worswick and Ady, op. cit.; R. Major, op. cit.; M. Fg. Scott, in Worswick and Ady, op. cit.; *Scot. Jnl. Pol. Econ.*, Feb. 1966, *passim*.

[2] We concentrate on the period 1958-1964, since it has been suggested by M. Panić and T. Seward (*Bull. Oxf. Inst. Ec. Stat.*, Feb. 1966, pp. 19-32) that the link between relative prices and trading success weakened in the 1960s.

1958=100

TABLE 23: INDUSTRIAL COUNTRIES' TRADE, 1964

Col. 1	2	3	4	5	6	7
	Imports		Exports		GDP	
Country (a)	Quantity	Price	Quantity	Price	Quantity	Retail Prices
Canada	132	112	156	108	129	108
Australia	154	104	165	112	131	111
U.S.A.	141	100	150	103	128	107
Switzerland	130	106	123	111	140	114
U.K.	142	104	123	107	126	115
Belgium-Luxembourg (b)	186	100	184	98	134	111
Sweden	156	106	168	105	136	119
France	187	113	174	119	136	129
New Zealand	126	98	124	127	—	115
W. Germany	202	94	172	102	149	114
Netherlands	187	98	172	102	138	119
Denmark	192	100	154	106	137	126
Finland	202	102	100	105	145	129
Austria	187	93	156	100	133	119
Norway	164	92	178	98	135	120
Italy	240	94	240	96	143	124
Japan	271	96	245	95	202	132

Source: U.N., *Monthly Bull. Stats.*, May 1966.

Notes: (a) Ranked in order of the ratio between the percentage rise in price of *imports* to that of *GDP* (i.e. of Col. 3 to Col. 7).

(b) GDP data exclude Luxemburg (no post-1960 data exist for her).

seller's domestic output. We suggest simply: the faster the growth of a nation's export prices from 1958 to 1964, the slower the growth of export volume. For the 17 industrial countries observed, between cols. 4 and 5 of Table 23, $r = 0.584$, significant at 1 per cent. Since $r^2 > 0.33$, variance of export prices is linked to over one-third of variance in export volume. Both hypotheses are thus supported by the evidence.

Professor Matthews' analysis[1] of U.K. trade and prices from 1855 to 1963 confirms the cross-section evidence for imports. He, too, measured relative import volume by the ratio of imports to GDP, both revalued at 1958 prices; relative import prices, by (a) expressing the prices in each

[1] In a lecture at the University of Sussex, January 1966, from which the following data are taken.

year of the 1958 import bundle as a percentage of its 1958 price, (b) doing the same for 1958 GDP, and (c) taking the ratio of (a) to (b); and relative import spending, by the current-price import/GDP ratio. His data show a big secular rise in relative volume, corresponding to a similar fall in relative price, to leave relative spending hardly changed. Year-to-year fluctuations in relative prices are also, in most cases, inversely related to those in relative volumes. As in Table 23, a sort of demand curve is identified; the smaller the price-ratio of imported to domestic products, the greater the quantum ratio.

Professor Matthews' analysis shows that the responsiveness of the U.K.'s volume ratio of imports to home output (to changes in price ratio) has declined since the war; this is fortunate, since otherwise the U.K.'s relatively fast inflation would have damaged the balance of trade more than it has actually done. The responsiveness or 'ratio-elasticity' has been lowered by full employment, which has made it less easy to reallocate resources to exploit relative price shifts. This has outweighed the increases in responsiveness due to the structural trends shown in Table 21; plainly, the more we import goods like those we make ourselves, the more readily can we substitute for imports when their relative prices rise, and *vice versa* when they fall.

Despite this declining responsiveness, overall import trends since 1959 are unfortunate in view of the excellent performance in 1945-58. In current prices, imports were 12 per cent of GDP in 1945, but 24 per cent in 1965. This is nowhere near the historic record of 1913 (32 per cent). But it is more than the U.K. can afford with her current capacity to export, invisibles position and requirements on capital account. This fact does not justify the protection of inefficient domestic producers by long-term import restrictions. Vested interests can be relied upon to magnify any case for protecting their own product; economists, whatever their politics, do well to succour the battered body of the principle of comparative advantage. If long-term import controls are ruled out and if output/cost ratios determine choices between domestic and foreign products, the case for some form of incomes policy—shorn of its investment-discouraging effects by measures to make machines cheaper, relative to labour, for British firms—becomes overwhelming.

For exports, it is less easy to find long-run links between price and volume in the British time-series. The price-ratio of exports to GDP fluctuated in sympathy with the volume ratio, suggesting a supply curve, in 1855-65, and again in 1945-50; but otherwise the (weak) tendency is in the reverse direction. Here we seem to be stuck with the cross-section data (Table 23), but these are powerful enough to make the case for output/cost ratios as the principal determinant of export trends.

Elasticity analysis confirms these views. Both for exports and for imports, long-run price-elasticity of demand is about -5.[1] This means that sterling devaluation of 10 per cent—assuming that higher import costs were not passed on (via recoupment of real wages or profits) to higher export costs, and that no other country devalued—would *ultimately* raise export volume by 50 per cent[2] and cut import volume by 50 per cent. Since import prices would be 10 per cent higher and export prices 10 per cent lower, this would mean a 35 per cent rise in export value and a 45 per cent drop in import value. Even serious erosion of the assumptions, and a long 'ultimately' (very slow reactions by buyers), could scarcely turn the effects of devaluation against Britain's balance of payments. True, one is devaluing other people's assets, endangering the mechanism of international payments, making incomes policy harder to sell (since rising import prices cut the worth of even the small rises in incomes that are allowed) and giving export help, and protection against imports, to efficient and inefficient producers alike. For all this, the crude balance-of-trade case for devaluation, and the underlying output/cost ratio explanation of trade trends, are very strong.

(e) Private service incomes

Even in money terms, col. 6 of Table 19 was lower in 1965 than in 1952-4. In 1938 private services paid for 8·4 per cent of goods imports, in 1955 for 3·9 per cent, and in 1965 for only 2·4 per cent—despite the reduced ratio of imports to income in the later years. This stems from London's decline as financial, commercial and imperialising centre of the economic universe. Can the private service account recover? This depends on the ability of British shippers, hoteliers, bankers and insurers not merely to improve on their past competitive performance, but to do it fast enough to overcome the erosion of their old colonial advantages.

In shipping the U.S. has shared with the U.K. the ebb tide from European and Japanese emergence. From 1952 to 1962, gross overseas earnings from shipping rose by 314 per cent for West Germany, 281 per

---

[1] Cf. *Scottish Jnl. Pol. Econ.*, Feb. 1966; J. R. Parkinson (p. 12) for exports, I. G. Stewart (p. 38) for imports. Neither tells us how long is the long run.

[2] Less in so far as exporters exploit devaluation to raise *sterling* prices; even this helps, making exports more profitable compared to home sales.

cent for Japan and 113 per cent for Italy—but fell 19 per cent for the U.S.A., and rose only 11 per cent for the U.K.[1] The balance deteriorated annually from 1952 (+£137m.) to 1956 (−£48m.) and the recovery of 1957-9 proved temporary. In the U.K. the industry is afflicted by small companies with low profits and hence little finance for modernisation. Moreover, the 1966 strike has meant permanent loss of business. Major's 1964 prediction of a −£100m. balance in 1975 is not unduly pessimistic.

The other part of transport account, civil aviation, has steadily gained since 1952, and since 1962 has outweighed the shipping deficit. Here, as in shipping, Governments face a policy choice. In these sectors, unlike visible trade, international convention permits large, if concealed, subsidies. These improve the balance of payments but distort domestic resource allocation. British lines to Timbuctu cannot make long-run sense. Exports, whether of services or goods, are means, not ends.

What of tourism and business travel? Table 24 presents an insufficiently dismal picture. Hotel and rail prices in the U.K. have far outdistanced the cost of living, which in turn has outdistanced overseas living costs. Thus Table 24, which is in money terms, understates the extent to which the volume of foreign tourism in Britain has been outpaced by British tourism abroad. In 1958 prices, expenditure by foreign tourists, etc., in the U.K. rose only 19 per cent from 1954 to 1964. Ominously, this volume indicator fell each year from 1961. Meanwhile, British consumer's expenditure abroad in 1958 prices rose 59 per cent.[2]

As Major points out,[3] some of this growth was caused by the easing of U.K. currency restrictions. This cannot be the main cause, however. Restrictions were greatly eased in 1954 and 1957, and had effectively vanished by late 1959; tourist spending by Britons abroad has grown fastest since 1962. British hoteliers contrast their own tax burdens with governmental subsidies to overseas rivals; but the relative position of British hotels did not obviously worsen in 1954-64. Since 1954, moreover, real income per person has grown more slowly in Britain than in most other substantial 'touring countries'. Since demand for

---

[1] Major, in Beckerman, op. cit., p. 129. Other data in this section also come from this paper.

[2] *Nat. Inc. Exp. 1965*, p. 28. A. E. Holmans, *Scot. Jnl. Pol. Econ.*, Feb. 1966, p. 54, shows that the number of visitors to the U.K. from abroad was 439,000 in 1938, 818,600 in 1953 and 2,158,600 in 1963. However, in view of the sluggish volume of spending (and the much faster tourist growth of competitors, despite their faster income rises), one cannot agree that 'Britain's tourist trade has been making a major contribution to the balance of payments' (p. 55).

[3] Beckerman, op. cit., p. 131.

holidays abroad is highly income-elastic, our tourist balance should have improved dramatically. Especially in view of the growth of information concerning package and budget holidays, one is forced towards Britain's relatively high and rising prices, both of hotels and of rail travel, as the main cause of our distressing performance. The very high income-elasticity of demand for comfort suggests that inadequate, slowly improving heating, cooling, eating, drinking, sleeping and bathroom facilities may also have played their part—the whole philosophy of 'sorry, Sir'.

It is hard to be sensible about 'other services', an amalgam of banking charges, some insurance earnings, films, royalties, etc. A plea for intelligent presentation of this enormous item, which in 1965 provided a favourable net balance sufficient to pay for 4·7 per cent of all goods imports, may be more useful than bogus analysis of an inchoate sponge. Official data provide no breakdown at all. Holmans[1] suggests that

TABLE 24: PRIVATE SERVICE INCOMES

(£ million + (−) net gain (loss) to balance of payments)

| Year | Shipping | Civil Aviation | Business travels tourism: | | 'Other services' (insurance, banking, etc.) | Total service income (b) |
			Britons abroad	Foreigners in U.K.		
						−10 for 3 yrs from tourism
1952-4 (a)	+87	+1	−91	+88	+162	+247
1955	−30	−3	−125	+111	+171	+124
1956	−48	−1	−132	+121	+179	+129
1957	+7	−3	−146	+129	+180	+167
1958	+43	+8	−152	+134	+195	+228
1959	+16	+18	−164	+143	+205	+218
1960	−32	+18	−186	+169	+207	+176
1961	−28	+22	−200	+176	+244	+214
1962	−12	+21	−210	+183	+247	+229
1963	−12	+25	−241	+188	+233	+193
1964	−25	+28	−261	+190	+248	+180
1965	−11	+31	−280	+188	+235	+163

Source: Economic Trends, June 1966, p. viii; *Ann. Abst. Stat.*, 1963, Table 268; 1965, Table 274.

Notes: (a) Annual average.

(b) To convert to Table 19, Col. 6, add net private transfers to the U.K.: −£2m. (1955), −£28m. (1956), −£20m., +£4m., O, +£3m., O, −£14m., −£23m., −£34m. (1965).

[1] In *Scot. Jnl. Pol. Econ.*, Feb. 1966, p. 56, using estimates by the Treasury for 1956 and by W. M. Clarke for 1963.

earnings from financial services—the City's argument for the status of sterling as an international currency—rose by over one-third from 1958 to 1963, to £155m.–170m., about 3 per cent of import value.

(ƒ) *The government balance*

The distinction between current and capital accounts, always arbitrary, is confusing and absurd when applied to Governmental activities abroad. Loans to underdeveloped countries presumably have the same aims as grants. Yet the former appear on capital account in the balance of payments, the latter on current account. Government subscriptions to the International Finance Corporation and the International Development Association are on capital account; most similar subscriptions are on current account. If the Government undertakes direct investment overseas, e.g. by building a barracks for British troops in West Germany (to yield the foreign exchange that would otherwise go in rent), this goes on current account! We therefore amalgamate the Government's accounts in Table 25.[1]

In 1938, the unfavourable Government balance added well under 3 per cent to goods-import charges. In 1955 this was 5·9 per cent, and in 1965 it was 10·6 per cent, i.e. some 2 per cent of national income. The two main reasons are the expansion of aid to underdeveloped countries and the acceptance by the U.K. of a permanent, growing military burden abroad. Neither trend seems reversible. Minor components of the explosion of net Government deficits—booming administrative and diplomatic costs (but not receipts), repayments of past U.K. loans such as Marshall Aid, rising pay for British troops abroad, reluctance of rich foreign countries to pay for their own defence—may decline but can hardly outweigh the trend towards more aid and more world-wide forms of defence. Therefore, if the Government balance is to look better in future, the international community must agree on ways for countries to meet such commitments with less strain upon foreign balances. The interests of debtor and creditor nations conflict—so do the interests of countries taking the strain of supporting an international currency (U.K., U.S.A.) and those of their luckier competitors (France, W. Germany). Such accord is therefore unlikely.

Table 26 gives some idea of the expansion of aid. Aid is hard to

---

[1] This is the Government's 'current and long-term capital account': short-term loans to the U.K., to tide us over balance-of-payments difficulties, are not shown. Nor are I.M.F. subscriptions.

TABLE 25: GOVERNMENT BALANCE

	1955	1956	1957	1958	1959	1960	1961	1962	1963	1964	1965
1. *Loans by U.K. Govt.*	−32	−9	−16	−21	−48	−61	−61	−62	−66	−84	−74
2. Loans to U.K. Govt.	—	—	+89	—	+37	—	+18	—	—	—	—
3. *Repayments by U.K. Govt.*	−48	−70	−30	−60	−183	−72	−82	−44	−45	−36	−16
4. Repayments to U.K. Govt.	+28	+29	+32	+37	+76	+41	+100	+15	+14	+19	+27
5. Other official long-term capital (*a*)	−10	−13	−9	−6	−2	—	−201	−4	+11	−6	−6
6. *Subscriptions* (*b*)	−9	−13	−10	−11	−17	−28	−30	−29	−39	−45	−64
7. *Bilateral Economic grants*	−62	−60	−61	−51	−52	−58	−73	−74	−69	−82	−88
8. *Military grants*				−13	−13	−8	−13	−12	−19	−31	−20
9. *Other transfers*						−14	−12	−12	−13	−14	−14
10. *Payments for military service* (*c*)	−152	−174	−157	−180	−167	−206	−225	−243	−249	−270	−279
11. For admin., diplomatic services	−21	−22	−25	−26	−29	−31	−36	−37	−42	−46	−47
12. *Receipts for military services* (*d*)	+58	+66	+80	+52	+40	+45	+36	+30	+35	+38	+26
13. For other services			+5	+2	+3	+4	+6	+7	+5	+7	+20
14. *Total Govt. balance* (*e*) (current + capital a/c.s)	−201	−240	−81	−274	−357	−388	−383	−466	−487	−550	−535

Sources: Economic Trends, Dec. 1964, June 1966; *U.K. Balance of Payments, 1965*, tables 1, 6. Notes (c), (d): Major, in Beckerman, op. cit., pp. 124-5.

Notes: (a) Loans by (−) and repayments to (+) quasigovernmental bodies (Atomic Energy Authority, Commonwealth Development Corporation, etc.), and 'loan-like' transactions such as purchase (−) or sale (+) of U.N. bonds.

(b) Whether officially entered on current or long-term capital account. Excludes I.M.F.

(c) W. Germany: £47m. in 1958, −£45m. in 1960, −£75m. in 1962, about −£90m. in 1965.

(d) Including expenditure by U.S. and Canadian forces in the U.K. (averaging £18m. yearly in 1958-63).

(e) Equal to Table 19, Col. 7 + Col. 10. In 1955-8, this differs from the sum of rows 1-13 by defence aid and related transfer receipts (+£47m. in 1955, +£26m. in 1956, +£21m. in 1957, +£3 m. in 1958 and 200 thereafter). *U.K. Balance of Payments 1965*, p. 7, last row but two.

measure: to assess potential benefit to recipients, one should add, to grants, only the discounted present value of interest foregone upon loans made at less-than-market rates of return.[1] Our concern here, however, is to assess yearly strain on the balance-of-payments; in this context the sum of loans and grants, whether made directly to a country (bilaterally) or channelled through multilateral agencies like the I.B.R.D., is the relevant figure.

TABLE 26: ECONOMIC AID BY U.K. GOVERNMENT

	Financial year		
	1956-7	*1960-1*	*1964-5*
Total (£m.)	75·4	*157·8*	*190·6*
Proportion bilateral (per cent)	*79·2*	*82·4*	*90·2*
Of bilateral aid: loans (per cent)	24·6	55·5	49·3
grants (per cent)	75·4	*44·5*	50·7
India (per cent)	0·3	21·9	17·8
Pakistan (per cent)	2·5	2·4	7·7
Africa (per cent)	43·6	43·6	47·4
America (per cent)	11·2	5·5	6·7
Asia (per cent)	22·3	34·5	34·4

Source: U.K. Ann. Abst. Stats. 1965, p. 245.

From 1945-7 to 1964-5, the primary strain of British aid on the balance of payments has risen over 2½ times. However, two secondary effects reduce this strain. Table 25, row 4, shows that repayments of past loans (mostly aid), after a big bulge in 1959-61, were at the same level (£25-30m.) in 1955 as in 1965; but the rise from a quarter to a half in the share of loans in total aid must raise future return from this source, correspondingly lowering the strain. Second, more and more aid is tied by the U.K. to purchases of British products—reflected in Table 26 by the falling role of multilateral aid, which is harder to tie in this way. It is tentatively estimated in Whitehall that, on present tying practice, around half U.K. aid finds its way back to the U.K. as *extra* demand

[1] A good discussion is P. P. Streeten, 'Rich and Poor Nations', in P. D. Henderson (ed.), *Economic Growth in Britain*, Oxford, 1965. The best account of the correct measurement of aid is J. Pinkus, *Economic Aid and International Cost Sharing*, Johns Hopkins, 1965.

G

for her exports.[1] Thus the addition to the balance of payments deficit
from the 1964-5 aid bill of £190·6m., was about half this sum, *less* £23m.
(average repayments of loans to the U.K., 1964 and 1965)—i.e., about
£60-65m., or some 1·2 per cent of our goods import bill.

This is still substantial, and the sum went on rising despite the running balance-of-payments crisis of 1964-66. Nevertheless, most people
(including politicians and economists) would wish the burden to increase.
Beneath the cold war and good business as motives for aid lies the
extension beyond national borders of the welfare state—the responsibility of the rich and powerful to help the poor and weak towards
decent levels of living. The growth of international aid, for whatever
motives, is the most hopeful feature of the post-war world, and perhaps
can lever into existence a genuine international community. It would be
economic, political and moral myopia for Britain to contract out of such
a community by failing to expand her aid outflows. The real task is to
find a way to give resources, not reserves—either by international
agreement or by 'super-tying'.[2]

The composition of aid is another matter. It is alarming to note that,
for all the decolonisation, almost half British aid in 1964-5 went to
Africa—a bigger share than in 1956-7. India and Pakistan get just over
half the amount of aid going to Africa; yet they have more than double
Africa's population, lower income per head, greater political stability
and economic expertise, and more determination and ability to enforce
planning decisions. India and Pakistan, moreover, face a problem that
is sensitive to aid: resource scarcity. In particular, they have small
reserves of foreign currency, but need complex machines at a stage of
development when they cannot economically produce substitutes
themselves. Most African states, especially the mineral exporters, have
substantial foreign exchange reserves and spare physical resources. On

---

[1] Tying does not automatically destroy the whole strain of aid on the balance
of payments, since recipients use some tied aid to buy donor's products that they
would otherwise have bought with their own foreign exchange; it is thus extra
demand that counts.

[2] The 'Stamp Plan' would, in effect, increase world liquidity by giving aid as
coupons which could be spent on the exports of any donor in the group. 'Super-
tying' means giving £X on condition that the recipient's balance (imports —
exports) with the donor worsen at least £X (or £X *plus* trend rate of deterioration
of the balance) in the year after the gift. In my view super-tying is a more hopeful approach. The Stamp plan conflates two enormous problems, a procedure
which seldom helps to solve either. If rich countries are unwilling to give aid,
they will not be fooled into doing so in order to solve their liquidity problems,
which arise almost entirely from their dealings with one another.

any criterion of aid (even the 'Communist threat'), it is hard to justify the allocation among countries—or the very large number of recipients over whom the little jam is thinly spread. If Britain, despite problems with her balance of payments, is to continue to expand aid, she must concentrate that aid where need, population pressure, political stability, administrative control and economic dynamism are greatest. For once, all the criteria coincide, and point to India and Pakistan.

With military spending, as with aid, the horse (policy objectives) must precede the cart (manipulation of the balance of payments). In neither case can the weight of the cart be forgotten entirely. No country has unlimited ability to overspend and overstretch. However, once the U.K. has decided her proper world role and counted its cost, she need not abandon it completely rather than export more, import less, improve the private-service account, or devalue.

However, the trend of Britain's military commitment is hard to justify. Since 1950, British GNP has been growing slower than, and her balance of payments worsening relative to, W. Germany, Japan, France and Italy. Yet British foreign-exchange military outlays have grown faster than in any of these countries. In 1965 they were 83 per cent above 1955 levels—and rather above our total foreign deficit (£279m. as against £249m.). While the Soviet threat in Europe has receded, the net foreign-exchange cost of British troops defending West Germany has risen from £47m. in 1958 to £90m. in 1965—36 per cent of Britain's deficit on the balance of payments. In view of the enormous strength of W. Germany—current account surpluses, huge resources uncommitted to any banker's role, living standards above the U.K.'s—this situation seems quite intolerable. British commitments east of Suez— most of the non-German component of Table 25, row 10—are a political issue, but if they are as important as their supporters believe, we can of course cut our mink coat to leave some cloth for them.

Some of the smaller components of the Government deficit have grown for less defensible reasons. Why has the cost of overseas embassies, etc. (Table 25, row 11), risen 129 per cent in 1955-65? Does the much lower level, and till 1965 the comparative stability, of analogous receipts (Table 25, row 13) indicate the undercharging typical of conventional prices and public utilities? Does the huge decline in receipts for military services stem from reluctance to incur the charge that British troops are mercenaries? All this leaves some scope for improvement. But the main components of the government deficit, aid and collective security, are costing more because of political decisions which imply that they should cost more still. These decisions may or may not be politically wise. Certainly they are not economically crippling.

(g) Foreign investment and property incomes

Short-term restrictions on capital movements may well be needed to meet short-term difficulties in the balance of payments. In the long run, a country's tax system should not (as Britain's did until the 1965 budget) encourage savers to put cash abroad if the real yield to Britain is higher at home. Yet there is a strong case for relatively free movements of international private capital. Until development of the world economy is subject to effective planning and co-ordination, the search for profit is the least inefficient allocative device. Countries should align their tax systems so that private investors, in choosing where to lend, are confronted with a structure of private yields approximately reflecting social benefits. Aid donors, like the U.K., should provide incentives to channel private capital flows towards aided countries. Within this framework, provided that foreign capital is subject to the same social and economic control as domestic capital, movements of cash among nations in search of profit can assist growth, for investor country and recipient country alike.

Theoretical considerations suggest that too much fuss is made about private capital movements in conjunction with British difficulties with the balance of payments. Foreign investment is of two types, direct and portfolio.[1] Decisions on both types depend on the risk that the currency yielded by the asset will fall in value, whether by inflation or by devaluation. Direct investment, and portfolio investment in equities, also depends on expected growth in economies among which the investor is choosing. Fixed-interest portfolio investments (Government securities, local authority loans) are insensitive to growth, but depend on prevailing interest rates. Thus, along every line of motivation, the private capital account—British investment abroad and foreign investment in Britain alike—is the creature of the current account.[2] A persis-

[1] Within a country, portfolio investment (purchase of shares, etc.) is not included in the national investment figures, since the asset—the claim on yield— is merely transferred, not added to the nation's asset stock. When I buy a French share, this is an extra asset for the U.K. and is counted as investment. Corresponding sales are disinvestment. These non-domestic investments do not form part of NNP.

[2] Devaluation would not change the balance of advantage between yields from British and (say) Australian assets. Here it is relative growth of profits that counts. Outside the sterling area, devaluation matters too.

tent current deficit generates fears of devaluation, and Government restriction of growth; hence Britons and foreigners alike are induced to sell British assets, real or paper, and to buy similar assets abroad. The ensuing sterling crisis is met by high interest rates, which pull back fixed-interest portfolio investment to Britain.

Table 27 does not suggest that the total effect of private capital movement has harmed the foreign balance. Earnings remitted to the U.K. from British holdings of overseas assets rose steadily, and in 1965 were 92 per cent above 1955 levels; meanwhile remissions abroad by foreign owners of U.K. assets rose about 87 per cent from the abnormally high 1955 level. The sluggish growth of Britain's economy was reflected after 1961 by a sharp fall in foreign investment in Britain, and an acceleration of the rise in British investment overseas. However, this meant that (indeed happened because) Britain's earnings from overseas rose much faster than foreigners' earnings here.

TABLE 27: PRIVATE CAPITAL MOVEMENTS AND YIELDS

| | British capital abroad | | Foreign capital in U.K. | | Net effect on current and capital accounts of balance of payments | |
	Investment	Income remitted to U.K.	Investment	Income remitted from U.K.	Value	Per cent of import value
1955	−182	+516	+122	−343	+113	3·3
1956	−258	+569	+139	−342	+108	3·2
1957	−298	+579	+126	−334	+ 73	2·2
1958	−307	+679	+164	−389	+147	4·4
1959	−299	+659	+172	−396	+136	3·7
1960	−316	+676	+233	−438	+155	3·7
1961	−304	+676	+426	−424	+374	9·3
1962	−236	+743	+247	−419	+335	8·2
1963	−335	+828	+278	−441	+330	7·6
1964	−399	+895	+132	−489	+159	3·2
1965	−312	+991	+175	−537	+317	6·3

Source: Economic Trends, June 1966, p. xii; *U.K. Balance of Payments 1965*, p. 1.

Big capital outflows, then, are the effect of British difficulties with growth and the current balance, rather than their cause. Trends in the distribution of private investment overseas, however, *are* disturbing. First, in 1963-4, only 27 per cent of private investment overseas went to underdeveloped countries, and the absolute figure was half the 1960-1 level.[1] Second, the distribution of U.K. assets among countries is no better related to profitability than to aid policy; in 1962, Canada and the U.S. accounted for 28·2 per cent of the book value of U.K. capital overseas, but only 14·6 per cent of earnings on such capital.[2] Third, some British overseas investment may be traditional, or automatic replacement, or just ill-informed about domestic opportunities; Major calculates that 'in 1962 and 1963 British investment overseas was earning just under 8½ per cent per annum and foreign investment in Britain about 10½ per cent',[3] despite the relative sluggishness of the British economy then.

The balance of payments statistics, then, suggest that capital account is effect rather than cause of current account positions; that the Government balance is a policy variable that we need not subordinate to our reserve position unless we so wish; that the trade balance, while far better than in 1900-39, has deteriorated since 1959 owing principally to excessive rises in costs per unit of output, both of exports relative to competitors' exports and of home output relative to imports; and that the private services balance has deteriorated owing to world political change, and (except for tourism) will gain little from guts, etc., in the U.K. All this suggests the slightly paradoxical conclusion that the trade balance, so much better than pre-war, is susceptible of improvement, while Government, services and capital accounts, so much worse than pre-war, are not to blame for our unsatisfactory foreign balance except in a purely arithmetical sense.

5. EQUALITY

(a) Some problems of the British data

We pass now to objectives of policy where methods of measurement are much more controversial, evidence scanty, and pre-war and foreign comparisons almost non-existent. These sections will be shorter and

---

[1] *U.K. Balance of Payments 1965*, pp. 14, 26.
[2] Major, in Beckerman, op. cit., p. 137.
[3] *Ibid.*, p. 136.

more tentative than the first four, though the objectives discussed are probably even more important.

To assess overall inequality, Lorenz curves of distribution for various years, and to various groups, should be examined. Different results are obtained for wealth, income from property (less related to effort, and hence more inegalitarian for the same Lorenz coefficient, than other income), total income, and spending. The basic data comes from Inland Revenue (IR) surveys (1949-50, 1954-5, 1959-60, and yearly since 1962-3); only recently has IR found that distribution estimates for years between surveys were unreliable,[1] so that some earlier studies are partly invalidated.

IR surveys concentrate on higher income groups. In 1963-4 all incomes below £275 are excluded, in 1949-50 all below £135. The national accounts (NA) data for distribution of personal disposable income take the limit down to £50, and include types of income (e.g. social security benefits) left out by IR; but NA is even more aggregative than IR, and, before 1963, includes at least three months based on unreliable non-survey IR data (because the IR tax year ends on 31st March, but the NA year on 31st December). None of these sets of data casts much light on income distribution among the bottom 70 per cent, even on the income receivers who *are* considered.

Relative price changes create a further problem. Given the distribution of money income, how does one allow for inflation, at different rates for different commodities? One must select a 'bundle' for each main income group. The choice of base-year, and hence of weights, makes an enormous difference to relative rises in real income for various groups.[2]

Even if all this is somehow solved, we should convert income into benefit before assessing distribution. Lydall (1959) allows for numerous types of benefit, but a major component of inequality is undistributed profit. Here one cannot do right. If it is added to income before measuring the distribution of benefit, we artificially increase measured inequality with something not affecting current spending power. If we exclude it, we artificially reduce measured inequality by completely failing to allow

---

[1] IR *108th Annual Report* (for year ended 31st March, 1965), p. 79.

[2] H. Lydall, Size Distribution of Income, *Jnl. Roy. Stat. Soc.* (A), 1959, p. 11, gets almost identical price rises for rich and poor households, 1938-49, on a 1953 base. D. Seers, *Levelling of Incomes since 1938*, Blackwell, 1951, p. 21, on a 1938 base (and somewhat different definitions—and price data that reflects different commodities for rich and poor) but for the same period, shows a 10 per cent faster price rise for the rich!

for the main possible source of capital gains.[1] The latter, when realized, do confer spending power, and their omission seems so serious that we prefer the second horn of the dilemma; but there is no right answer.

Further, an entire book has been devoted to two types of gap between income and benefit necessarily unrecorded in even the finest adjustments of IR-NA data:[2] demographic and tax-evasive. The demographic issues are:

(i) the 'population of tax units' is shifting and uncertain, and the tax unit is an unhappy compromise between individual and family;

(ii) some of the apparent gain in relative income by poorer tax units stems from their more rapid growth of family size, wiping out some of the relative improvement;

(iii) in so far as the relative improvement in income by poorer families since 1938 stems from reduced unemployment, and higher activity rates among women, it conceals relative reduction of leisure time. Titmuss documents many types of tax evasion, but nowhere shows that they (a) are a greater share of income than pre-war, (b) represent a larger share of tax liability for rich than for poor, or (*a fortiori*) (c) have retarded the movement towards equality by becoming available faster to the rich than to the poor.

(b) Distribution of income

After allowing for many forms of incomes untaxed, or otherwise un-allocated by IR-NA data, Lydall concluded that the share of the top per cent of income units in post-tax personal benefit fell from 12·6 per cent in 1938 to 8·0 per cent in 1949, 6·9 per cent in 1954, and 6·4 per cent in 1957. If we include undistributed profits on securities, the corresponding percentages are 15·2, 10·5, 9·6 and 9·1.[3] These attri-

---

[1] See the discussion by T. Barna, Lydall and others, loc. cit., pp. 29-31, 37-39.

[2] R. Titmuss, *Income Distribution and Social Change*, Allen and Unwin, 1963.

[3] Lydall, loc. cit., p. 31. One's faith in this is increased by the rise in the ratio of *employees'* income (including employers' contributions to National Insurance, but excluding income from self-employment) to *total personal income*. This ratio rose from 59·5 per cent in 1938 to 65·2 per cent in 1946, 69·0 per cent in 1950, and over 71 per cent in 1955-64 (*Nat. Inc. and Exp.*, 1956, p. 5; 1961, p. 5; 1965, pp. 4-5; *Mon. Dig. Stat.*, May 1966, pp. 2-3) partly due to higher employment levels. Barna's objection to Lydall—that the ratio of *employment* income to GNP changed little—fails because employment income includes the returns of rich self-employed doctors, lawyers, farmers, etc.—and GNP excludes 'egalitarian' social-service spending. The ratio of employee income to total personal income is therefore a more relevant indicator of 'equality'.

butions allow for changes in prices paid by each of the income groups, but even the second fails to allow for undeclared incomes obtained by tax evasion, especially bogus gifts, transfers and covenants. And the data end in 1957.

In 1957-64, there were some unequalising changes in the tax laws. Incomes became liable to surtax at £5,000 a year instead of £2,000, and it became simpler to evade death duties through gifts *inter vivos*. The Labour Government has passed several measures designed to reverse these trends, including the capital gains tax and the 40 per cent corporation tax—though the betting levy probably affects the poor more than the rich.

More important have been non-tax developments. Since 1956, rent decontrol has steadily raised the share of GNP accruing to landlords. After 1964, a prices and incomes policy that succeeded in holding price rises to about 4 per cent yearly, while earnings grew 8 to 10 per cent and output only 1½ to 2 per cent, meant two years of steady erosion of the profit share.

It is thus high time that Lydall's pioneering work was brought up to date. We do not pretend to do this here.[1] Lorenz curves, however, are given for post-tax income on various definitions (Figs. 14 to 16) and are confined to years now classified by IR as reliable. There is evidence of slight overall income equalisation between 1949-50 and 1953-4, especially at the highest income levels. On IR data, the wealthiest 2·41 per cent after tax received 10·69 per cent of post-tax income in 1949-50; the wealthiest 2·51 per cent in 1963-4 got 'only' 9·22 per cent.[2] On the wider NI concept of disposable incomes over £50 a year, the top 1·75 per cent (of 26,100,000 tax units) in 1949 received 14·5 per cent of disposable income; in 1963 the top 1·81 per cent (of 27,300,000 units) got 'only' 7·78 per cent. The extent to which this huge apparent reduc-

---

[1] Just before this book went to press, the gap was filled by R. J. Nicholson, The Distribution of Personal Income, *Lloyds Bank Review*, Jan. 1967. He showed that the Conservatives' 'tax changes underline the ending of the movement towards equality'. After tax, the top 1 per cent of income recipients got 6·4 per cent of income in 1949, 5·0 per cent in 1957, but 5·2 per cent in 1963; the top 5 per cent received, respectively, 17·7 per cent, 14·9 per cent and 15·7 per cent; but the bottom 30 per cent got 14·6 per cent in 1949, 13·4 per cent in 1957, and only 11·8 per cent in 1963.

[2] This is, of course, spurious accuracy—given only to make it clear that the trend is unambiguously (if very slightly) equalising. Sources as Table. The totals of taxable incomes were close (20,842,500 in 1963-4, and 20,050,000 in 1949-50). Many poor households, however, are excluded from both sets of data.

G*

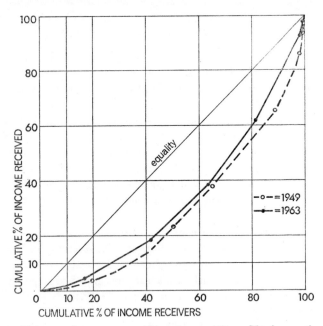

Figure 14 Lorenz curves for post-tax 'disposable incomes' (National Income concept) over £50 a year after tax. Some increase in equality, especially among higher incomes.

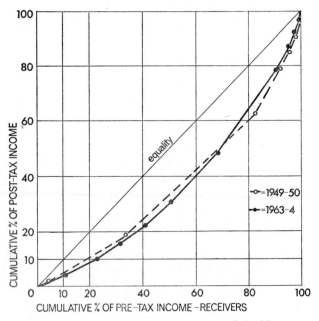

Figure 15 Lorenz curves, 1949–50 and 1963–64: Inland Revenue concept (taxable incomes). Clear evidence of increasing equality among very high incomes; some suggestion of less equality among lower incomes.

tion in inequality is bogus—attributable to demography, changes in the tax base, or evasion—must be a matter of opinion; mine is that it cannot be total.

Other, more partial indicators confirm this view. We compared hourly and weekly earnings of 18 main industrial groups in the periods 1948-65, for men and women. Since 1960 only, the rank correlation

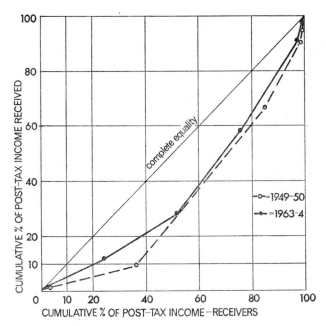

Figure 16 Lorenz curves: post-tax receivers and post-tax income; Inland Revenue concept. Slight equalisation at all levels.

coefficients between initial levels of earnings and their rates of change are uniformly significant and negative. In the period from April 1960 to October 1965, for example, over 56 per cent of ranking of industrial groups by *growth* of male hourly earnings is associated with ranking by *lowness of initial levels* of such earnings.[1]

[1] Data from *Statistics of Prices* . . ., Min. of Lab., June 1966. The *simple* correlation coefficients, April 1960-October 1965, between initial levels and growth rates, are: male weekly earnings, −·594; hourly, −·409; female hourly, −·296; weekly, −·124.

The pre-tax rewards of many identifiably underprivileged groups, too, have risen faster than disposable income as a whole. From 1952 to 1965, personal disposable income per head rose by 144 per cent, but retirement pensions by 167 per cent for a single person and 160 per cent for a couple.[1] True, the price of typical consumer goods also rose rather faster for pensioners in this period,[2] but selective price rises are avoidable by substitution in a more real sense than 'Let them eat cake' cynically suggests. Moreover, the burden of taxes is smaller upon very low incomes. In 1948-49, direct and indirect taxes took 24·8 per cent of incomes below £135 per year, 34·3 per cent of incomes of £750 to £1,000, and 89·1 per cent of incomes above £20,000.[3] Since 1953 taxes on essentials have been much reduced. This equalising effect must be set against any possible unequalising results of relative price movements, and the greater jerkiness of pension rises and hence their relatively more severe erosion by gradual price inflation.

In the long run, price movements in a growing economy must be equalising. As incomes grow, demand rises for butter relative to margarine; margarine therefore become relatively cheaper, so that the real income share of margarine-eaters rises relative to their money income share. Seers estimates that from 1938 to 1949 'upper-middle class prices' rose 113 per cent, 'lower-middle class prices' 85 per cent, and 'working-class prices' only 81 per cent.[4] (This reinforces the long-run links between growth and equality; see pp. 233-7 below.)

(c) Distribution of Wealth

Table 28 summarises our limited information. It suggests that:

(i) Wealth is distributed much less equally among persons than income;

(ii) Inequality of wealth has declined, but the decline has been mainly confined to the very rich;

[1] *Ann. Abst. Stat.*, 1965; *Mon. Dig. Stat.*, May 1966, pp. 11, 2; *Nat. Inc. Exp. 1961*, p. 5.

[2] J. Hughes and K. Alexander, *A Plan for Incomes*, Fabian Research Series no. 247, 1965, p. 7, state that pensioner households' prices rose 60 per cent from January 1952 to January 1964, and high-income households' prices only 40 per cent, as against 48 per cent for retail prices as a whole. Calculations by T. Lynes suggest a price rise of 83 per cent for retail prices and 99 per cent for 'low-income-group' prices, 1948-65: M. F. W. Hemming, Social Security in Britain and Other Countries, *Nat. Inst. Ec. Rev.*, Aug. 1965, p. 64.

[3] D. J. Robertson, *Economics of Wages and the Distribution of Income*, Macmillan, 1961, p. 174.

[4] Seers, op. cit., pp. 21-2.

(iii) Although post-tax income is more evenly distributed in the U.K. than in the U.S., capital is much less equally distributed here.

The first finding is not confined to the U.K. It is hard to be happy about it. Inequality of earned income reflects one's own effort and usefulness; of wealth, of those of one's ancestors. The effect is worsened

TABLE 28: ESTIMATES OF CAPITAL DISTRIBUTION

Date	Source	Coverage	Proportion of wealth considered that was owned by:		
			Top 1%	*Top 5%*	*Top 10%*
1911–13	MR	U.K.	69	87	92
1911–13	LT	E.W.	65·5	86·0	90·0
1924–30	LT	E.W.	59·5	82·5	89·5
1936	LT	E.W.	56	81	88
1936–8	MR	U.K.	56	79	88
1954	LT	G.B.	43	68	79
1951–6	LT	E.W.	42·0	67·5	79·0
1960	MR	U.K.	42	75	83
1960	IR	U.K. estate-owners	30	53	63
1964	IR	do.	28	48	58
1924	LT	U.S.	32	—	—
1929	LT	U.S.	36	—	—
1954	LT	U.S.	24	—	—

Sources:
MR = J. Meade, *Efficiency, Equality and the Ownership of Property*, Allen and Unwin, 1964, p. 27, based on work by J. Revell.
LT = H. Lydall and D. Tipping, Distribution of Personal Wealth in Britain, *Bull. Ox. Univ. Inst. Stat.*, 1961, pp. 90-92.
IR = Inland Revenue analysis at of estates passing at death (cf. Appendix and Diag. 12).
Coverage: E.W. = England and Wales
G.B. = E.W. plus Scotland
U.K. = G.B. plus N. Ireland

because 'the rich obtain a higher yield . . . partly because better informed . . . (and) partly because with large properties risks can be taken and spread more easily'. Thus at the start of the 1960s the top 1 per cent, 5 per cent and 10 per cent of adults owned, respectively, 'only' 42 per cent, 75 per cent and 83 per cent of wealth, but received 60 per cent, 92 per cent and 99 per cent of property incomes.[1]

The second finding is thrown into relief by Lydall's estimate that, in England and Wales in 1954-6, the bottom 80 per cent of persons aged

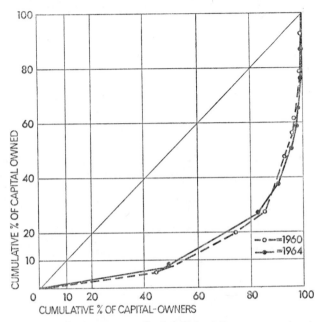

Figure 17 Lorenz curves: Capital (Inland Revenue sample of estates).

25 and over owned only 11 per cent of personal net capital.[2] It is further supported by Harbury's analysis of the wealth of *fathers* of the very rich in 1956-7. He compares his results with Wedgwood's in 1926-7, and shows that for huge estates—over £500,000—the father's wealth had become a much less important determinant of the size of the son's estate, but that this diminution in the role of inheritance became less marked as the size of estate fell.[3] Fig. 17, based on IR data available since

[1] J. E. Meade, *Efficiency, Equality and the Ownership of Property*, Allen and Unwin, 1964, p. 27.

[2] H. F. Lydall and D. G. Tipping, Distribution of Personal Wealth in Britain, *Bull. Ox. Univ. Inst. Stats.*, p. 92.

[3] C. D. Harbury, Inheritance and the Distribution of Personal Wealth, *Econ. Jnl.*, 1962, esp. pp. 853-7. The huge rise in property values distorts some of Harbury's results, but this one appears to survive.

1960, show that the trend continues; 13·2 per cent of wealth was shared among 0·15 per cent of estate-holders in 1960, but 0·22 per cent in 1964.[1] Titmuss, Lydall and others suggest that much of this high-level equalisation stems from gifts *inter vivos* made to escape death duties. Such gifts, however, genuinely increase equality of capital holding, unless the receivers live abnormally long.

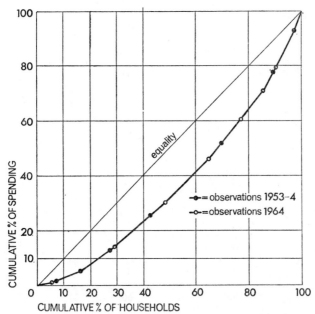

Figure 18 Spending: Ministry of Labour, sample of households. The tiny apparent increase in equality is far smaller than the margin of error of the data (which are much more reliable than those for income or (*a fortiori*) capital distribution.)

(d) Distribution of spending

Since most saving is done by the richest, while the poorest spend more than they earn, expenditure is much more evenly distributed than income. Since 1953-4, the Ministry of Labour has carried out household expenditure surveys, which show total spending and its distribution for various income groups.

[1] See Appendix. Spurious accuracy does not invalidate the result. Equality seems to exceed the Meade-Revell data, but only because IR data exclude the very poor, who leave no estates at all.

These surveys show great equality among households. Since richer households include more persons, equality is even greater among persons. In 1964, the 1·7 per cent of persons in the very poorest households did 1·4 per cent of total personal spending. The best-off 13·7 per cent of persons spent only 21·8 per cent.

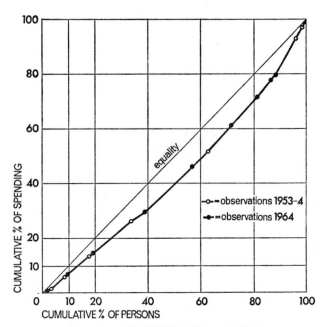

Figure 19 Spending: Ministry of Labour, sample of persons. Big households are richer households. Therefore, spending is distributed among persons even more equally than among small households. Changes in interpersonal distribution of spending 1953–64 are negligible. Prices, however, probably rose much faster for goods bought by poor people!

Things cannot be this good, and they are not. Many rich people own their house. They thus enjoy, rent-free, accommodation at a much higher standard than the poor in their rented dwellings. The rich also own more access to other consumer durables, yielding them benefits unrecorded in expenditure surveys—from cars, television, gardens, libraries, gramophones, yachts. It would be desirable in future surveys to include, in a family's expenditure, imputed spending on some of these (at the going rental or hiring rate for housing, cars, etc.).

The 1964 survey suggests that ownership of consumer durables other than houses is widespread. In London, 78 per cent of households had a television set—even 65 per cent of households with under £10 a week. In rural areas the figures were 78 per cent and 48 per cent. Car ownership was much more sensitive to income. In Greater London only 1 per cent of households earning under £10 per week owned cars, 36 per cent of those with £20 to £30, and 63 per cent of those with over £30. In rural areas the figures were 7 per cent, 50 per cent and 80 per cent respectively.[1]

None of these data refutes the notion of a submerged group without consumer durables, maintaining primitive living standards only through chronic debt.[2] The 1964 survey[3] revealed 5·1 per cent of households, containing 1·7 per cent of the population, in squalor. These people were mostly lonely old women (104 persons per 100 households, of whom 78 were over 65, and only 22 men). They received, on average, £4 2s. 10½d. per household per week, but spent £5 7s. 10d.

Figs. 13-14 show no recognisable shift in distribution of money outlay, among either persons or households, between 1953-4 and 1964. Prices, however, have risen faster for lower income groups (p. 190). Thus real spending, while quite egalitarian due to debt, may have been growing less so. On the other hand, rising and slightly more evenly distributed incomes have meant much wider distribution of consumer durables. It is equalising for over 70 per cent of households to receive TV programmes.

(e) *Equality: conclusions*

There is plenty wrong with the data, but the message is clear, and the reasons plain. The message: growing equality during the period 1938-57. The reasons: full employment and hence strengthening of labour *vis-à-vis* capital, and elimination of the huge dole class that were the main cause of extreme poverty; to a small extent also surtax and death duties. The evidence: employee income, and social security payments, rising faster than other incomes; and the following table:

---

[1] Ministry of Labour, *Family Expenditure Survey 1964*, p. 28. The distribution among *persons* is again far more egalitarian than among *households*.
[2] See *inter alia*, Cole and Utting, *Economic Circumstances of Old People*; P. Townsend, *The Last Refuge*.
[3] Ministry of Labour, loc. cit., Table 2.

TABLE 29: EQUALISATION SINCE 1938

Item	Share of top 1 per cent		Share of top 10 per cent	
	About 1938	About 1960	About 1938	About 1960
Property income	?	60·0	?	99·0
Capital	56·0	42·0	88·0	83·0
'Personal benefit' (a)	15·2	9·1	?	?
'Personal benefit' (b)	12·6	6·4	?	?
Post-tax income	16·2	8·0	38·0	28·0
Household spending	?	3·7	?	20·8
Personal spending	?	2·8	?	18·0

Sources: Lydall, *J.R.S.S.* (A), Part 1, 1959; Meade, op. cit., p. 27; Ministry of Labour, *Family Expenditure Survey 1964*; Lydall and Tipping, *Bull. Ox. Univ. Inst. Stats.*, 1961, no. 2.

Note: (a) includes, (b) excludes undistributed profit.

(*f*) *Appendix*

The following tables show how the Lorenz curves were obtained.

APPENDIX TABLE I: LORENZ CURVES, POST-TAX INCOME DISTRIBUTION

Figure 16 — 14 — 1949 NA		Figure 16 — 15 — 1949-50 IR (General % of)		Figure 15 — 15 — 1949-50 IR		Figure 16 — 14 — 1963 NA		Figure 16 — 1963-4 IR (General % of)		Figure 15 — 15 — 1963-4 IR	
Post-tax receivers	Post-tax disp. income	Post-tax receivers	Post-tax disp. income	Pre-tax receivers	Post-tax disp. income	Post-tax receivers	Post-tax disp. income	Post-tax receivers	Post-tax disp. income	Post-tax receivers	Post-tax disp. income
49·96	23·70	3·96	1·58	3·69	1·46	16·34	4·55	24·66	11·65	2·13	0·73
88·81	65·14	35·64	19·28	32·54	17·12	41·10	18·24	51·82	32·32	11·51	4·61
96·55	80·09	85·00	66·93	81·72	62·67	63·15	38·37	75·80	57·67	21·19	9·62
98·24(a)	85·42	97·59(b)	89·31	92·81	79·16	81·26	61·23	97·49(b)	90·78	30·73	15·59
99·66	93·41	99·55	96·64	95·84	85·07	98·19(a)	92·11	99·57	92·23	40·69	22·91
99·98	98·65	99·97	99·70	98·03	90·66	99·68	97·63	99·92	99·32	50·21	30·92
99·999	99·898	99·999	99·993	98·83	93·33	99·95	99·47	100·00	100·00	68·32	49·07
100·00	100·00	100·00	100·00	99·44(c)	96·01	100·00	100·00			91·03	78·83
				99·78	98·10					95·98	87·54
				99·94	99·42					98·27	92·72
				99·999	99·873					99·36(c)	96·33
				100·00	100·00					99·37	98·93
										99·98	99·75

Sources: National Accounts (NA) from *Nat. Income and Expenditure,* 1959, table 87; and *108th Report* ...; Cmd. 8726 of 1953, table 87; and *108th Report* ..., Cmd. 2876, table 60.

Note: IR data cover income over the lower tax exemption limit: £135 pre-tax in 1949-50, £275 in 1963-4. NA data include, further, £1,571m. of exempt income for 1949 and £4,308m. in 1963, in particular (a) incomes between £50 per year and the IR limit; (b) social-security benefits; (c) scholarships, etc., and (d) income in kind of agricultural workers and domestic servants.

Before 1962, IR data are reliable only for years starting on 31st March, 1949, 1954 and 1959. NA data are based on IR data for over 90 per cent of the income covered. See Commissioners, *108th Report,* Cmd. 2876 of 1966, p. 79.

(a), (b), (c): these three pairs show unambiguous changes—all equalising—in income distribution. At the later date, in each case, a smaller group, of the relatively poor, is getting a bigger income share. The tax base, population and income are all different, however.

APPENDIX TABLE 2: LORENZ CURVES FOR INHERITED ESTATES

Cumulative percentage of

Owners 1960	Estate value owned 1960	Owners 1964	Estate value owned 1964
50·22	7·50	44·22	5·41
82·67	27·12	73·48	19·73
90·15	37·27	85·50	32·13
95·50	50·75	93·73	47·52
97·25	58·32	96·20	55·56
98·06	63·10	97·33	60·97
98·54	66·93	97·97	64·95
99·49	78·44	99·26	77·23
99·85	*86·91*	*99·78*	*86·92*
99·96	*92·79*	*99·94*	*92·80*
100·00	100·00	100·00	100·00

Source: Dept. of Inland Revenue, *Annual Report: No. 108* (Cmd. 2876 of Feb. 1966).

Italicized rows show unambiguous (but tiny and unreliable) equalisation.

APPENDIX TABLE 3: LORENZ CURVES FOR EXPENDITURE

Cumulative percentage of

1953-4			1964		
Households	Persons	Spending	Households	Persons	Spending
5·79	2·11	1·63	5·09	1·73	1·41
15·69	8·37	6·24	*16·09*	7·76	6·15
26·82	17·89	13·65	28·79	18·71	14·33
42·55	33·42	26·47	48·21	38·88	30·05
69·08	61·78	52·70	64·15	56·52	45·98
89·05	85·32	78·37	76·85	70·87	60·57
97·30	96·30	92·65	84·92	80·94	71·53
99·40	99·20	97·55	90·04	87·26	79·20
100·00	100·00	100·00	100·00	100·00	100·00

Source: Ministry of Labour, *Family Expenditure Surveys*, 1953-4, Table 8; 1964, Table 2.

Italicised totals enable unambiguous (unequalising) comparisons to be made in the row in which they occur.

6. COMPOSITION OF OUTPUT

No single variable and no agreed set of variables can measure the good-ness of a nation's composition of output. We have seen, however, that certain productive activities and certain uses of income tend to be under-valued in mixed economies.

(i) Maldistribution of income underprices goods bought by the poor, and hence discourages their production—a trend reinforced by growing affluence in the community as a whole.

(ii) Advertising *may* discourage personal saving, and form opinions implicitly hostile to forms of activity that are hard to advertise (health, education, research, roads)—especially if they are financed by taxation of incomes otherwise spent on advertised goods.

(iii) Lack of information on the effects of certain forms of consumption (e.g. cigarettes), together with habit, *may* cause such forms of consump-tion to be over-valued by comparison with others.

(iv) Preference for the present over the future *may* cause under-investment.

In this context, we examine three relevant uses of resources: social security, advertising and investment.

(a) Social security

'Provision for medical care is now more comprehensive and generous in Britain than in most other countries, but as regards cash support [during] interruption and cessation of earnings Britain no longer stands in the vanguard . . . Family allowances . . . in most European and the older Commonwealth countries [are] considerably more generous than in [Britain] . . . The proportion of national resources devoted to social services is very much lower in this country than in any of the Common Market countries.'[1]

For instance, the ratio of unemployment and sickness benefits to normal earnings is lower in the U.K. than in W. Germany, France, Belgium or Italy. The shares of GNP devoted to social cash benefits (social insurance, national assistance and family allowances) in 1960 were: W. Germany 10·4 per cent, Australia 9·2, Sweden 9·1, France 8·3, Italy 7·9, U.K. 6·4, Canada 6·3, U.S.A. 4·1. Users of private beds and public schools are thus mistaken in their belief that the U.K.'s

[1] M. G. W. Hemming, Social Security in Britain and certain other countries, *Nat. Inst. Econ. Rev.*, Aug. 1965. If free school milk and subsidies on school meals are included, British family allowances are much closer to Continental levels.

'poor' performance *vis-à-vis* W. Germany, France and Italy springs from recklessly feather-bedded social services.

The share of British efforts devoted to helping those in need, if still low by European standards, has been rising. Social cash benefits were 4·6 per cent of GNP in 1938, 5·1 per cent in 1957 and 6·8 per cent in 1963. After we make allowance for faster inflation in goods bought by the poor, we find that a sick or jobless man, married with two children, receiving insurance benefit enjoyed only 38·1 per cent of the real earnings of his healthy, working counterpart in 1948, but 47·0 per cent in 1965.[1]

Public outlays on health rose accordingly, from 3·3 per cent of GNP (in current prices) in 1955 to 3·9 per cent in 1963 and 1964. Most of the expansion came from new hospital building, sadly neglected until the early 1960s. Other forms of Government outlay designed to spread opportunities have also outpaced GNP. The share of GNP spent on education was 3·4 per cent in 1955-6 and 4·2 per cent in 1964-5, though in both periods only 0·6 per cent was for investment. The share of GNP spent by the Government on libraries, museums and the arts had rocketed to 0·2 per cent by 1965.[2]

(b) *Advertising, consumption and saving*

Money devoted to advertising corresponds to use of scarce resources of printing equipment, businessmen, copywriters, newsprint and television time. The share of GNP devoted to all forms of advertising and sales promotion in 1964 was 2·2 per cent,[3] less than in the U.S.A. (2·9) but about twice as high as W. Germany and three times as high as France. This rate was significantly above earlier levels (2·0 per cent in 1938, 1·5 per cent in 1950), and concentrated on promoting economically unimportant products: 15 to 20 per cent of toiletry costs are for advertising.[4] About half these outlays are for non-controversial, largely informative advertising (trade, classified, financial, etc.)[5]. Part of the rest—and a growing part—is downright anti-economic, conferring subjective glamour upon products physically and chemically identical with cheaper substitutes. Far too much national effort goes to make,

[1] Hemming, loc cit., pp. 65, 67. Earnings *after* tax, plus family allowances.

[2] All data are in current prices. Changes may partly reflect changes in relative prices. *Nat. Inc. Exp. 1965*, Table 48; *Economic Report for 1965*, H.M. Treasury, 1966.

[3] *The Times*, 13 May, 1965.

[4] *The Economist*, 17 July, 1965.

[5] M. Corden, *A Tax on Advertising?*, Fabian Society, 1961, p. 3.

or buy from abroad, overpriced and oversold duplicates of cheaper petrols, aspirins, Epsom salts and soap powders. Some effort, too, is wasted absolutely on useless products, such as baldness 'cures'. This is no fault of the advertisers, but of the products they support.

Advertising has raised its share in GNP, and has promoted wasteful competition among identical products (petrols, detergents) to the detriment both of cheaper identical substitutes and of rival forms of competition in price, service and genuine differentiation of product. Advertising has certainly not, however, outweighed the pressures towards higher personal saving. With State commitment to full employment, and problems of excess demand for domestic and imported goods alike, a rising ratio of personal saving to personal disposable income is a substitute for higher taxes (forced, public saving)—and an unambiguous improvement in the composition of resource use. This ratio steadily grew from 4·2 per cent in 1955 to 8·1 per cent in 1964.[1] New savings outlets like life insurance and unit trusts, rising interest rates, and growing affluence have outweighed the discouragements to personal saving provided by advertising, leisure and the Joneses.

The make-up of consumption depends on free choice modified by indirect taxes and the state of information (or delusion). Most smokers wish they were not; the fact that spending on tobacco (at 1958 prices) fell steadily, by 9·4 per cent, from 1961 to 1965 represents a clear improvement. Moderate consumption of cigarettes causes moderate increases in the risk of lung cancer, bronchitis and coronary thrombosis; moderate drinking is probably harmless, so the steady rise—at the pace of total consumption—in real spending on alcohol (one-third from 1955 to 1965) need not cause too much concern. Consumer spending on alcohol and tobacco in 1965 was worth 8·5 per cent of GDP (in constant prices of 1958)—as against 9·2 per cent in 1955.[2] Of course most of this is a transfer to the Government, via taxation. However, most people would regard it as too large a share of consumer spending.

'Too small', and declining, is spending on books, papers and magazines—no higher, in 1958 prices, in 1964 than in 1955, and only 1·2 per cent of 1964 consumer outlay. Happily growing is the volume of consumer spending abroad—almost 79 per cent up in volume from 1953 to

---

[1] *Economic Trends*, Oct. 1965, p. xii; *Economic Survey 1965*, p. 7.
[2] *Nat. Inst. Econ. Rev.* May 1966. The shares of consumer spending—also in 1958 prices—were for tobacco, 6·7 per cent in 1955 and 5·3 per cent in 1965; for alcohol, 6·1 per cent at both dates.

1964. If only foreign spending in the U.K. kept up with this! In general, the growth of consumer information (if largely confined to the middle class and hence 'unequalising') has reduced buyers' regret substantially, and probably improved output composition somewhat.

(c) Investment and sacrifice

'In most countries, the ratio of the value of capital to yearly gross output is between 3 and 4. In industrial economies, about 3 per cent of capital stock—10 per cent of gross output—wears out each year. A country investing only 10 per cent of gross output can, therefore, expect no growth. For each 3 to 4 per cent of yearly gross output invested above 10 per cent, it can expect growth of around 1 per cent yearly. In the mid-1950s, Germany and Japan devoted over 25 per cent of GNP at current factor cost, to gross investment; Italy, 23 per cent; France and the U.S.A., about a fifth; and the U.K. around 16 per cent. Subsequent growth performances are thus explained.'

Thus argues the capital-centred model, which is the basis of very many criticisms of British output composition. Careful study of the data modifies it almost out of existence, because

(i) it is out-of-date in view of Britain's rising ratio of investment to output since 1954;

(ii) it ignores the special and increasing cheapness of investment in the U.K. relative to consumption;

(iii) it neglects investment composition—directed much more towards production in the U.K.;

(iv) it concentrates on physical investment, ignoring Government civil spending with similar effects upon output.

Behind these facts lie two theoretical points. The capital-centred model neglects labour inputs, and economies of scale. Thus it cannot explain Beckerman's finding that faster-growing economies (and sectors within a single economy) have lower requirements of extra capital per extra unit of output.[1] Second, the model works with values of capital and output; Professor Joan Robinson has often pointed out that the relation between these values cannot be treated as any sort of production function, since capital value depends on expected yield, which depends partly on expected output, which in turn depends on current and past output.

[1] Beckerman, op. cit., pp. 27, 31.

In Table 30, we try to allow for (i)—(iii) above. The corrections reinforce the theoretical points, since they show that the true addition to productive capital stock, as a proportion of GNP and in 'standard' prices, has not differed nearly enough to explain variations among countries in growth rates. However, it remains true that extra capital produces extra output—that no economy operates with fixed factor proportions in all sectors and completely immobile factors among them.

(i) Despite Britain's slow growth in 1955-64, she showed enough guts,

TABLE 30: SHARES OF GROSS INVESTMENT IN OUTPUT

(Gross domestic investment as percentage of gross
national product at market prices)

	1	2	3	4	5	6
					'European'	
	Current prices		*1958 prices*		*prices of 1955*	
	1955	*1964*	*1955*	*1964*	*1955*	*1964*
France						
Total	17·9	20·9	17·6	21·8	17·7	22·1
Equipment	8·0	8·8	7·5	9·4	9·2	11·3
Construction	9·9	12·1	10·1	12·2	8·5	10·6
Germany						
Total	22·2	26·4	21·8	25·7	22·3	26·3
Equipment	11·7	12·5	11·4	13·9	11·4	13·9
Construction	10·5	13·9	10·4	11·8	10·9	12·3
Italy						
Total	19·9	21·1	19·6	21·2	20·9	22·7
Equipment	8·8	7·6	8·5	8·9	7·6	7·9
Construction	11·1	13·5	11·1	12·4	13·3	14·9
U.K.						
Total	14·5	17·6	14·2	18·4	15·6	20·2
Equipment	7·4	8·5	7·3	9·0	9·2	11·3
Construction	7·2	9·2	6·8	9·4	6·4	8·7

Sources and methods: Current-price and 1958-price data: O.E.C.D., *Statistics of National Accounts 1955-64*, Paris, 1966, converting French and German 1955 data to the 1964 basis at 1960 $\frac{\text{new area}}{\text{old area}}$ ratio for W. Germany (data excluding and including Saar and W. Berlin from *Statistisches Jahrbuch, 1965*, p. 560) and 1959 postrevision/prerevision ratio (both sets of data from O.E.C.D., *Statistics of National Accounts 1950-1961*, Paris, 1964). European-price data: M. Gilbert et al., *National Products and Price Levels*, O.E.C.D., 1958, p. 87 for 1955, correcting French and German data as above; for 1964, Gilbert's data were multiplied by the national ratios, for each component, of 1964 to 1955 values at constant prices of 1958.

etc., to sacrifice much current consumption. The U.K. raised the ratio of investment to output more than any European competitor (Table 30). On the capital-centred model, this should have brought a great upthrust of real incomes. 1950-55 featured a ratio of gross investment to GNP at factor cost of about 15 per cent; 1960-65, around 20 per cent. Thus *net* investment rose from around 5 per cent to 10 per cent, so that the growth rate should have doubled. Instead it has fallen, while the European economies, with far slower accelerations of net investment since 1955, have maintained growth.

This conclusion is strengthened if investment and output are measured in national prices of 1958 (col. 3 and 4 of Table 30). It becomes stronger still when each country's investment and output are measured in standard prices.

(ii) In 1955, M. Gilbert revalued the outputs of several European economies at standard prices. He valued both investment and total output of each country at the European average price of the goods and services concerned. Thus comparisons can be made in real terms.[1] Poorer countries have relatively abundant labour and scarce capital. Both capital-intensive goods and investment goods themselves are therefore dearer relative to GNP. Even in 1955, this effect was modified by investment subsidies and by purchase taxes on consumer goods. Nevertheless, the true investment ratio in the U.K. in 1955 (Table 30, col. 5) was less unfavourable for the U.K. than the crude ratios (cols. 1 and 3), especially for equipment. By 1964, the U.K. had made investment goods even cheaper, relative to consumer goods, than before—by out-inflating Europe in consumer goods but not in producer goods. Again the movement of 'relative price relatives' was sharpest for investment in equipment. Thus not only did the U.K. improve her investment/output ratio in constant national prices (cols. 3 and 4) faster than her current price ratio, while competitors performed less well; at standardised European prices she did better still (cols. 5 and 6) by comparison with France, Germany and Italy.

(iii) Hardly any investment is completely unproductive. Some forms are more productive than others—and some investment yields benefits not wholly counted as part of GNP. Several analysts have excluded dwellings from investment when assessing its impact on GNP, a strange

---

[1] M. Gilbert and associates, *National Products and Price Levels*, Paris, 1958. Following his methods, we show proportions of GNP at market prices in Table 30, though factor cost, as in Table 31, might be more appropriate (why?).

procedure, since dwellings produce an output of servic⸍
rents (or, for owner-occupied homes, imputed rents) wh′
in GNP. Whenever the real rate of return on allegedly
investment is calculated, it turns out to be astonishingly ｌⅈ
market rate, even in the public sector.[1] It remains true, howe⸱
some investments (schools, hospitals) are made for their intrinsic
well as their instrumental value. Because they yield human happiness
not measured in national accounts data, a sub-normal addition to GNP
per £ of investment is acceptable and accepted. This does not apply to
plant and machinery—'equipment'.

A crude but tolerable approximation can thus be made by treating
equipment as proxy for ultra-productive, purely instrumental investment, and construction as proxy for intrinsic, low-yield projects.
This is better than the division into dwelling and non-dwelling investment.
Many non-dwelling constructions are largely intrinsic (though docks and
roads are not). Even new, pleasanter factories include an element of
disguised wage rises.[2]

When this distinction is followed out, Britian's share of effort devoted
to ultra-productive investment in 1964, as in 1955, compares favourably
with the bigger European competitors. The notion that Britain fritters
away her investment effort on unproductive purposes, while her rivals
install new machines, is a myth. It is in constructional investment that
Britain lags far behind Europe. Moreover, the depreciation rate in
Europe and Japan is 11-12 per cent of GNP, as against 9-10 per cent in
the U.K. Equipment depreciates much faster than buildings. So British
ultra-productive investment, net, is probably *higher* than that of our
main European rivals relative to GNP. It is our use of investment which
is less satisfactory, and its allocation among industries.

(iv) A parallel myth is that sacrifices from private consumption in
Britain are wasted in current public spending. The part of this item that
contributes to output is shown in col. 3 of Table 31. Most of this raises
future production—through education, health, maintenance of roads,
etc. Such uses of resources have as much right to be treated as productive sacrifices out of current consumption as have most forms of
constructional investment. Teachers' pay, like that of builders of

[1] See, for example, M. E. Beesley and C. Foster, *Jnl. Roy. Stat. Soc.* (*A*),
1963, on the Victoria Line; or M. Blaug, *Manchester School*, 1965, on secondary
education.
[2] A point made by Sir John Hicks in conversation.

TABLE 31: 'SACRIFICE' OUTLAYS AND OUTPUT STRUCTURE, 1956-64

(Percentages of GNP at factor cost)

Country	Prices	Year	1 Gross domestic investment — Equipment	2 Gross domestic investment — Construction	3 Govt. civil spending (current)	4 Total of 1 to 3	5 Govt. defence	6 Balance of payments surplus (current account)	7 Stock investment	8 Total of 5 to 7	9 Total of 4 to 8
France	Current	1956	9·8	11·6	8·7	30·1	7·6	−1·5	2·1	8·1	38·2
		1960	9·9	12·0	9·1	31·0	6·5	−2·0	2·8	11·3	42·3
		1964	10·5	14·3	10·6	35·4	5·2	−0·1	2·0	7·1	42·5
	Constant of 1958	1956	9·9	13·3	10·2	34·0	8·7	−1·9	2·5	9·3	43·3
		1960	11·1	12·4	8·7	31·0	6·7	−1·5	2·8	11·0	42·0
		1964	13·6	14·5	9·2	34·8	5·3	−0·9	2·2	6·6	41·4
Germany	Current	1956	13·9	12·5	11·9	38·0	3·1	3·4	2·4	8·9	46·9
		1960	13·9	13·7	12·1	39·7	3·7	2·8	3·4	9·9	49·6
		1964	14·4	16·1	12·8	43·8	4·5	1·8	1·3	7·6	50·9
	Constant of 1958	1956	13·3	12·4	12·1	37·8	3·1	4·1	2·2	9·4	47·2
		1960	14·4	12·6	11·9	38·9	3·6	2·5	3·5	9·6	48·5
		1964	16·1	13·6	12·2	41·9	4·3	−0·2	1·6	5·7	47·6
Italy	Current	1956	10·4	13·0	11·3	34·7	3·8	−1·3	0·8	3·7	38·4
		1960	10·7	14·6	12·7	38·0	4·2	0·3	1·7	5·8	43·8
		1964	8·7	15·3	15·2	39·2	3·6	0·6	0·6	5·1	44·3
	Constant of 1958	1956	10·1	12·3	11·2	33·6	4·2	−0·9	0·8	4·1	37·7
		1960	11·1	14·5	12·0	37·0	3·6	−0·1	1·9	5·4	42·4
		1964	10·2	14·2	12·4	36·8	2·9	−0·3	0·6	3·2	40·0

Country	Type	Year										
U.S.A.	Current	1956	6·8(a)		12·9	8·1(a)	27·8	10·5	1·0	1·1	12·6	40·4
		1960	6·5(a)		11·9	9·7(a)	28·1	9·9	0·9	0·8	11·6	39·7
		1964	6·8(a)		11·7	11·5(a)	30·0	8·9	1·4	0·7	11·0	41·0
	Constant of 1958	1956	7·0(a)		12·8	8·3(a)	28·1	9·8	1·2	1·1	13·2	41·3
		1960	6·6(a)		12·0	9·3(a)	27·9	8·9	0·9	0·8	11·5	39·4
		1964	7·2(a)		11·4	10·4(a)	29·0	8·9	1·6	0·7	11·2	40·2
Japan	Current	1956		25·1		9·0	34·1	1·7	0·2	7·7	9·6	43·7
		1960		33·5		8·0	41·5	2·4	0·6	6·1	9·1	50·6
		1964		36·6		8·2(a)	44·8	1·2	−0·5	5·7	6·4	51·2
	Constant of 1958	1956		23·4		9·1	32·5	1·7	1·4	7·5	10·6	43·1
		1960		34·1		8·1	42·2	2·4	−0·7	6·3	8·0	50·2
		1964		41·0		8·6	49·6	1·1	1·4	6·7	9·2	58·8
U.K.	Current	1956	8·6		8·2	10·4	27·2	8·4	1·5	1·4	11·3	38·5
		1960	9·4		8·6	11·5	29·5	6·9	−0·6	2·6	8·9	38·4
		1964	9·6		10·4	12·2	33·2	6·7	−0·6	1·8	7·9	40·1
	Constant of 1958	1956	8·5		7·9	10·6	27·0	8·6	2·1	1·2	11·9	38·9
		1960	9·7		8·9	10·8	29·4	6·7	−0·4	2·7	9·0	38·4
		1964	10·2		10·7	10·7	31·6	6·2	−0·2	1·9	7·9	39·5

Sources and Methods: Data form O.E.C.D., *Statistics of National Accounts 1955-64*, Paris, 1966, amended as follows:

France—1956 data made comparable with later data by multiplying each component by its 1959 $\dfrac{\text{new method}}{\text{old method}}$ *current-price* value ratio from O.E.C.D. *Statistics of National Accounts 1950-61*, Paris, 1964.

Germany—1956 data made comparable by multiplying each component by its own 1960 $\dfrac{\text{new area}}{\text{old area}}$ value ratio from *Statistisches Jahrbuch . . . 1965*, Bonn, 1966, pp. 560, 552-4.

Italy—Government defence expenditure from *Nippon Times*, 28 Feb, 1956; *Japan Times*, 14 Jan., 1960, 29 Dec., 1964. For Japan and Italy, the ratio of civil to military Government outlays at constant prices is assumed to be the same as at current prices. The same is done for GNP factor-cost/market-price ratios where only market-price data are available at constant prices in the O.E.C.D. data.

Note: (a) U.S. Government expenditure on equipment is included in its current civil spending, not in equipment investment.

concert halls, is partly but not mainly designed to raise future output; both are financed out of the pay of mixers of ice cream.

In 1964, Germany spent 12·8 per cent of current GNP (at factor cost) on Government non-investment civil spending; Italy 15·2 per cent; and Britain 12·2 per cent. Japan (because poorer) and the U.S. (partly for ideological reasons) spent smaller proportions. It is certainly false to say that slow growth in Britain stems from underinvestment in industrial equipment. In so far as a crude explanation in terms of inadequate self-sacrifice makes sense at all, it is productive spending in *lower-yield* sectors that Britain has understressed—current Government outlays and constructional investment. To put it another way: given our labour shortage, British capital costs are too high relative to wages.

The productive sacrifices a country can afford depend on her initial living levels, their growth rate, and the *un*productive sacrifices she makes. In 1955 Britain's initial living levels were higher than her large European rivals'. By 1963 France and W. Germany had overtaken Britain's per-head income (though not Britain's endowment of social capital—homes and roads). Britain's growth we know about. Britain's commitment to unproductive sacrifice is shown in Cols. 5-8 of Table 31. The data, especially Col. 5, speak for themselves.

It is open to anybody to argue that Britain ought to continue to devote 6·7 per cent of GNP at current factor cost to defence, while her major rivals' percentages are 1·2 (Japan), 3·6 (Italy), 4·5 (Germany) and 5·2 (France), as in 1964. But one should not be surprised if such sacrifices, in a fairly free economy, are reflected in lower shares of GNP spent on construction and Government current outlays together (U.K. 22·6 per cent, Italy 28·5, Germany 28·9, France 24·9 per cent). Free consumers will insist on consuming. Competent businessmen, private and public, will choose those investments, in plant and machinery, giving the highest rate of return. Governments will tax to finance construction and civil outlays, but are limited by electoral reality. So these outlays lag behind. When they are *complementary* to spending on equipment, as they are in the training of skilled mechanics or the maintenance of good roads, their neglect makes the yield on new equipment disappointing.

7. CHOICE

Choice is both the process of deciding and the act of selecting. 'Has the range of choice widened or narrowed in post-war Britain?' is thus really two questions. Has the process of reaching decisions become more informed and intelligent, or less so? Has range of choice—the number of decisions that can be implemented—grown or shrunk? In each case we must be clear who we are talking about. It is quite likely that some people's range of choice widened while other people's narrowed. Further, we must limit the areas of choice that we consider, or we shall write an encyclopedia. Some choices (when and whom to marry, how many children to have) are not primarily economic. Some economic choices are not very important. We shall consider two choices: of job and of commodity.

(a) Job choice

Few obvious things—apart from generally rising educational standards —have happened since 1945 to affect the process of deciding what job to seek. The number of decisions that can be implemented depends on training, job availability and demographic factors. Growing specialisation has made it much likelier than in 1939, or even 1959, that a worker will find only one or two employers requiring his particular skill, especially if he is tied to one area by house or school. More slowly, growing educational opportunity has widened the range of jobs to which young people can aspire. For people over thirty, scarcity of re-training opportunities (and hardening of the flexible mental arteries) must reduce the choice of jobs in an increasingly specialist economy.

Less speculative are the effects of job availability in widening the area of choice. In periods and regions of unemployment, people without savings—over half the working population—must take what jobs they can get. When and where unfilled vacancies for an occupation exceed applicants, the only limitation on choice (apart from lack of information) is the similarity of the allegedly alternative jobs. This depends partly on the specificity of a worker's training—a serious restriction on choice of job in Northern England, with its tradition of craft apprenticeships (often in declining industries) and its shortage of high-quality general secondary education.[1] But, given full employment and the range of alternative jobs, the real difference made to a worker by choices within the range depends on the degree of business concentration in the industries offering the jobs.

[1] Of all children aged 13 in 1962, the percentage still at school on the same day in 1964 was: Metropolitan London, 52·2; S.E. England, 47·7; S. England, 43·1; N.W., 32·7; Yorkshire, 29·9; N. England, 24·2. The regional gap has steadily widened since 1953. *Abst. Reg. Stats. 1965*, p. 46.

The balance of evidence on this disputed question suggests a steady increase in industrial concentration over the whole period 1908-66 in the United Kingdom, possibly reversed slightly in 1938-50. The definition and measurement of 'concentration' affects the results. We can measure profits, assets or employment of each firm in an industry. Whichever we measure, we can indicate the share accruing to the biggest three or four firms or else the whole distribution, as indicated by the Lorenz coefficient—plotting, say, the cumulative percentages of building profit (*y*) against the cumulative percentages of firms in the building industry (*x*). Our measure should depend on why we want to know about concentration. In considering job choice, concentration of employment is appropriate. The Lorenz coefficient would be the best indicator, but unfortunately we are forced to rely on data for shares of leading firms, designed to indicate market power. These do at least show the extent to which three or four firms dominate the job market.

From 1935 to 1951, the share of employment offered by the three biggest firms rose in 27 industries and fell in 14.[1] However, concentration in the U.S.—despite the much bigger population, area and market, and harsher anti-trust laws—was greater. In 1951, only 0·2 per cent of British employees (but 4·5 per cent of U.S. employees) worked in industries where over 90 per cent of jobs were with three or fewer firms.[2] The most relevant comparison, West Germany (similar population, area, income and structure), is not available. News of mergers in motors, aircraft, retailing, newspapers and brewing suggests reduction in the average British worker's job choice since 1951, but concentration is news and disaggregation is not. Statistics often confute hunches. The biggest fifty firms had a bigger share of *profits* in 1938 than in 1950, and the Lorenz curve of firms by *market valuation of assets*, while showing steadily rising concentration in 1885-1939, equalised in 1939-50 to its 1924 level.[3]

[1] P. S. Florence, *Economics and Sociology of Industry*, Watts, 1965, p. 84, citing Evely and Little.

[2] W. G. Shepherd, Comparison of Industrial Concentration in the United States and Great Britain, *Rev. Ec. Stat.*, 1961, p. 71.

[3] P. Hart and S. J. Prais, The Analysis of Business Concentration, *Jnl. Roy. Stat. Soc. (A)*, 1956, p. 155; P. Hart, Business Concentration in the U.K., *Jnl. Roy. Stat. Soc. (A)*, 1960, p. 52. However, Hart shows that the top 1 per cent of firms raised their share of corporate profits from 54 per cent in 1927 to 60·5 per cent in 1949 (p. 53) and warns trend-spotters that 'it is necessary to assume that inflation or depression do not favour or disfavour large firms compared with small firms' (p. 51); surely more *small* firms are likely to go bankrupt in depression?

Behind business concentration lie long-run economies of scale. Almost all recent work on production functions, for industries or advanced economies, testifies to their existence.[1] Florence has analysed the technology of production causing such scale economies—the insurance provided by offsetting risks, the transport economies (twice the volume can be carried in a cubic container made of much less than twice the material—why?), etc.[2] The link between specialisation of job, learned efficiency, and standardisation of product means pressures towards industrial concentration that, unless checked, reduce job choice and choice of goods together.

If workforces at two factories are dominated by trade unions with distinct policies, the package of conditions, pay and hours may vary, providing more worker choice. The growing concentration of trade unions, therefore, provides another powerful reducer of job choice. In 1938, there were 1,024 trade unions in the U.K., with 6,053,000 members, of whom 334,000 were in tiny, almost inevitably democratic unions of under 2,500 members each, and 4,391,000 in huge, almost inevitably bureaucratic unions of over 25,000 members. In 1963, the 596 U.K. trade unions had 9,917,000 members (still well under half the number of employees), of whom 236,000 were in unions with under 2,500 members, but 8,609,000 in unions with over 25,000 members. The proportion of unionists in giant unions (over 100,000 members) had risen from 49 per cent in 1938 to 68 per cent in 1963.[3] This doubtless raises the unionist's corporate bargaining power, and helps him to cut hours, raise income and thus increase his range of choice of commodities; but, together with other monopolising union practices (closed shop, the fight against small rival unions, the emphasis on national agreements), it reduces the extent to which, by choosing another employer, a worker can change his conditions of work. The power of shop stewards—apart from their function in adapting over-rigid national agreements to local or industrial scarcities of labour—provides more chance for workers to choose between genuinely different jobs, especially if they can migrate.

Demographic factors are powerful determinants of work choice. Britain's young labour force, produced by the 1945-50 baby bulge, is relatively mobile. Urbanisation means a wider choice of employers

[1] A good summary is A. A. Walters, Cost and Production Functions, *Econometrica*, 1963.

[2] P. S. Florence, *Logic of British and American Industry*, Routledge 1961, pp. 48-55.

[3] *Ann. Abst. Stats., 1954*, p. 115; *1965*, p. 128.

H

within one's area of residence. Against this, the growing rôle of married women in the workforce (p. 129) militates against mobility. They can seldom travel far to a new place of work.

Choice of job is a complex matter, not reducible to a few statistics. Full employment has massively increased the range of choice. Demographic forces are powerful but uncertain in direction. Little can be said about the most important factor of all—choice *at* work. Full employment, shop stewards, more professional managers and more educated workers all increase such choice. However, the same scale economies that caused industrial concentration have produced a big secular fall in self-employed workers as a share of the labour force. Meanwhile the ratio of directly productive workers to clerical workers, and hence the proportion of people who can see the direct relevance of their job to an end-product, has declined.[1] Even workers directly connected with the production process are often assembly-line automata.

These results of specialised, integrated processes are universal, independent of political systems. The answer to the problem of choice at work is participation by workers in controlling the production process, not reversion after the style of William Morris to simple, inefficient primary crafts. How trade unions, shareholders, or public corporations can be induced to transfer power efficiently to workers is the central problem of modern industry, not of growth nor of any -ism. The alternative to solving it is the confinement of choice to consumption and leisure, and growing disaffection of people at work from a process of production that they are patronisingly regarded as too stupid to understand and too insignificant to control. Creative use of leisure is unlikely to be compatible with deprivation of creative choice at work.

(b) Commodity choice

Suppose that the British market demands X pairs of shoes at a certain price, whatever the number of factories or styles. Now the choice of styles when a single factory makes all X *need* not be smaller than when X-production is split among two or twenty plants. However, economies of scale due to standardisation are a major cause of amalgamation of plant; and big, concentrated plant goes together with concentration of firms in an industry,[2] as bigger firms have the cash and the administrators

[1] *Ann. Abst. Stats.*, and Florence, *Economics and Sociology of Industry*, Watts, 1965, pp. 15, 21-2.
[2] P. S. Florence, *ibid.*, pp. 82-3.

to run giant factories. Probably, therefore, concentration of newspaper publishers, brewers and car-makers reduces the number of decisions that can be implemented by buyers of such things.

Sometimes this does not reduce choice, because the products that vanish were effectively identical with those surviving (patent medicines, petrol, detergents, toothpastes). In some cases, such as electric plugs, variety is a nuisance and standardisation welcome as well as merely efficient. Usually, however, concentration of firms genuinely reduces choice by consumers. Indeed, the increase in control over price that accrues to firms with market power is a major reason for growing central restrictions upon monopolies and mergers; this control stems from reduced price-elasticity of demand via elimination (or co-ordinated pricing) of substitutes, formerly marketed independently.

It is a huge question, not relevant here, when scale economies cut costs enough to outweigh growing market power, so that mergers cut rather than raise prices. The point here is that these two results of business concentration (growing market power and scale economies), opposed in their effect on prices, join to reduce the range of purchasable commodities. Suppression of inventions, which is not practicable without a certain amount of concentration, is an extreme and probably very rare case. Comparison of groceries in France, the U.K. and the U.S. is more instructive. Rising scale and market power have meant the progressive disappearance of distinctive tastes in strawberries, beef and cheese. In France, free-range chicken is still generally available; in Britain, mass-produced cardboard chicken dominates; in the U.S. there is no other.

One must retain balance in face of annoyance. If (as with chicken) a protein-bearing food is made much cheaper through the standardising effects of economies of scale, millions of people increase the range of effective choice; only a few suffer. In India the net benefit would be obvious. It is in rich nations, however, that complex, labour-intensive, subtle products are vanishing. They are hard to restore even when the mass market becomes rich enough to afford them. Shall we become a community of millionaires living on colourful cubes of processed plankton?

If the technology and economics of concentration reduce the range of choice, the development of new commodities, mostly by the huge research departments of monopolies, increases it. The great inventions that enhanced choice since 1950 were mainly made before 1939 (television, refrigerators, washing machines, cars). Their post-war irruption into the mass market has two causes. The first is growth itself; the most powerful enlarger of all sorts of choice is real income. The second is 'learning effect' in making new products, substantially cutting production costs. The price of durable consumer goods rose hardly at all after 1956, as against the huge rise in other prices (Table 17). Choice has thus been substantially increased by the appearance of old inventions as marketed innovations, and by cost reductions and income rises enabling consumers to buy them. Paradoxically these last two desirable tendencies can conflict; as income rises, people become less interested in price cuts, and less prepared to search for them, reducing businessmen's incentive to cut costs.

Perhaps the most important influences on the range of commodity choice are nothing to do with commodities themselves. Earlier marriage and childbearing, and the trend to larger families, mean a big but unmeasurable increase in men's choice, and reduction in women's. Women now cook, launder and keep house, at well below market rates, for men who would otherwise have had to fend for themselves. Women's growing participation in the civil labour force similarly reduces their leisure and choice, especially since under a quarter of women are unionised as against almost half the men.[1] Conversely, women's leisure has been increased by a great range of labour-saving household gadgets, owned by more and more people (p. 195); and family leisure, which immensely increases the range of choice, has increased steadily with the falling working week since 1955 (p. 142), though less than in Europe. This rising range of choice, strengthened by the spread of durable consumer goods complementary to leisure (cars, television) has found expression in all sorts of new purchases. Foreign holidays are perhaps the best-known example.

What of the rationality that guides buying decisions? The most important and least recognised influence is urbanisation. In a shopping centre, a housewife can compare several shops, choosing the combination of price, quality, service and convenience she likes best. In a big store with heavy turnover, it pays to carry a wider range of competing examples of many commodities. Urban consumers thus have possibilities of choice brought to their attention; isolated villagers must take what they can get, or at best acquire information at considerable cost in time, energy and perhaps a local ill-will. With easier choice comes the

[1] 1963 data. *Ann. Abst. Stat. 1965*, p. 128.

danger of impulse buying. This, however, is something most people learn either to like or to curtail.

Most, but not all. And there are other ways in which information has been supplied selectively to the intelligent, and misinformation to the stupid—a regressive process, raising the share of richer sections of the community in total consumer satisfaction. In August 1966, *Which?* had a circulation of 405,000—mostly those informed middle-class people who, through credit accounts, membership of professional associations and similar arrangements, were already buying cheaply and intelligently. While the mass market succumbs to petrol advertisements appealing to sado-masochistic motives of which they know nothing, the better-off buy the identical product $7\frac{1}{2}$ per cent cheaper with an unadvertised name. The choice of the rich is rationalised while that of the poor is perverted.

CHAPTER FOUR

Interactions among Economic Aims in Recent British Experience

I. TYPES OF INTERACTION

In Chapter Two, we suggested the following 'economic aims' as largely agreed:

1 Growth in income per person
2 Full employment
3 Price stability
4 Balance of payments: balance or small surplus
5 Improved output composition
6 Less unequal income distribution
7 Choice

To what extent will progress towards any one of these aims affect the others? We cannot discuss every possible interaction here; 21 pairs of aims could be selected from the seven listed above. What is more, each pair involves at least four relationships. Consider 1 and 7. Growth may reduce or increase the possibilities for choice; an increasing range of individual choice may accelerate or retard growth; a policy directed towards growth has side-effects on choice; and a policy aimed towards choice has side-effects on growth.

Where it is not too misleading to measure achievement of an aim with a series of quarterly figures, we have made statistical tests of whether aims have been attained together. Some of these are reported below. Such tests are often imperfect because they do not separate the four causal sequences mentioned. Something can be done about this;

we can, for instance, find whether a quarterly indicator of growth accounts for more variation in the balance of payments in the current, previous or subsequent quarter, and hence make some inferences about causal sequence. But these conclusions are never more than suggestive. For instance, the next quarter's growth, anticipated in this quarter, may lead to accelerated imports now in order to supply expected future demands. Temporal sequence does not infallibly indicate causal direction. Theoretical discussion cannot be replaced by statistical testing.

To simplify the discussion, we use a notation for considering these effects. The effect of achieving an aim on performance in another aim will be called a *direct effect*, and written as a row of numbers: thus [27] will mean 'the effect of fuller employment on choice', [72] 'the effect of increasing choice on employment levels', [742] 'the effect of fuller employment, via changes in the balance of payments, on employment levels', and so on. The side-effect of policies, directed mainly towards a certain aim, upon other aims will be called a *policy effect* and written as a column of numbers: thus $[\frac{2}{7}]$ means 'the effect on choice of measures designed to raise employment levels'. The two notations can be combined: thus $[\frac{2}{4}\ _7]$ would mean 'the effect of employment-creating policies, through side-effects on the balance of payments, upon choice'. It is simple to incorporate + and − signs for the direction of all these effects. Thus $[2\bar{7}]$ would mean, according to context, 'the harmful effects of fuller employment on choice', or else 'fuller employment has, in general, harmful effects on choice'. The usual arithmetic of signs works, provided that effects excluded from a particular sequence do not invalidate it; then (for instance) $[2\bar{4}]$ and $[4\bar{7}]$ implies $[2\overset{+}{7}]$.

The twenty-one pairs of aims, related by four effects (e.g., 12, 21, $\frac{1}{2}$ and $\frac{2}{1}$) for each pair, would form an over-long, yet inadequate, discussion. Over-long, since many effects, like 74, are relatively small; inadequate, because many three-aim effects, like $[\frac{4}{2}\ _1]$, are extremely important in recent British experience. Moreover our statistical evidence usually relates a pair of aims without telling us anything about the causal sequence—whether direct or policy, which way, and whether involving a third (or fourth, etc.) aim. Statistics alone will seldom distinguish $[\frac{4}{2}\ _1]$, [41], [14], etc. We shall discuss the statistical evidence on compatibility; consider the relations between growth and each other aim; and finally deal with a few of the major relations among aims other than growth.

2. STATISTICAL DATA

We cannot do much about direct measurement of aims 5, 6 and 7. For growth, employment, prices and the balance of payments, however, plenty of data are available. Yearly data will not do for a correlation analysis, however. When the analysis was done, data were available for only 13 fairly homogeneous (post-Korean) years, 1953-65. Since we are interested in the effects of past and future, as well as current, achievement of each aim on current performance in other fields, 1953 and 1965 will be useless for most purposes, and 1954 and 1964 for many. That would leave only 9 complete sets of yearly data. With so few observations, we could hardly ever be reasonably (say 95 per cent) confident that any statistical relation between aims had not arisen by chance.

Fortunately, since the start of 1955, quarterly data for GDP, exports and imports are available in constant (1958) prices.[1] These real data are what matter for output (though net national product data would be preferable if available), since only after eliminating the effects of inflationary price rises, and relative price shifts, can we assess growth of welfare. For exports and imports, 'real' data are also essential. It is extremely unlikely, in the long run, that a small country can make world prices subject to national policy. Changes in export (or import-substituting) effort, as opposed to movements of domestic and world prices, can be indicated only by volume data.

We are concerned with possible effects of attainment of each aim upon other aims in the past and future as well as the present. Quarterly data do not start till 1955/I. Thus no rate of growth of real GDP, exports or imports (over the previous quarter) is available till 1955/II, and no figure for the previous quarter's growth rate till 1955/III. When the raw data were fed to the computer, figures up to 1964/III were available; thus data for next quarter's growth rate went up to 1964/II.

In Appendix Table A, we tabulate the 36 sets of observations, one for each quarter 1955/III-1964/II, of real GDP in current, last and next quarter; real imports; real exports; and two indicators of balance-of-payments effort. To this are added indicators of employment achievements—unfilled vacancies *less* unemployed as a percentage of labour force in quarter—for current and past quarter, and of percentage rise

---

[1] Exports and imports of goods and services (not counting property incomes to or from abroad) throughout. 'Net national' data, a better welfare indicator (p. 43), are not available on a quarterly basis.

in price in quarter, currently and for last and next quarter. All data are adjusted to eliminate seasonal variations.

3. CORRELATION ANALYSIS

The policy-maker, trying to discover whether aims are compatible, is concerned with three sorts of correlation coefficient (CC): simple, multiple and partial. In each case, he must know the risk that the relation arose by chance (the significance level), and preferably the causal mechanism involved.

The simple CCs are listed in Appendix Table B. They indicate the proportion of deviation from its mean, of each variable correlated, linked with deviations of the other variable. For 36 observations (quarters), a CC of ·525 or above[1] indicates a probability smaller than 1 in 1,000 that the association is chance; ·424 or above, below 1 in 100; ·386, below 1 in 50; ·329, below 1 in 20; and ·278, below 1 in 10.[1]

Apart from the uninteresting definitional correlation between our two balance-of-payments indicators (App. Table B, Col. 5 and Row 4), and the *autocorrelation* of employment (Col. 12, row 11) the following simple CCs are of interest:

1. *Very highly significant* (probability of chance relationship under 1 in 1,000): growth of real GDP and of real exports (·670), and growth of real exports and of real imports (·615), in same quarter (Col. 3, rows 1, 2).

2. *Highly significant* (1 in 100 to 1 in 1,000): growth of real GDP and of contemporary real imports (·500, Col. 2, row 1); growth of real GDP and *slow* growth of exports in next quarter (−·449, Col. 7, row 3).

3. *Significant* (1 in 50 to 1 in 100): fullness of employment and (i) next quarter's rate of price inflation (·407, Col. 12, row 6, or, for a slightly different group of quarters, ·403, Col. 11, row 10); (ii) current success on the balance of payments, by both measures (−·409, Col. 12, row 5; ·387, Col. 12, row 4); and, on one of two possible groups of quarters, (iii) current price inflation (·390, Col. 12, row 9).

4. *Somewhat significant* (1 in 20 to 1 in 50): Full employment and (i) current price inflation on the other possible group of quarters (·367, Col. 11, row 6); (ii) inflation six months later (·346, Col. 12,

---

[1] Method described in Moroney, op. cit., p. 311; t-tables from Goulden, *Methods of Statistical Analysis*, Wiley, 1952, p. 145.

H*

row 10). Also export growth and next quarter's inflation (·335, Col. 10, row 3).

5. *Probably significant* (risk 1 in 10 to 1 in 20): inflation and (i) slow real growth of current GDP ($-$·280 or $-$·282, Col. 9, row 7, and Col. 10, row 8); (ii) slow real growth of current imports ($-$·311, Col. 6, row 2); (iii) next quarter's demand for labour (·304, Col. 11, row 9).

To interpret these links, we shall examine partial and multiple CCs too. A *partial CC* $r_{xy.z}$ shows the proportion of variance of x linked to variance of y when z is held constant. If z had simple CCs of opposite sign on x and y—i.e. if z pulled x and y in opposite directions—holding z constant brings out the strength of any positive link between x and y, and allows us to assess the weakness of a negative link. For example, the simple CC between current employment (variable 11 in Table B) and inflation (variable 6) is ·367. Next quarter's rate of inflation (variable 10) pulls current employment up (Table B, Col. 11, row 10), and current inflation down (Table B, Col. 10, row 6). Therefore, by taking the partial CC of current employment on inflation with next quarter's inflation held constant, we raise the degree of explanation. The partial CC goes up to ·4743 (see Table E, Col. 1, last row but one). The reader should trace out analogous examples. Of course, if z pulls x and y in *identical* directions (CCs of same sign), $r_{xy.z}$ will exceed the simple CC, r_{xy}, if r_{xy} is negative, and fall short of r_{xy} when r_{xy} is positive.

As we shall see, the difference between partial and simple CCs often reflects an economic effect. In taking partial CCs (as in interpreting simple CCs) we must, however, beware of *autocorrelation*. A link between variables can be artificially induced by time, because both series are growing steadily (e.g. wireless licences and car accidents). We can test for autocorrelation by the simple CC of a series to its own previous value—and, in most cases, insure against it by linking quarterly growth rates, not absolute levels, of variables suspected to be severely autocorrelated. Only one variable gives trouble, demand for labour (Table B, Col. 12, row 11). So there are no 'wireless licences' for these 'accidents' to be spuriously linked to! However, we must not take a partial CC between variable 11 (or 12) of Table A and some other variable, holding variable 12 (or 11) constant; variables 12 and 11 are too much alike.

A *multiple CC* tells us how much of the variance of x is linked to variances of y and of z.[1] In using these, we must beware of *collinearity* between our explanatory variables y and z, ideally independent (simple CC zero). If y and z have a high simple CC, then much of z is linked with y. So, if we explain changes in x by changes in y, and then add changes in z as a further explanation, we are counting part of the effect of y on x twice. If z then varies alone, without any change in y, our multiple CC will lead us to expect more change in x than will actually take place; how much more we cannot know until we have verified hypotheses about the causal (and not merely statistical) sequences linking x, y and z.

In the rest of this book, we shall consider some theoretically possible links among aims and examine the statistical evidence. We must bear in mind that the whole correlation exercise assumes linearity, e.g. (roughly) that twice the import growth will cut the rate of inflation (other things being equal) exactly twice as much. We shall check this assumption by examining extreme situations, both of success and of failure. We must also see if the sustained achievement of any one aim has a different effect on other aim variables from a briefer success; again the linear correlation model is not useful, though Table A is.

4. GROWTH AND OTHER POLICY AIMS

(a) Employment [1 and 2]

In Appendix Table B, none of the simple CCs relating real growth to demand for labour is significant even at 10 per cent. Partial CCs are even less significant. It is, however, both surprising and unlikely to be a matter of chance that all six simple CCs (Table B, Cols. 11 and 12, rows 1, 7 and 8) are negative. In Britain today, very high levels of demand for labour are *not* typically accompanied by more rapid growth in the previous, current, next or next-but-one quarter. Between the wars, these aims *did* go together. Why is full employment different? To restate the mystery of 1964-6, why did rising levels of employment do so little to raise real output?

Wilhelm Busch has written:

> *Vater werden ist nicht schwer;*
> *Vater sein dagegen sehr.*[2]

[1] If the multiple CC is 0·8, then 64 per cent of variance is explained (0·8² = 0·64).

[2] Easy to become a father;
  Being one is harder, rather.

The sequence [21] (see pp. 216-7) illustrates. While men and machines stand unwillingly idle, the economy grows by putting both to work. Near full employment, however, further growth is impeded by rising unit costs and price-inelastic factor supplies—overtime rates, the employment of inexperienced workers or fatigued metal, and so on. The nearer one gets to full employment, the less growth can be achieved by further increases in demand for labour. The process of becoming a fully employed economy is [2 $\overset{+}{1}$]; the state of being one, [2 $\overline{1}$]. Diminishing returns to variable factors of production are more severe when full capacity and full employment increase the number of fixed factors, and lengthen the period over which they remain fixed.

In rich economies—with slow population growth, full-employment policies, strong unions, and a high marginal rate of substitution of leisure for income as income rises—growth requires the replacement of labour by capital. The employment-destroying effects of automation have been overstated (workers make machines and even automatic control systems), but exist to some extent.

Full employment, moreover, destroys the normal positive policy effects [+ $\overset{2}{1}$], which familiarity with Keynesian public-works reflation might mislead us into suspecting. When employment gets very full, inflationary pressure builds up, since overtime rates have to be paid (and less able workers employed) to get an addition to output that previously was got for less extra income. Then the difficulty or expense of home purchase turns buyers towards imports. These dangers to price stability and the balance of payments lead Governments to deflate, reducing employment levels—and growth. Thus the negative correlation between employment now and growth later is largely created by deliberate policy.

What happens if we abandon the linear assumptions of regression analysis, and instead examine situations of very good or very bad performance on either employment or growth fronts and see what was happening to the other aim? Not much: the nine quarters of very rapid growth (above 1·75 per cent, seasonally adjusted, in a quarter) range from 1955/3, with its high demand for labour, to the slack employment situation of 1963/2. The seven quarters of serious decline in GDP (over −0·75 per cent in one quarter) range from the high demand for labour of 1955/2 to the climatically abnormal, low demand of 1963/1.

There are clear periods of trend in labour demand: steadily rising in 1955, 1957/1-3, 1959/1-1961/2, and 1963/2-1964/3, otherwise steadily falling. Growth was far jerkier. Even seasonally adjusted data show only one period of positive growth for longer than three quarters: 1959/2 through 1961/3. This coincided almost perfectly with the longest consecutive period of rising labour demand. Both trends signified recovery from the doldrums of 1957-8. One example proves nothing, but it suggests how difficult it is, in an economy with a tiny agricultural reserve, to grow without some sustainable boost to labour input, or to labour's ability (or incentive) to shift to more productive activities.

The links between growth and employment are, therefore, mildly negative, but of doubtful statistical significance; and this is because policy and causal, and especially static and dynamic. interactions are pulling in opposite directions. Pessimism about the employment effects of automation receives little support from the statistics. The view that growth and employment go hand in hand, even after full employment has been approached nationally, even with labour immobile, receives no support at all. Suggestively, however, the only period of sustained growth coincided with expansion of employment, and this growth was stopped by rising unit costs near full employment *before* the counter-inflationary measures of Mr Selwyn Lloyd. Indeed, these were in response to the employment situation. If growth runs up against the full employment ceiling, and labour is immobile, further growth requires overtime and/or absorption of less able workers. This means that extra monetary demand (incomes) outruns supply—even without rises in hourly rates of pay! Then prices, or net imports, rise. Deflationary policies are required, not by the rapid growth of money incomes, but by the failure of real outputs to keep pace with this growth.

(b) Price stability [1 and 3]
The tables give no support to the suspicion of a general correlation between inflation and growth. The only single CC that may be statistically significant, that between growth and current inflation (Table B, Col. 1, row 6; Col. 7, row 9; Col. 8, row 10) is negative. None of the lagged or led correlations, and none of the first-order or second-order partial CCs, is even suggestive.

This does not suffice to disprove that running the economy flat out (i.e. 'over-rapid' growth) is responsible in part for inflation. Sustained series of figures or extreme cases might tell a different story. But they do not (Table A). The only period of sustained growth, 1959/2 to 1961/3, began with the longest post-war period without a quarterly price rise over 0·5 per cent (1959/1 to 1960/3). The effort of firms to sustain growth, well after many areas and industries had reached the full-employment ceiling, then produced the only sustained post-1955 series of unusually rapid price rises. However, the link between current growth and inflation 3 or 6 months later (Table B, Col. 1, row 10; Col. 7, rows 6, 10) is negligible. Other periods of rapid inflation, e.g. 1955/2-1956/2, had little to do with growth, whether as cause, effect, or policy consequence.

Nor do the extreme cases suggest that growth causes inflation. The most rapid quarters for growth were 1963/2, 1963/4, 1959/2 and 1955/3, in falling order of rapidity; the worst three, in falling order of badness, were 1957/3, 1955/2 and 1957/4. Table A shows that neither directly nor with a lag could these quarters be linked to any special price performance. Of the worst price performances, 1955/4 came during decline of GDP (though after a quarter of very fast growth); 1956/2 came during a period of bad growth performance; 1962/2 during a quarter of good growth in the middle of a longish bad patch; and 1964/2 during a period of rather ordinary growth. The quarters of particularly stable prices show equally diverse rates of growth, except for the striking period 1959/1-1960/3, already discussed.

Few subjects have generated more opining than the relation between growth and inflation. The U.K. statistics give no support to any of the general hypotheses advanced. Foreign experience is similar. Galbraith suggests that the U.S. in the 1950s sacrificed price stability to the frantic pursuit of growth. In fact, during the period he discusses, the U.S. experienced exceptionally slow growth and exceptionally slow inflation, by the standards of her past and of comparable economies.[1] In the post-war world, advanced industrial countries exemplify growth without rapid inflation (W. Germany), inflation without rapid growth (U.K. for most of the period), inflation accompanied by rapid growth (France), and price stability without rapid growth (U.S.A.). No correlation between the two phenomena exists.

This is just what theory predicts. Forget about all the institutional complications (a growing concentration of unions and firms, and hence the possibility of cost-push inflation when demand-pull is absent). Leave aside even the vital issue of labour immobility, which enables excess demand for the products of certain industries and regions to

[1] See pp. 47-9 above.

coexist with falling employment levels in others. Then, very crudely, real growth is of both *monetary demand for* and *physical supply of* commodities. If extra demand outstrips extra supply, further growth is stimulated (since demands remain, for businessmen to satisfy profitably) and prices rise. If extra supply outpaces extra demand, except in so far as exogenous demands for output (e.g. of defence equipment) maintain growth of supply, prices fall. Real growth rates (Table A, Col. 1) tell us nothing of the balance between increasing supply and increasing demand. Hence they are not significantly linked to inflation rates.

As long-period growth, with immobile productive resources, presses against supply ceilings, or is sustained at rising average cost, either inflation or pressure upon foreign exchange (diversion from exports or higher imports) is likely to be felt. But there is no link between accelerated growth and inflation. Supply grows as well as demand. Economies of scale exist as all factors grow; diminishing returns prevail as a fixed factor is saturated with a variable one. These elements have to be weighed sector by sector before predictions can be made.

In steel, there is usually spare capacity expensively carried, save in high boom, and labour costs are a tiny proportion of total costs; growth should lower unit costs, prices (even for profit maximisers; why?), and hence input costs for other, steel-using sectors. On the other hand, labour-intensive consumer-goods makers like housepainters or food processers, in regions of high activity, would find the pressure of spending could be most profitably met by higher prices rather than by sharp rises in output levels.

There is no reason why all this should add up to a coherent one-way relation between growth and price stability. It depends on the composition of output that grows, the distribution of income paid out to makers of the extra output, and the way such income is spent. (Unfortunately we know, in Britain, almost nothing about sectoral multipliers—how workers in each region and industry will spend additions to income.) The causal sequence [13] is of uncertain sign and operates via 5 and 6, and alternately to [14], i.e. in so far as growing demands are allowed to make their impact upon foreign countries, they will have less inflationary effect at home.

What about the policy sequences [$\frac{1}{3}$] and [$\frac{3}{1}$]? This is part of stop-go, which is not the old trade cycle, rather the reverse: deliberate counter-cyclical policy, restraining demand (even at the cost of slower growth) near full employment to safeguard prices and the balance of payments, and stimulating demand when it appears so slack as to threaten employment levels. The complaints are that it has been (i) ill-timed, so that intended disinflation produced its main, delayed effect (see p. 8) when the downturn was already well under way, (ii) a blunt instrument, deflating the depressed regions as much as the overstretched ones, hospital building more than casino operation, purchasing power over butter more than over caviar. These are complaints not against stop-go itself, but against its inefficient execution—an inefficiency caused partly by statistical series that reminded Mr Harold Macmillan of 'last year's Bradshaw', but mainly by the lack of any reliable information about the origin of industrial inputs and the spending of incomes by regions, and an apparent lack of will to seek such information or to use what exists.[1]

A more fundamental criticism is that stop-go is wasteful. Investment resources are built up by sacrifice of current consumption, then allowed to stand idle or half-built during periods of pause. Smoother growth, by avoiding such waste, could get as much addition to future productive resources with less current sacrifice. In other words, greater smoothness would get more growth from the same sacrifice of current consumption.

Stop-go has policy consequences for compatibilities between 1 and 3. Policies designed suddenly to stabilise prices and/or the balance of payments tend to retard growth: $[\frac{3}{1}]$. Go is less unpleasant; the reflating takes place when some slack exists around the economy, so that there is little $[\frac{1}{3}]$. Stop-go is asymmetric. Stop-tactics, at very high levels of employment, aim to stabilise prices and the foreign balance, but retard an already faltering rate of growth. Go-tactics stimulate demand while some spare resources exist. The extra employment at this early stage (e.g. 1959) means real growth, and little harm to price stability.

(c) The balance of payments [1 and 4]

British economasochism is such that we take the intrinsic value of the unpleasant for granted. Repeatedly since 1951, we have tolerated measures depressing growth, in order to help the balance of payments. It is sometimes alleged that foreign lenders impose this upon us. They want (a) their money back, at high real value and with substantial interest, and (b) no disruption of international flows of money and goods. Both concerns are damaged by chronic weakness in Britain's balance of

---

[1] We have Ministry of Labour *Family Expenditure Surveys* yearly from 1953-4, but no matrix multiplier; and no input-output table later than 1954! The 1963 table is mainly intelligent extrapolation from 1954.

payments. But bankers are not mad. The evidence of repeated failures suggests that the retardation of growth does not produce long-run improvement in the foreign balance, at least in Britain. Does the retardation of growth at least provide short-term relief?

There is a crude policy link. Higher interest rates pull in short-term foreign money, strengthen reserves and reduce the risk of devaluation; speculative crises are thus averted by measures which make borrowing more expensive for business, and thus retard growth. But this is not really [$\frac{4}{1}$], because short-term money flows are not balance-of-payments improvements unless linked to actual rises in exports or falls in imports. The central case for stop-go as a balance-of-payments corrective is: [$1\overline{34}$], therefore [$\frac{\overline{1}}{3}\,_4$]. Growth, it is argued, pushes up demand ahead of supply at full employment, straining resources and raising prices, so that buyers turn to imports, and sellers from exports to the 'soft' home market. Retard growth, and the foreign balance improves.

There is no statistical evidence for the existence of this crude gold-standard equilibrium system. The simple CC between growth of real GDP and of real exports is ·670, whereas the above argument suggests it should be negative. That between real growth and real import growth is only ·500 (Table B).

When we look at partial CCs, suspicion mounts. Table D lists all statistically significant first partials relating real growth rates of output, exports and imports. It shows that the link between output growth and import growth is a statistical accident. Imports and exports tend to rise and fall together, because of our growing tendency to import the same sort of things that we export (see pp. 169-170). So we must ask: is the link between growth of output and of exports accidental—caused by the link of import growth to both? Is the link between growth of output and of imports accidental—caused by the link of export growth to both?

When variations in export growth are allowed for, the link between real growth of output and of imports becomes statistically insignificant (Table D, Col. 1, row 3: 0·1496). Conversely, however, the link between real growth rates of output and of exports survives allowance for variations in imports; the relevant first partial (Table D, Col. 2, row 2) is significant at 0·3 per cent. Real growth helps exports more than it raises imports in the same quarter. As the consistently significant CCs between Cols. 3 and 7 of Table A (see Tables B, D) show, acceleration of output growth usually means fall-back of export growth three months later. Thus the balance of payments suffers, not during real growth, but when it slows down. *This* is when money incomes go on rising, home output is outpaced, and British manufacturers divert potential extra exports to the hungry home market.

Stop-go does rather more, in the short run, to affect the level of imports than of exports. Accelerated growth promptly turns consumers towards imports. But the crude fact that exports are part of output, and grow when output grows, outweighs the alleged diversion of the *current* quarter's potential exports to home consumers. Scale economies (and wage-push in boom and slump alike) tend to moderate increases in export prices during growth; this suggests a further favourable relation between growth and exports. Admittedly, if firms expect restrictions designed to improve the balance of payments, they stockpile imports and curtail exports in advance of Government action to make such activities dearer —and hence compel such action.[1]

The statistics amalgamate [14] and [41] sequences. Exports are inflationary, money now without goods now; imports, the opposite. Exports stimulate, and imports depress, home demand before real home supply. While labour is unemployed, *or mobile towards more productive jobs*, exports stimulate real growth in proportion to size, and imports retard growth similarly. When labour is fully employed *and immobile*, only money growth (inflation) can be thus stimulated or retarded. Some of the link between real growth of output and of exports is certainly due to this 41 effect during slack periods.

Since 1945, faster-growing countries have been more successful in building up a sound balance of payments (pp. 171-2). We have seen that favourable [41] sequences can operate via employment; the [14] sequence is via 5 and 6. If growth is geared towards export sectors [15] and steps are taken to prevent extra income from being spent on imports [16], then (tautologously) growth helps the balance of payments. With growing sales, exporters find that higher rates of investment pay—and can be paid for. This makes lower unit costs, relative to slower-growing competitors, likelier in the long run, owing to the increasing expensiveness of labour relative to capital in any economy where income rises (so that capital is easier to accumulate, while the incentive needed to persuade workers to sacrifice leisure rises).

---

[1] Beckerman, op. cit., ch. II. Conversely, an expected easing of restrictions produces a temporary improvement in the foreign balance. The enormously favourable balance of trade in November 1966 was caused by importers holding back orders, in advance of the removal of the import surcharge.

Furthermore, the faster output rises, the more politically practicable does it become to divert increases from consumption towards exports, and investment in export sectors; and the faster real expenditure rises, the softer is the screaming when such expenditure is directed away from imports towards domestic products. Such export-oriented, import-replacing growth has been seen in most European economies, and in Japan, since 1955. Favourable interactions between growth and foreign payments have been assisted in these economies by the absence of speculative strains caused by use of their currencies for trade and reserves, and by the presence of a mobile *flow* of labour, channelled with ease (and small incentives) towards exporting or import-substituting sectors where necessary.[1]

Light is shed on [14], or on [¼], by the simple CC of −0·449 (highly significant, and retaining significance as a first partial: see Table D) between growth of GDP and next quarter's export growth—despite the +0·670 correlation between growth of GDP and of current exports. As for price movements, so for exports: the evil that growth does lives *only* after it. As full-employment ceilings are approached or anticipated in a few areas and industries, so, first, imports are raised, though exports initially share in the growth of total output and thus rise as fast as imports. Later, goods are diverted from exports to the home market.

The delay—the fact that in a quarter of rapid growth exports are likely to rise, and only in the next quarter do they fall off—is an expression of the same Buschian phenomenon observed for prices. The approach to the ceiling features growth in supply at least *pari passu* with demand, but along the ceiling the economy features high-level creeping stagnation, with a mixture of deficits on the balance of payments and rises in prices as consumers buy to satisfy demand. This sequence has more to do with causal than policy sequences—policy in this matter has usually been belated response to the inflationary or import troubles involved in (or rather after) growth. Imports do not lag, as exports do, in their [14] impact; it is easier and more profitable to respond to a shortage by raising imports than by cancelling an export contract.

What of extreme situations for either growth or payments (Table A)?

---

[1] Beckerman's fascinating analysis of export-propelled growth really fails to distinguish it from growth-propelled exports, or from policies propelling both at once. W. Beckerman and others, *The British Economy in 1975*, Cambridge, 1965, ch. II. He is fully aware of the problem, of course (cf. pp. 64-7).

We have noted the marked, severe decline in the balance of payments on current account after 1960/1; 1955-9 is so different from 1960-4 that separate treatment is required. In 1955-9, GDP grew fastest in 1955/3, 1957/1 and 1958/3, without exceptional trouble on current account. In 1960-4, growth was fastest in 1963/4, 1963/2, 1961/1 and 1962/2, whereas the really bad foreign balances materialized in 1960/2-1961/2 and in 1963/3-1964/4.

The extremely rapid expansion of the second and fourth quarters of 1963 created a group of shortages that could not be met from home resources.[1] The same happened on a smaller scale in 1959-61. In 1959-60, twelve months of growth at 8 per cent per annum started by taking up the slack from the recession of 1957/2-1959/1; investment, being half public-sector, is largely stabilised during recessions, so that the new equipment is all ready to respond to initial boom demands. The drain on current account did not become really severe until mid-1960. If import and export prices had stayed at 1958 levels, the U.K.'s current balance would have been in the red for every quarter since 1959/4, except 1963/1. Only favourable movements in the terms of trade made things less bad[2] in value terms. During the last nine months of 1963, the economy grew at almost 11 per cent a year in real terms. Partly this was because there was a long period of preceding slack (1961/3-1963/1) and thus some unemployed men (and many optimistically invested machines) to use. But this alone does not suffice to explain the exceptional severity of the balance-of-payments crisis following the later growth spurt. Of 1964's deficit of £745m., £360m. was current-account.

We have seen (pp. 162-84) that most of Britain's balance-of-payments troubles come from current account. How has growth affected capital-account movements? These movements are, in the main, the balance between British purchases of foreign plant and shares, and foreign purchases of British plant and shares. The better British growth pros-

---

[1] The impending and disastrous 1964 balance-of-payments crisis, almost universally predicted by economists, was ignored by the Chancellor, Mr Maudling. There was a general election in October 1964. It would be sad if the link between growth and *current* exports, which has sound statistical support, were discredited as a basis of policy by the neglect, electorally motivated, of the equally established danger that the slowing-down of growth brings about an import expansion.

[2] Arithmetically! On the normal assumption that traded goods are price-elastic, the fact that our inflation was faster than that of our trading partners ('favourable' movements in terms of trade) *caused* the unfavourable movements in the balance of trade. See above, pp.170-74.

pects are thought to be, relative to other countries', the more willing are businessmen to put their money into British (as opposed to foreign) firms. A substantial deficit on private capital account means that prospects abroad are regarded by those who move funds as more favourable, relative to those in the U.K., than before.

This is not all there is to it. If you rate British and American growth prospects, taxes, etc., equally, but expect sterling to be devalued in terms of U.S. dollars, it pays you to sell sterling-bearing assets and buy dollar-bearing ones. 'It may sound anti-British and derogatory to sterling, but it makes sense to me.'[1] This behaviour, by increasing the supply of sterling and the demand for dollars (for the asset-shifter will sell the sterling, got for his British asset, to buy the dollars needed for the U.S. share), makes likelier the devaluation it anticipates. This growing likelihood causes more asset-shifting. This is destabilising speculation.

Thus capital-account fluctuations (for Government military and aid outlays seem to be on a steady trend, irrespective of the rate of growth) depend chiefly on (i) the expected yield of British as against foreign assets—above all, anticipated growth in Britain and abroad, but also relative confiscation and tax risks, profit shares, etc; (ii) expected command over goods and services of sterling relative to other currencies, i.e., the effect, on devaluation dangers, of current-account movements. Years when the prospects for the balance of payments on current account and for growth both seem sustainably good are likely to be inflow years on private capital account too. For devaluation risks are set up primarily by big unfavourable current balances, i.e. big excess of supply of sterling-to-buy-foreign-currency (by British importers to pay for their purchases) over demand for sterling-paid-for-with-foreign-currency (by foreign importers to buy British exports). Thus bad current accounts make for bad capital accounts by causing speculation against sterling.

However, the converse does not apply; a deficit on private capital account helps current account. First, net purchase by Britons of assets abroad means a net rise, in future years, in currency earnings from these assets. Second, if holders of British assets sell them and buy foreign ones, they make sterling (and hence means to purchase British exports) more plentiful and other currencies (and hence means to buy exports of Britain's rivals) less plentiful.

[1] Mr W. J. Keswick, a Governor of the Bank of England, advising Lazard's customers in September, 1957. It was, of course, Mr Keswick's duty to give this advice.

A good growth performance and potential, associated with a healthy current account, will benefit capital account. The big drains on U.K. capital account in 1960-1 and 1964 resulted from our apparent inability to sustain growth without (a) incurring big current-account deficits, (b) stemming them by ending growth, and hence (c) improving the likely future yield of foreign assets relative to British assets.

(d) Output composition [1 and 5]

The numerous changes in output composition (pp. 199-208) cannot produce a simple effect on growth; but most links appear to be favourable. Undoubtedly the huge rise in investment/output ratios has helped growth. Net investment means more capital; replacement investment means faster innovation. The expansion of welfare, too, has aided growth (especially during labour shortage) by providing a better-trained, healthier labour force. In many fields (free crèches for working mothers, retraining on full pay) more would be spent on welfare if we allowed for the understatement by low wage rates (and thus by calculations of 'lost' wages of mothers, the redundant, etc.) of real labour scarcity. Certainly one can find changes in output composition with big ill-effects on growth, notably the rise in the share of spending devoted to alcohol and gambling. Most of the major [51] sequences, however, seem to have been favourable.

For several reasons, the rising share of welfare outlays in GDP is likely to speed up economic growth. Sociological enquiry shows that the productivity of labour responds much more favourably to security than to threats. Studies of rate of return in the U.S. and U.K. (p. 204-5) show that education, especially secondary, is at least as socially profitable as investment. The National Health Service costs much more than the old panel system, but the excess is more than repaid by saved labour-time in any given year. Further, if foreign exchange is scarcer than its sterling price indicates, social security (which costs hardly any overseas currency) is cheaper than it seems. And if stability assists growth (pp. 116-7), so does the welfare state, since many welfare payments are counter-cyclical.

[15] sequences bring us to the muddled notion of a 'growth sector'. Some people believe that minimal intervention is the best contribution that the State can make to growth. They claim that growth sectors will emerge and, subject only to control of monopoly, should be allowed to expand. Now a growth sector (with no monopoly and for a given income

distribution) is merely a sector with income-elasticity of demand above unity. There is no mechanism to ensure that luxury production encourages *future* growth. Many growth sectors are growth-restricting. Advertising, whatever its virtues, is a once-for-all diversion of resources from producing to selling. Boats, cars, restaurants, and in general all products making leisure nicer, make work less attractive. The sequence is $[15\bar{1}]$!

However, $[\frac{1}{5}]$ is almost certain to be favourable with a modicum of intelligent central control. More rapid growth makes the improvement of composition politically easier—however one defines 'improvement'. All the policies previously discussed—stimulation of exports and import substitutes, deployment of resources to alleviate tomorrow's inflationary shortages—are special aspects of $[5]$. Availability of statistics, and the usual way we think of aims, made us list price stabilisation and an improved balance of payments separately; but they are really part of output composition.

Growth and an improved composition of production are not mutually maximising. They are, in general, mutually helpful. Sensible policies, by reducing the importance of existing income distribution in determining future output composition, can make the interaction even more favourable.

(e) Equality [1 and 6]

Though we have no single measure of equality (pp. 85-8), interactions between equality and growth are perhaps the most interesting area of controversy in political economy today. There are three main effects in 61 and $\frac{6}{1}$: through incentives, demand and saving.

Equalisation dampens incentives; that is the main overt reason for opposition to it, especially among advocates of rapid growth. The argument does not apply to equalisation of inherited wealth. Professor Milton Friedman and his colleagues at Chicago typify the most honest and intelligent advocates of *laisser-faire* in the U.S.A. They condemn income redistribution by Governments because it interferes with the free-market mechanism for transferring factors among uses, but—how different from our own pragmatic Right!—advocate large death duties and even, sometimes, capital levies. Though the wish to hand on assets to one's children is part of the urge to make money, incentives can hardly justify large inherited wealth. It is a disincentive to effort, both for inheritors, who need not work to live well, and for non-inheritors, who lose the chance to earn those claims on national income which accrue to inheritors of assets. An honest advocate of incentives, who is sincerely sad when he rejects income equalisation because of disincentives to growth, can be recognised by his willingness to make death duties much more effective (e.g. by the Rignano plan or punitive duties upon gifts *inter vivos*).[1]

More important than the sincerity of the view is its correctness, even as regards income. Few would deny the need for some income inequality to stimulate labour mobility. But how much inequality is needed? The U.S. has more labour mobility than the U.K. despite considerably greater overall income equality. The difference in rewards for occupations in Britain has more to do with past social hierarchies than with present labour markets;[2] how many professors would become dustmen, if dustmen's pay were tomorrow multiplied tenfold? Earnings indicators (p. 189) show no variation in differentials from 1949 to 1960, but a considerable contraction since; has labour become substantially less mobile as a result?

In any event, the immediate, dynamic effect of equalising policies offsets static disincentive effects. Consider two fully employed countries, A and B, identical except that post-tax hourly pay for relatively scarce workers is (to promote equality) lower in A, while plentiful unskilled labour does worse in B. Certainly one would expect less essential and more inessential work to be done, and hence less total output, in A than in B: [61].

But it does *not* follow that, within one country, lower hourly returns for a well-paid job will lower work done in that job. If a living standard has been adopted (and even more if commitments, such as H.P. payments, have been entered into) by people in that job, a reduction in hourly income—e.g. by a rise in income tax—may mean that longer hours are worked, so as to maintain the previous income level. This is most plausible for earners of high incomes, who are likeliest to have fixed commitments, such as mortgage payments and school fees, that are large relative to income. These people often hold positions where short hours and long holidays have become normal, work less strenuous, and labour-input expansible. Thus [$^6_1$], the dynamic policy effect, may well be

---

[1] C. A. R. Crosland, *The Future of Socialism*, Cape, 1958.

[2] G. Routh, *Occupation and Pay in Great Britain 1906-1960*, Cambridge, 1965; B. Wootton, op. cit.

positive for equalising changes in tax structure, balancing the static disincentive effect [61].[1]

The demand and saving effects of redistribution are opposite sides of a single coin. It was once argued, against income equalisation, that growth required investment, which could be financed only by personal and company saving; but, since such saving comes mainly out of the incomes of the very rich, redistribution would destroy its source and hence curtail growth. Keynes, an advocate of moderate equalisation, attacked that argument by showing how, during unemployment caused by demand deficiency, excessive thrift (and hence the inequality that caused it) would reduce the growth rate. More saving, from a given income, means less consumption; and consumption inadequate to require full use of existing plant would deter investment in new plant.[2] There seems to be a paradox here. Saving is good *and* bad for growth: good because it finances saving and thus provides the *ability* to invest, and bad because (by reducing consumer demand) it lessens the *incentive* to invest. It all depends on employment. At any given employment level, capacity to invest depends on saving (plus the temporary prop of import surplus),[3] so saving helps growth. If employment is not assumed constant, an increase in thrift lowers it by cutting consumer demand. Thus Keynes was right; demand-induced unemployment weakens the case for thrift, and hence for inequality to produce thrift.

But the commitment to full employment seems to revive the pre-Keynesian case for inequality. If the level of employment and the import surplus are given at 98-9 per cent of labour supply and zero respectively, the ability of an economy to invest (and hence grow) is limited by its ability to save—and hence by its degree of inequality? This is where the argument really breaks down. First, the difference between saving/income ratios in different income groups is much smaller than was once thought; saving levels have other, more important determinants than income differences.[4] Second, important routes to saving by the less wealthy have recently opened up—building societies, life insurance,

---

[1] Further, (a) lower tax rates for lower income-earners counterbalance the incentive effects of higher rates for higher earners, (b) income tax is not the only way to equalise—one could also tax car commuters and diners at the Savoy Hotel.

[2] J. M. Keynes, *General Theory of Employment, Interest and Money*, pp. 372-3.

[3] Remember $Y = C + I + X$ (output); $Y = C + S + M$ (spending); therefore $I = S + (M - X)$: investment equals saving *plus* the surplus of imports over exports.

[4] A good summary of the evidence is R. Ferber, Research on Household Behaviour, *Amer. Econ. Rev.*, March 1962, pp. 19-63. See pp. 95-98 above.

superannuation schemes, arguably even hire-purchase. Third, there are other paths to growth than investment.

Above all, the process by which the Government has taken responsibility for maintaining aggregate demand at the level needed to preserve full employment has been the socialisation of investment. This has removed the dependence of the investment level upon *private* savings. About half U.K. investment is by nationalised industries and local and central Government—mostly financed by surplus of current revenue over current expenditure. Deficiencies in private saving, whether caused by equality or otherwise, can be made up by public saving through higher taxes, lower current public expenditure, or bigger surpluses on nationalised industries. This argument defuses both the defence that inequality is necessary for savings, and the Keynesian plea for equality to provide extra consumer demand to induce new investment. Where the volume of saving and investment are decided primarily by the Government, they cease to be possible side-effects of any chosen distribution of income.

The prevailing degree of inequality in Britain, especially of wealth but also of income, cannot be defended on grounds of incentives, and other [61] sequences about balance out. Nevertheless, richer countries have more equal income distribution, among sexes, races, regions and overall (Lorenz),[1] than the poorer ones. This is principally because (a) growth makes equality easier to attain; the poor, as they become educated and articulate, press harder, and the rich resist less forcibly because labour is stronger and scarcer—and because, given growth, they can permit equalisation without themselves suffering absolute income decline; (b) growth *is* equalisation.

True, in the early stages of growth, income distribution becomes less equal; big profits are accumulated for reinvestment, while the ex-agricultural labour force presses down urban wages. But as agricultural labour reserves are used up, and as affluence renders leisure more valuable relative to yet more income, earnings rise; and as capital is accumulated marginal returns diminish. More fundamentally, in a very poor country, the poorest villagers are tied to the soil by their lack of information, skill, literacy, transport and cash. The shortage of adequate offices, transport, and every type of complex service confines industrialists to existing, richer centres.

---

[1] T. Morgan, Distribution of Income in Ceylon, Puerto Rico and the U.K., *Econ. Jnl.*, 1960; H. F. Lydall, *Economic Weekly* (Bombay), June-July 1960.

However, in mature growth, mobility among regions and jobs becomes much greater. There is abundant evidence, both from the history of particular countries and from international comparisons, of the equalising force of this growth sequence. In a mature economy with scarce labour resources—especially if it is hard to raise levels of investment—[61] is not only positive: the sequence is almost the only way to rapid growth. Workers have to be got to move from the poverty of Wales, Scotland and Northern Ireland to the South and East of England, in search of higher rewards; or (perhaps preferably?) machines and plant must be set up in the poorer areas, where workers are available and unit social production costs lower. This process of equalisation *is* growth. More accurately, it is *long-run* growth that converts *short-run* growth from an unequalising to an equalising process.

(*f*) *Choice* [*1 and 7*]

A celebrated article, P. J. D. Wiles's *Growth versus Choice*,[1] summarises a great debate: is the antithesis valid? Few deny that *affluence* assists choice in an economy with higher per-head income—more people can choose among a wider variety of goods and services, can choose more leisure without risking hunger, and so forth. But does rapid *growth* require policies that curtail choice?

Most of these $[\frac{1}{7}]$ sequences are alleged to operate because Governments try to reconcile growth and other objectives. If Governments use current surpluses to replace the investment finance lost by taxing high-income savers, they transfer private spending power (and decisions) to Governments. But this will reduce consumption choice only if private consumption actually falls. A fall in the share in GDP per head, as opposed to the absolute value, of private consumption per head does not establish $\frac{1}{7}$. There is no sign of such an absolute fall during *mature* growth. At no time since 1945 did any advanced country's total real private consumption per head, let alone personal disposable income, fall for any prolonged period. The decision to replace lost private investment finance by public surpluses, at once reinvested in the public sector or made available to the private sector, did not prevent the increase of private consumption, even in the short run.

$[\frac{1}{6}]$—unfavourable effects on choice of policies aimed at growth and improved output composition at once, 'the man in Whitehall knows best'—is another common fear. However, it is based on a psychologically

---

[1] *Economic Journal*, June 1956, pp. 244-55.

misleading golden-age myth: an ideal consumer who, with no central pressures on output composition, would make uninfluenced choices, determined only by a completely spontaneous preference structure. In a world of ignorance, brand-image advertising, tastes formed by family and neighbourhood, and pressures to irrationality of every kind (whether in buying sleeping pills or petrol, choosing a doctor, borrowing money, or in any other major economic activity related to consumption), this is a piece of naïve theorism.

A related objection is that growth, centrally or privately determined, produces (and largely proceeds by) standardisation of product; but how genuine was the choice among hundreds of identical toilet-cisterns? Is choice more seriously restricted during growth by the great standardisation of elementary products, than it was hampered at lower income levels by the lack of leisure, vacuum cleaners and cars? True, some groups feel some aspects of growth-linked standardisation acutely. Mass production and marketing in the U.S. food industry have reached such proportions that in my experience it is impossible to buy chickens, and difficult to buy strawberries or apples, with any taste at all. It is not just that the exercise of some types of consumer choice becomes expensive; in certain respects it becomes impossible. But, on the other hand, mass production techniques applied to fishing have made fresh lobster accessible to poorer people in the U.S. than anywhere else.

Choice means ability by producers, as well as by consumers, to choose. Growth in advanced economies seems to involve big expansions of purposive State action. But flat assertions that this restricts Individual Choice are propaganda, abusing the emotive connotations of choice in a context where its descriptive meaning is not clear. Choice by whom? If an industry's investment volume, pricing policy or costing systems are subjected to governmental and parliamentary scrutiny, control or even ownership, workers and consumers neither lose nor gain choice in any obvious way. Nationalisation is probably necessary for *substantial* increases in workers' managerial power and influence,[1] but it is not sufficient. Gas workers lost some control over their conditions of work on nationalisation in 1946: coal miners probably gained. Consumers' pressure on a nationalised firm through M.P.s need be no less effective than on a private firm through letters to its public relations officer,

---

[1] Rentiers do not buy shares (rather than bonds) so that risks may be taken by the workers in their own interests.

despite the alleged independence of nationalised Boards from Parliament in day-to-day operations.

What of shareholders? Their reserve power, exercised at annual meetings, may be reduced if governments scrutinise or control a firm in the interests of growth, as was done through the Iron and Steel Board; but industries thus controlled usually consist of huge firms, where power has long been in the hands of the directors.[1] In any case, democratic governments can be turned out at elections. Greater central control of industry, whether taken to make growth compatible with desired output composition, with equality, or for any other reason, means more direct influence by voters on industrial policy. Those who speak of the 'restriction of individual choice' required by centrally planned growth often mean the restriction of a few directors' power to choose *for* many managers, workers and consumers, and the transfer of that power to democratically elected governments.

5. RELATIONS AMONG AIMS NOT DIRECTLY INVOLVING GROWTH

(a) Full employment and inflation

All the simple CCs between Cols. 11 or 12, on the one hand, and row 6, 9 or 10, on the other, have some statistical significance. The multiple CC between demand for labour and inflation in current *and* preceding quarters is ·4823.[2] In every case, aims conflict; the fuller employment, the faster is present and future inflation; the faster an inflation, the greater is present and future employment.

Both Keynesian and neo-classical effects produce this result. On the neo-classical approach, the expectation of rising prices for output leads to the employment of workers who would otherwise produce too little to be profitably hired; and rising demand for labour bids up its price, pulling up variable costs and hence equilibrium prices of output. On the Keynesian approach, excess aggregate demand reflected in high employment pulls up real output and prices, the balance between

---

[1] P. S. Florence, *The Economics and Sociology of Industry*, Watts, 1965, pp. 132-5: 'Shareholders as a whole cannot be expected to govern their company. They are an extension of the "sleeping partner" . . . In this conflict [between directors and owners] the board of directors is probably gaining in strength . . . The larger the company, . . . the wider the divorce of management from control.'

[2] Col. 11 in rows 6 and 9, from Table A. Formulae from Spiegel, *Statistics*, Schaum, 1961, p. 271.

growth and inflation depending on initial levels and mobility of factor employment. Neither plain CCs nor the alleged historical demand curve for labour derived by Phillips and Lipsey (U.K., 1875-1957)[1] tell us whether employment causes inflation or *vice versa*—or how far the mechanism works through prices as opposed to incomes. These are the questions that policy-makers need to answer.

Since we are trying to sort out directions of causation, the time-sequences of Table E are of interest. The biggest simple CCs link inflation with the previous quarter's demand for labour; next comes the link to current employment levels; then with the level two quarters before (last column of Table E); and, last and least, with next quarter's inflation. This suggests that [2̄3] is more powerful than [3̄2].

The partial CCs reinforce this judgment. Since the simple CCs between inflation in various quarters (variables 6, 9 and 10 of Table B) are negligible, the partial CCs holding one quarter's inflation constant, while varying another's, are meaningful. When we hold next quarter's speed of inflation constant, variation in speed of current inflation is linked with about half the variation in the level of current employment (Table E, Col. 1, holding constant 10; Col. 2, holding constant 6). Success in holding back prices in a quarter is weakly linked to failure in the previous quarter, and strongly linked to lowness of demand for labour in the previous quarter.

From Table E, then, we tentatively conclude that variance in the levels of demand for labour is linked to 15 to 25 per cent of variance in the rate of inflation in the current and in the subsequent quarter.[2] Rising exports happen when inflation is relatively mild, and raise employment levels; rising imports, the reverse; thus holding either exports or imports constant strengthens [2̄3]. While [2̄3] and [3̄2] are negative for all time-periods up to six months, the 'neo-classical' and employment-to-inflation links seem, on the evidence presented here, to be stronger than the 'Keynesian' and inflation-to-employment links. The writer would add his own opinion that this is because full employment, as Government policy, limits the extent to which the second sort of

[1] *Economica*, Nov. 1958 (Phillips) and Jan. 1960 (Lipsey). They show that differences in the *rate of change* of money wages in the period are largely explained by variations in the *level* of employment. For a critical discussion, see A. J. Hagger, *Theory of Inflation*, Melbourne, 1964.

[2] A simple or multiple CC of x implies a degree of explanation of x^2, which is numerically smaller than x because $-1 < x < +1$.

link can work; and his value judgment that full employment is much more important, relative to price stability, than the technical literature, reflecting the views of fully-employed economists and their price-conscious wives, seems to suggest.

(b) Inflation and the balance of payments [3 and 4]

Compared to her rivals, Britain's poor performance since 1958 on current account can be traced to her high *ratio* of domestic to import-price inflation, and to her high *rate* of export-price inflation. Tables (pp. 172-3) covering all 16 advanced industrial countries showed that 33-50 per cent of their variance in export and import growth was explained by such price variance. Moreover, non-price explanations special to the U.K. proved flimsy (pp. 166-74).

Before examining the evidence of Table A, we summarise the relations between the aims of restraining inflation and improving the foreign balance. There is no simple contradiction.[1] Slower inflation makes the foreign balance better; but an improving foreign balance makes inflation worse. Hence policy against inflation helps the foreign balance, but policy to improve the foreign balance makes inflation worse. That is: [34], [43], [$\frac{3}{4}$], [$\frac{4}{3}$].

Inflation worsens the foreign balance through income effects, and probably through price effects. Income effects: more cash in people's pockets mean more demand for imports; it also raises the pressure of home demand, encouraging producers to satisfy it at the ultimate expense of exports; since inflation is fastest near full employment, both effects are intensified by the difficulty of making more exports or import substitutes. Price effects: domestic price rises turn British consumers towards imports (unequivocally [$\overline{3\ 4}$], whatever the elasticities); export price rises turn foreign consumers away from British exports—probably [$\overline{3\ 4}$], because more and more of our exports are processed manufactures (just like our customers' home output and their imports from elsewhere) so that the period over which demand for our exports is price-elastic gets shorter and shorter.

Improvement in the foreign balance (other things, especially real growth, being equal) harms price stability mainly via incomes. Extra exports (or fewer imports) transfer *money incomes* from foreign to British

---

[1] 'And if you've got this balance of payments problem *and* inflation, the one makes the other worse: it's as bad as having eczema on top of shingles.' K. White-horn, Deckchair Economics, *The Observer*, 21.8.1966, p. 8.

pockets, and *goods and services* from British to foreign shops. If the extra exports are part of real growth, the extra domestic cash bids up the prices of the same amount of *domestically available* output. If the extra exports are diverted from the home market without real growth, a smaller amount of commodities is bid up by the same amount of cash as before the export drive.

True, unemployed and mobile labour can make extra exports, though some multiplier effects will leak into price rises. Anyway, this is irrelevant in Britain now. Politicians devoted to guts, etc., seem unaware that each nose to the export grindstone is *ipso facto* a shoulder to the inflationary wheel.

These effects are complicated and long-run; not much hint can be expected from short-run CCs. What few mildly significant results we get point in the expected direction. Just over 10 per cent of variance in the rate of inflation is positively linked to variance in the preceding quarter's rate of growth of real exports (Table B, Col. 10, row 3, significant at 3 per cent; $0.335^2 = 0.112$); this result is fairly insensitive to the holding constant of other variables[1] and reflects a little of the multiplier effect of exports on domestic spending. Rather under 10 per cent of variance in import growth is linked to variance (in the opposite direction) in current inflation (Col. 6, row 2; significant at 7 per cent, and retaining sign in all first partials);[2] income effects seem to outweigh immediate price effects.

This view is strengthened by the fact that variance in the foreign balance seems to be associated with about 16 per cent of current variance in fullness of employment. (Table B, Col. 12, rows 4, 5). 'The better the foreign balance, the more employment is generated' is the only plausible explanation of this. And, as we know, very high levels of demand for labour are linked to inflation.

Reversion to Table A, Cols. 4 and 6, shows that neither extremes of good or bad performance on either aim nor long sequences of above- or below-average quarters help much. The relation is too complex, and too long-run, for that. It affects all four aims tabulated in our quarterly

---

[1] This cannot be said for the superficially surprising (if not statistically significant) link of inflation to the preceding quarter's *imports* (Col. 10, row 2); fortunately for economic logic, the first partial, when the preceding quarter's exports (row 3) are held constant, is negative.

[2] Again not true of the other trade link; Col. 6, row 3 becomes almost zero if current growth is held constant, but just acquires the positive sign that suggests income effects outweigh price effects in the very short run.

series. First, assume there is no policy, save 'fullish' employment. When employment is high relative to real growth, domestic spending outpaces real output, since wages and overtime rise relative to profits, out of which the propensity to save is greater. The rise in effective demand tends to raise imports, cut export growth, and push up prices, which hampers the foreign balance once more. The worsening balance begins a downward multiplier spiral of money incomes, moderating inflation; both shortage of cash and slower-rising domestic prices help the foreign balance to recover.

Stop-go affects all this, as we have seen. Instead of considering policy sequences, perhaps we should consider our priorities. In the 1920s and 1930s, a balanced or suplus *budget*, over the period in which the Earth goes round the Sun, was the shibboleth to which employment and growth were sacrificed. A wage cut was unlikely to stimulate employment, as it cut purchasing power if prices did not follow wage-costs down, and failed to cheapen labour if they did—in neither case was there much incentive to employ workers. Is a balanced or surplus *foreign account*, over the period in which the Earth goes round the Sun, a similar shibboleth for Britain in the 1960s—with political fixity of *exchange-rates* replacing economic ineffectiveness of varying *wage rates*?

If Britain undertakes military and developmental duties overseas, these are real and not ritual commitments; they *do* require some surplus on the current foreign balance. Moreover, foreign deficits represent future claims on our real wealth, as budget deficits do not. So the analogy is not perfect. The conflict of aims, however, is analogous—only the shibboleth is not. In the 1920s our main domestic worry was deficient demand, which could have been cured by a 'forbidden' budget deficit. In the 1960s it is inflation, which could be cured by a 'forbidden' import surplus. Only the shibboleth has changed; we have good reason to want an export surplus, but not to tie ourselves to an exchange rate that makes our exports too dear or unprofitable (and our imports too cheap) for such a surplus to be practicable.

Whatever exchange rate Britain adopts, growth of real GDP can resolve the conflict between full employment, price stability and balanced payments. If the rate of growth of machinery and plant were such that, when full employment of labour was reached, real output still rose as fast as spending—*then* there would be no upward pressure on prices, and no price or income effects diverting spending towards imports, or exports towards the home market. Not only have we seen that

I

real growth is compatible *with* other policy aims—the simplifier of the tasks of stabilising prices, exporting, equalising, and improving choice and output composition; it also softens the conflicts *among* these policy aims. What a pity that Britain, almost alone among industrial nations, has found it impossible to turn stability and high rates of re-equipment into more rapid real growth of output!

(c) Equality and inflation

We looked at [36] on pp. 57-8, when deciding whether inflation was a Bad Thing, and saw that—under modern conditions of industrial organisation—the effects were about balanced. Unfortunately [63] is fairly certain. It is the full-employment replacement for [6$\overline{1}$], which has been outdated by massive Government finance of its own investment to replace the lost thrift of the 'equalised' rich. However, it remains true that workers (and, even more, pensioners) save a lower proportion of income than company directors. Equalisation thus means that the same extra money income, paid out in correspondence to the same extra real output, has more impact on aggregate demand.

Neither tax nor savings arrangements have yet been adapted to the replacement of [6$\overline{1}$] by [63]. Income tax rates can be changed only once a year; they are unprogressive, and hence non-stabilising when money incomes rise, over the whole range of incomes taxed at the standard rates. Encouragements towards saving are still aimed mainly at the traditional savers; tickets for neither a state unit trust nor a national lottery are offered to the workers on the first Friday of their bigger pay packet. With [63], just as with [4$\overline{3}$], our legislators have not yet progressed beyond exhorting people to achieve contradictory targets.

(d) Equality and output composition

Our general principle for output composition suggested a hierarchy: needs, wants, endogenous demands, stimulated desires. The satisfaction of need plays a larger part in the spending of poorer persons. In this sense [65] is likely. However, the demand of the poor is usually relatively ill-informed, suggesting [6$\overline{5}$]. In so far as further equalisation is likely, the extension of consumer information (and the prohibition of misinformation, which always fools the poorest worst) is particularly important.

6. AFTERWORD

Growth is not 'a cure for all diseases, an end to all distress'. But it makes other aims easier to attain, and softens conflicts among them. If incomes grow faster than output, then either the balance of payments or the stability of prices must suffer (because there is no mechanism to siphon off the extra income into saving). Much depends on the composition of extra output, and the distribution of extra income; incentives and controls can stop extra incomes from being spent on imports, and can encourage the use of extra output for exports or import-substitution.

Mobility of labour is emerging as the conceptual hero of this book. It makes all the aims easier to attain, and softens conflicts among them. If a boom threatens the foreign balance, workers can be steered towards exports. Changing the goods produced by machines is a longer job.

But labour mobility can be expensive, and humanly painful. Economists cannot avoid analysing any plan to make labour more mobile by looking at the costs and benefits, private and social, in cash terms. But this should be supplemented by listing the gains and losses for the agreed aims of economic policy: growth, full employment, price stability, an improved composition of domestic product and balance of payments, equality and choice. Such agreed values do not imply political consensus; the proper balance among them is as controversial as the proper methods to achieve them. But we have seen that each value can be roughly measured, though there is much scope for improving the measures.

We have used the measures of our agreed values to analyse, with historical and international comparisons, the performance of the whole economy. We have not yet applied them to particular sectors. The reader might well ask what can be done to 'improve' railways or building, in the sense of increasing their contribution to national growth, equality and so forth. If each government department had a research worker, making international comparisons of past performance, and assessing proposed policies in the light of these agreed criteria, micro-economic policy would be much more closely linked to macro-economic objectives. But that subject needs another book. This book has tried to show the application of marginal, linear and Keynesian methods of Analysis to the assessment of British economic performance as a whole.

APPENDIX TABLE A: SELECTED AIM VARIABLES, 1955-64: QUARTERLY DATA

Year Qtr.	1 GDP Growth	2 Import growth	3 Export growth	4 Balance of payments	5 Excess import share	6 Inflation rate	7 Last quarter's growth	8 Next quarter's growth	9 Last quarter's inflation	10 Next quarter's inflation	11 Demand for labour	12 Last qtr's demand for labour
1955 3	2·96	11·06	9·71	−4	0·35	1·12	−1·70	−0·02	1·37	2·45	0·86	0·70
4	−0·02	−1·75	0·09	17	−1·51	2·45	2·96	0·90	1·12	0·22	0·81	0·86
1956 1	0·90	−0·36	0·79	30	−2·68	0·22	−0·02	0·45	2·45	2·09	0·68	0·81
2	0·45	1·52	2·17	72	−6·52	2·09	0·90	−0·63	0·22	−0·39	0·51	0·68
3	−0·63	0·45	−1·53	49	−4·42	−0·39	0·45	0·65	2·09	0·91	0·38	0·51
4	0·65	−1·53	1·90	88	−8·06	0·91	−0·63	2·31	−0·39	1·16	0·29	0·38
1957 1	2·31	6·23	2·80	53	−4·57	1·16	0·65	0·30	0·91	0·64	−0·06	0·29
2	0·30	−3·45	−1·32	77	−6·88	0·64	2·31	−1·92	1·16	1·37	−0·04	−0·06
3	−1·92	2·95	−0·33	40	−3·47	1·37	0·30	−1·10	0·64	1·22	0·10	−0·04
4	−1·10	−2·69	−0·22	60	−5·35	1·22	−1·92	1·33	1·37	0·34	0·03	0·10
1958 1	1·33	0·53	1·10	67	−5·94	0·34	−1·10	−2·37	1·22	1·51	−0·30	0·03
2	−2·37	−1·60	−5·10	20	−1·80	1·51	1·33	2·55	0·34	−1·16	−0·68	−0·30
3	2·55	5·95	6·61	33	−2·81	−1·16	−2·37	−0·50	1·51	1·29	−0·77	−0·68
4	−0·50	0·17	−3·31	−9	0·76	1·29	2·55	−0·20	−1·16	0·49	−0·92	−0·77
1959 1	−0·20	0·17	−0·60	−18	1·53	0·49	−0·50	3·08	1·29	−0·94	−1·03	−0·92
2	3·08	2·97	3·27	−15	1·23	−0·94	−0·20	1·07	0·49	0·24	−0·76	−1·03
3	1·07	0·41	0·41	5	−0·41	0·24	3·08	2·25	−0·94	0·21	−0·41	−0·76
4	2·25	4·73	1·88	−30	2·35	0·21	1·07	1·03	0·24	0·03	−0·28	−0·41
1960 1	1·03	4·17	3·21	−51	3·81	0·03	2·25	0·84	0·21	0·55	−0·27	−0·28
2	0·84	2·09	−1·63	−100	7·32	0·55	1·03	0·39	0·03	0·21	−0·08	−0·27
3	0·39	1·02	0·87	−103	7·46	0·21	0·84	0·84	0·55	1·05	−0·02	−0·08
4	0·84	0·58	−0·39	−116	8·21	1·05	0·39	1·77	0·21	0·54	0·03	−0·02
1961 1	1·77	1·30	3·93	−84	5·97	0·54	0·84	0·70	1·05	1·25	0·06	0·03

	1	2	3	4	5	6	7	8	9	10	11	12
2	0·70	−3·41	−1·13	−51	3·75	1·25	1·77	0·50	0·54	1·26	0·09	0·06
3	0·50	−1·62	0·38	−24	1·80	1·26	0·70	−0·53	1·25	1·13	0·04	0·09
4	−0·53	−0·52	−0·53	−24	1·80	1·13	0·50	−0·80	1·26	1·00	−0·11	0·04
1962 1	−0·80	1·65	−0·15	−48	3·55	1·00	−0·53	1·77	1·13	2·13	−0·28	−0·11
2	1·77	1·63	3·83	−20	1·46	2·13	−0·80	0·11	1·00	−0·46	−0·44	−0·28
3	0·10	2·69	1·33	−75	5·32	−0·46	1·77	−0·44	2·13	−0·03	−0·72	−0·44
4	−0·44	−0·99	0·37	−56	4·01	−0·03	0·11	−0·74	−0·46	1·15	−0·85	−0·72
1963 1	−0·74	−2·00	2·31	3	−0·22	1·15	−0·44	3·93	−0·03	0·91	−1·16	−0·85
2	3·93	3·73	1·02	−34	2·39	0·91	−0·74	0·53	1·15	−0·71	−0·95	−1·16
3	0·53	4·01	0·07	−90	6·09	−0·71	3·93	3·87	0·91	0·74	−0·87	−0·95
4	3·87	0·61	2·52	−64	4·31	0·74	0·53	−0·75	−0·71	0·90	−0·56	−0·87
1964 1	−0·75	4·04	0·14	−104	6·73	0·90	3·87	0·76	0·74	1·84	−0·26	−0·56
2	0·76	1·88	0·07	−150	9·52	1·84	0·75	1·00	0·90	0·78	−0·13	−0·26

Sources: Cols. 1-3: *Economic Trends*, Oct. 1964, p. viii, to 1961/IV; *ibid*, Jan. 1965, p. v. Col. 6: *Monthly Dig. Stats.*, retail price index, three-month averages; where the base-year changed, the percentage rise in Col. 6 is the average of the increases on the two sets of monthly data available. Col. 11: 1955-6, J. C. R. Dow and L. Dicks-Mireaux, *Oxf. Econ. Pap.*, Feb. 1958, p. 33; 1957, *Nat. Inst. Econ. Rev.*, March 1959, p. 43; 1958, *ibid*, Jan. 1960, p. 49; 1959, *ibid*, Jan. 1961, p. 53; 1960-1, *ibid*, Nov. 1962, p. 52; 1962-4, *ibid*, Nov. 1964, p. 61.

Method: 'Growth' means 'percentage difference between last quarter's and current quarter's figure'. Cols. 1-3 are each quarter's growth in GDP at factor cost, imports and exports, in 1958 prices. Col. 4 is each quarter's exports *less* imports, both at 1958 prices; Col. 5, each quarter's excess of imports over exports as a percentage of imports, all at 1958 prices. Col. 6 is the growth of the price level in the last quarter. Col. 11 is employment *less* unfilled vacancies as a proportion of civil labour force, all averaged over 3 months. Col. 7 is last quarter's Col. 1, Col. 8 next quarter's Col. 1, Col. 9 last quarter's Col. 6, and Col. 12 last quarter's Col. 11. For price inflation and excess demand for labour, seasonal adjustments were made by multiplying each quarter's result by the ratio, to *that* quarter averaged from 1955 to 1964, of the average of *all* quarters in the period (correction factors were negligibly different from unity). For all other columns, seasonally adjusted data from the original sources were used.

APPENDIX TABLE B: SIMPLE CORRELATIONS BETWEEN PAIRS OF VARIABLES

	1	2	3	4	5	6	7	8	9	10	11	12
1	1·000	0·500	0·670	−0·110	0·121	−0·249	−0·252	−0·197	−0·018	0·017	−0·027	−0·172
2		1·000	0·615	−0·223	0·236	−0·311	−0·140	−0·038	0·159	0·175	−0·024	−0·125
3			1·000	0·077	−0·065	−0·152	−0·449	−0·115	0·111	0·335	0·184	0·105
4				1·000	0·995	0·097	−0·254	−0·211	0·128	−0·009	0·247	0·387
5					1·000	−0·111	0·251	0·219	−0·134	−0·156	−0·272	−0·409
6						1·000	−0·004	−0·045	−0·150	−0·101	0·367	0·407
7							1·000	0·129	−0·282	−0·280	−0·019	−0·099
8								1·000	−0·167	0·190	−0·266	−0·264
9									1·000		0·304	0·390
10										1·000	0·403	0·346
11											1·000	0·935
12												1·000

Source: Table A (where variables 1-12 are listed), via IBM 7090 computer.

Note: Simple correlation coefficients between two variables, if *squared*, show the proportion of variation of each, about its average, that could be predicted from knowledge of variation of the other about *its* average. All entries below the diagonal would be symmetric with those above it, if they were entered, e.g. Col. 1, row 2 = Col. 2, row 1; and the diagonal entries are, by definition, all 1.

APPENDIX TABLE C: SIGNIFICANCE LEVELS, 36 OBSERVATIONS

Minimum value of	*Risk of chance link not above:*				
	I in 10	*I in 20*	*I in 50*	*I in 100*	*I in 1000*
Simple (and Multiple) correlation coefficients	·2784	·3288	·3860	·4240	·5253
1st partial correlation coefficients	·2901	·3462	·4063	·4482	·5611
2nd partial correlation coefficients	·2946	·3493	·4122	·4545	·5694

Sources and methods: t-tables from Goulden, *Methods of Statistical Analysis*, Wiley, 1952, p. 443, at ·1, ·05, ·02, ·01 and ·001 significance levels; for simple and multiple CC, we inverted the formula $t = \dfrac{r\sqrt{N-2}}{\sqrt{1-r^2}}$ for the t-values at the stated significance levels with $N = 36$ and hence with 34 degrees of freedom (Moroney, op. cit., p. 311) to find r-values for the above table. For partials, we calculated the standard error of Fisher's Z, $(1/\sqrt{N-k-3})$, where $N = 36$, k is the number of variables held constant (1 for 1st partial, 2 for 2nd partial); we then found the value of r for which the t-statistic, applied to the ratio of Z to its standard error, gives the relevant significance level with $(N-k)$ degrees of freedom. (For calculation of Z, see R. A. Fisher, *Statistical Methods for Research Workers*, Olive and Boyd, 1944 (9th ed.), pp. 183, 197). In effect, $r = \dfrac{M-1}{M+1}$, where $M = $ antilog$_e \left(\dfrac{2T}{\sqrt{N-k}}\right)$, and T is the relevant significance level of t with $(N-k)$ degrees of freedom.

APPENDIX TABLE D: FIRST PARTIALS, GROWTH ON
EXPORTS AND IMPORTS

Variable held constant	Value of first partial correlation coefficient between		
	1 and 2	*1 and 3*	*3 and 7*
1	—	—	—·3900
2	—	·5307	—·4648
3	·1496	—	—
4	·4904	·6846	—·4457
5	·4885	·6841	—·4483
6	·4587	·6602	—·4553
7	·4847	·6437	—
8	·5025	·6645	—·4412
9	·5092	·6761	—·4387
10	·5046	·7049	—·4434
11	·4994	·6867	—·4536
12	·4893	·7022	—·4436
None	·500	·670	—·449

Source: Computed on IBM 7090 from Table B. The first partial correlation coefficient of A on B, holding C constant, may be obtained from the simple correlation coefficients by the formula

$$r_{AB.C} = \frac{r_{AB} - (r_{BC}r_{AC})}{\sqrt{(1 - r_{BC}^2)(1 - r_{AC}^2)}}$$

and statistical significance calculated from the z-transformation (see Table C).

APPENDIX TABLE E: FIRST PARTIALS,
EMPLOYMENT ON INFLATION

Variable held constant	*Value of first partial correlation coefficient between*					
	6 and 11	*9 and 12*	*6 and 12*	*10 and 11*	*9 and 11*	*10 and 12*
1	·3721	·3928	·3817	·4037	·3037	·3543
2	·3784	·4184	·3903	·4137	·3119	·3766
3	·4066	·3828	·4303	·3686	·2869	·3317
5	·3522	·3707	·3987	·4326	·2806	·3751
6	—	·4995	—	·5009	·3365	·4359
7	·3669	·3795	·4089	·4063	·3113	·3394
8	·3685	·3175	·4104	·3550	·2732	·2938
9	·4380	—	·5118	·3713	—	·2791
10	·4743	·3520	·4979	—	·2533	—
None	·367	·390	·407	·403	·304	·346

Source: As Table D. The effect of holding 4 and 5 constant is almost identical; 11 and 12 are too highly correlated for one to be held constant while the other is 'varied' in correlation. Notice that the first two pairs of columns must be compared with care, due to lags; for example, the partial of 6 and 11 (holding 1 constant) is like the partial of 9 and 12 (holding 7 constant), and so on.

INDEX OF SUBJECTS

INDEX OF NAMES

42 Equation ? = Identity

160 Cost push of demand pull. Machines are not too "dear". Friction far more important

107 Australia a slow grower?
Note 1 incomprehensible

169

50/1 Tony Posey GNP but the economist "can"
provide
but his "constraints" are really
unquantifiable value judgements
quantified

64. Ask Karunda what he wd. do without support
revenue

20/5 ?

121 ? ?

149 Inf. slow & smooth because cost push
& not demand pull